I0165634

THE PARADOX
of
ETERNAL LIFE

Discourses with Master Teacher

ENDEAVOR ACADEMY
Certum Est Quia Impossibile Est

©2010 Endeavor Academy
The Paradox of Eternal Life - Discourses With Master Teacher

International Standard Book Number (ISBN-10): 1-890648-07-8
                                    (ISBN-13): 978-1-890648-07-7

Published By:
Endeavor Academy
501 East Adams Street, Wisconsin Dells, WI 53965, USA
Phone: +1 608-253-1447
www.themasterteacher.tv
Email: publishing@endeavoracademy.com

Contents

Introduction

In these enlightening discourses given through the revelatory mind of The Master Teacher of A Course In Miracles, you are directed to your own inescapable self-inclusion in the singular reality of Eternal Life, revealed through the illumination of your conceptual thought forms.

You are individually verified as the entire cause of this apparent separation from reality, and presented with the manner of your personal escape from this world of pain and death through the unqualified affirmation of the resurrection of our Brother and Savior Jesus Christ, who reminds you that this nightmare of separation is yours alone, and vividly describes and explains His own physical resurrection.

Atonement remedies the strange idea
that it is possible to doubt yourself,
and be unsure of what you really are.
This is the depth of madness.
Yet it is the universal question of the world.
What does this mean except the world is mad?
Why share its madness in the sad belief
that what is universal here is true?
Nothing the world believes is true.
It is a place whose purpose is to be a home
where those who claim they do not know themselves
can come to question what it is they are.
And they will come again
until the time Atonement is accepted,
and they learn it is impossible to doubt yourself,
and not to be aware of what you are.
Only acceptance can be asked of you,
for what you are is certain.
It is set forever in the holy Mind of God, and in your own.
It is so far beyond all doubt and question
that to ask what it must be is all the proof you need
to show that you believe the contradiction
that you know not what you cannot fail to know.

The Integral Philosophy of Your Being

The *Course In Miracles* is an integration of a philosophical endeavor based on Greek philosophy, or the meaning of life, which is what all philosophies are. If you want to come up close to me and exchange with me — I'll use the word *Socratic.* We'll talk about Socrates for a minute. And we'd have to get into Plato, and we would get into Aristotle, and we would get into the great *Philosophia Perennis.* We would do all sorts of things in the philosophy of us in the relationship with the Universe. In that sense, the human condition is nothing but a philosophical animal. He has one very fundamental question. What is it? He says: *"What am I?"* "What is the purpose of me?" "Who am I?" That's the condition of the human being, isn't it? And if he asks the question, he must answer it somewhere within his association because he is in a consciousness association. Of course!

The whole basis of every philosophical association you will find in so-called higher forms of learning, in any condition, are nothing but an attempt to determine what you are. Why are you here? What is the purpose of life? You asked those questions from the time you were two years old. You were looking for something heavy. This is heavy — you are a manifestation of consciousness. You've got a name, haven't you? Here you are stuck with a name; you have, apparently, a purpose for being here; everything you see is an existent form of your reality. You have a philosophy by the time you're four years old if it's only "I've got to obey my teacher and go to school." That's a philosophy.

I know it's complicated because you need six years of Philosophy to determine this. That is crap. It's basically and fundamentally crap because the only purpose of a consciousness state of awareness would be to determine what he is. How would I handle that? I would begin to teach why in hell wouldn't you know who you are? Certainly you have a right to say "Who am I?" "What am I doing here?" Somewhere within your discernment of yourself, you have tried to struggle with a process of recognition of your condition that must fundamentally be based on the alternative. In other words, you know that there has got to be an answer somewhere to be found. If you don't know what your problem is, that must be an alternative. Yes or no? If you don't know who you are, you have to have an alternative. We call that religion. We're not concerned about what the religion of your philosophy is, but only what? This is *A Course In Miracles*, only what? You have asked the fundamental question: "What Am I?" That's what a human being is.

Say to me, "What am I." That's your problem. And also the solution to that is you sitting here doing the things that you are to justify what you are. And you like that. Next question. You've answered what you are. You are that. That's what I declare.

Now there's nothing unique about what you've accepted. You guys think that somehow you're unique. You're only unique in one regard. Class? Who knows why you are unique? Tell me. Who knows? *You haven't been able to find the answer!!* Yes or no? Talk to me. Or what the hell are you doing here? I'm not denying whatever you think you are in the association; but if you've got the answer, why the hell are you coming to me? I never had the answer. Can you hear that?

I didn't have the answer. I couldn't accept the answers that I was offered in association with what I was told I was. That's not hard. There's no analyzation involved in it. Do you hear what I'm saying?

The philosophy of Homo Sapiens is an existent association in an environment that sets the terms for his existence. It doesn't solve the problem of what you are in the entirety of your relationship, but certainly it gives you a purpose for occupation of your own existence. Do you hear that? "My purpose in life, my philosophy in life, is to be a human." Talk to me. Isn't that so? What's wrong with that? I have no idea what's wrong with it. Obviously you must be answering the question "What am I" somewhere in your mind, and are not satisfied with it. You have to be answering it somewhere in your mind because the question "What am I" must be answered somewhere. Listen to me.

Don't you wonder who you are? You have to wonder who you are, don't you. Try music, take Mozart. Listening to Mozart helped me because I feel the genius of the human mind and it indicates to me that whatever a human being is, he must be more than that. Otherwise, the human would just be satisfied with what he is. If you think "well that's certainly a philosophy or psychology," no, it's the *condition* of the human being. It's the invention of the human. Not only that, it is impossible for there to be a civilization that doesn't have at least a sacred tree. It is not possible! It's asking the purpose for its association that somewhere — and I hate to use the word "transcends" — but gives a meaning to life; that at a minimum it doesn't know what it is, and constructs a theology or a mythology in regard to it's own purpose. That's called God.

This is not complicated. There's nothing complicated about what the *Course In Miracles* actually says. Now, if you want to say to me, "I want to study about the philosophy of *A Course In Miracles.*" Why not? *A Course In Miracles* should be taught in the philosophy department of all the universities because in the sense that you subtract yourself from the association, it is a philosophy and it is a psychology of that philosophy. Now, let me say this: Since there is nothing new under the sun, there is nothing in *A Course In Miracles* that I cannot, as a philosopher, compare with other philosophical associations. So when I went to school, I rejected all the various philosophies and said I'm going to take a class that integrates the philosophies, that shows me a way of life, perhaps, that will make me more happy in the conclusions that I am reaching about myself. You can call it the philosophy of life. Everything that you do indicates a fundamental acceptance of some condition that you've got in association with the consciousness of yourself, your consciousness mind. And that is your dilemma.

The question, once more, is what? First: What am I? Then: What is the meaning of life? Who am I? Why am I here? When am I here? You guys think I'm going to trick you into something. Those are the questions you said you asked in association with yourself, aren't they? And you answer them. It would be impossible for you to have a question without an answer somewhere in your mind. You may end up, of course, saying "I don't know." That does not preclude your existence on earth. You simply have a question, presuming that you do. You are still going to have to get up and exist in your association with the applications that command your attention to consuming food, screwing, doing whatever you do in your life. And you are saying to me: "I don't know the answer" aren't you? That's a human philosophy, a human condition.

The acceptance of that condition: "I don't know who I am, but I know that I must do this" is the conclusion of an alternative that would be transcendent to the association in order to define himself. Do you understand that? In other words, if you are in the philosophy of human being whose meaning of life is his existence in his association, that's what it will be. Class? Good morning! Talk to me! It's impossible that you haven't got a meaning to your life. You can say, "Well, I don't know what the real meaning is, but in the meantime, I have to exist and eat and have an occupation, don't I? I have to study, take on a vocation, be a drop out, be a hippie — I have to do something." And that would be what? What my life is. So now the meaning of my life is to exist and try to be happy in a place where I know and consent to die and lose the things that I love. Will you just look at it with me? Are you afraid to look at it with me? I'm not offering you anything you don't know perfectly well. You know that's true. All humans know that's true, don't they? Of course! All humans exist in the association of their consciousness identity.

Then you say, "What about it?" I don't know. What about it? It pisses me off. If not knowing who you are doesn't piss you off, then you are gratified by the philosophy of your own existence. Ask me questions. You better start asking me questions if you don't hear this. All this is is what you say — you've been here six years, ten years, a hundred million years. All you would end up with is the determination of objective philosophy that gratifies you more — don't avoid the word "reason" — in your association with the reason of what you are to the ultimate purpose of the Universe, and that may include passion, faith, determination — all of the attributes of your self identity. You call that psychology. Psychology is nothing but the acting out of the philosophy of who you think you are. Raise your hand if you can hear that. We have the philosophy of the *Text* of the *Course* and we have the psychology of the *Workbook*. That's what it is. The psychology is to teach you a new way to view yourself in relationship with the philosophy of Neo-Platoism, which is what the *Course In Miracles* is. If you read *A Course In Miracles*, you'll see it's Neo-Platoism. I knew that.

I used to have little sessions with some what we call mindful associations — guys who can think. I always needed to integrate my own process with thinkers — and sometimes passionately. That is, I demanded to know, like most of you in this room: What the hell is the meaning of this? We were gratifying the meaning of life into philosophies that made what they do in the universities look like nothing. I can guarantee you that the new philosophy and the psychology of the emergence of your mind is a provision or a reasoning that's so beautiful I don't know what to do, because my mind is reasonable. There is absolutely no question that the meaning of life in my life had to have reason. And the solution that I was offered was always what? Unreasonable! Never mind that it was unreasonable that I didn't know who I was. I had to assume that that was the nature of my consciousness condition. Could you hear that? In other words, the question "What am I?" has to be initially a legitimate question, because that's the condition in which you find yourself. There's no sense in philosophizing what doesn't know what it is. It doesn't have any meaning. It can't go anywhere. The question still remains: What am I?

Questioner: "But there's no answer to that." You aren't listening to me. I'm trying to give you the answer. You don't want to hear it. You are so determined that you are going to organize it in association with this because you… now you've got me in Plato. You've trapped me in Plato which is the Greek philosophy that says because I am a perceptual association of myself, I can reason to the answer of the meaning of life. That is perfectly sensible, and it's perfectly possible. Here's the difficulty, this is Platoism, actually it's Socrates, the idea of the reasoning process by any what you would call acute discernment must involve the use of a power of the mind — any reasonable association can see the unreasonableness of separate existence. This is Plato. Therefore, all I may have in me, the reasoning determination of finding out who I am, I must be employing a single entirety of association that may or may not offer the terms for what I am, but certainly is an admission of the use of that mind. That's Platoism. Have you got it? Do you understand me?

Socrates, who was a step above that, was more of an inquirer. He said that I can determine my relationship with myself by us confronting each other in the purpose of our lives. But to pursue that confrontation you could admit that you don't know. And that admission that you don't know, which is called ignorance, is the whole *Course In Miracles*. The beginning of salvation is simply the reasoning more and more to wondering why I'm here. That's the beginning of salvation. The continuing assertion by a reasoning process is that you can't arrive at the conclusion of what you are — that's what a miracle is. But you still require the process of reasoning to the determination of what you are. The reason that there aren't a million people here very simply is because they are gratified in their existent association. They have the religion of existence. Who heard that? Their religion is their boss. Their religion is a weekend in the country. Their religion is being a family. Their philosophy of life is being in a body occupation and dying. It's not ultimately reasonable to them, but they're not concerned about that. They have evolved a vocabulary of communication symbolically to which they have given meaning and purpose to their relationship with themselves. This is the reasoning process in the entire *Course In Miracles*. The *Course In Miracles* does not avoid a single thing in the elements of your reasoning process.

So we have a philosophy of life that is Platoistic in that it says that my mind, by the process of reason or discernment, can arrive at conclusions that will justify me in my relationship with my environment. They will give me a broader range — should we use "self recognition?" Certainly the philosophy of Plato is going to be involved in self recognition. Here we have a dilemma. This is the dilemma that is expressed by all reasoning human beings. The dilemma is that I have reason in my association with myself, and the factors of geometry, history, science — I see spatial references in regard to man, I have intellectual capacities to determine the result of my own mind. I may or may not be happy with that, this is pure Platoism, but that's the way that it is. Okay.

If you have any questions, ask. You say, "Well, Plato is very complicated, I'm going to read the *Republic.*" That's all crap. What I'm telling you is that there is a way you can come together and harmonize better than in other associations. All that is nothing but that human beings in their separate associations have a common denominator that can be expressed in the harmony of their own life. This is great stuff. This is *Course In Miracles* in an intrinsic association. It says that somewhere through a reasoning process of our own associations with ourself and each other, we can find harmony — we'll call it Utopia — and that the human mind is evolving to a point where that harmony can be discerned. This is not difficult, just because it's Plato and because it's whatever thousand years old, doesn't have anything to do with it. Does anybody not understand it? It's nothing but an association looking for a gratification of happiness contained within the existent mind.

Okay, here's the problem, and it occurs intrinsically in the idea that the problem has to be solved. There is a fallacy somewhere in the idea that first, the problem has to be solved; and second, that you can solve the problem. Inevitably Platoism will be reduced to Aristotelian. Inevitably, the singular aspect authenticated or admitted to by Platoism, in a connection with conceptual possibility, is reduced by Aristotle to: the solution is in the perceptual possibility. Plato says fundamentally that if there is a singular totality in the Universe, if there is a single total cause of everything, dualism or separation is impossible. This is *Course In Miracles!* That's exactly what it is.

Now Socrates has a better facility; he took some hemlock and fooled around with it — no, but Socrates could see the subtlety of the action of psychology that Plato finally couldn't get away with because he was too passionate in his association. So we have Aristotle who says that Plato is absolutely right, we are human beings and in our own discernment, we can figure out who we are. We can figure out who we are and what we're doing here. What aspect has he forgotten about? He's forgotten that there is an admission of a totality of singular association that must involve and include your dualistic nature. Yes or no?

The fundamental question then arises, that I am going to determine this reasonably, which my mind absolutely demands. There's no way that you can tell me that Jesus Christ is my savior unless I experience it; that's absurd, do you hear me? I'm not gratified by the fact that Jesus died on the cross for my sins. You may be, but I'm not. I never was. How did that solve my problem? My problem is of the mind. The *Course In Miracles*, Jesus resurrected, teaches that your problem is of the mind. For those of you getting here late, the question is: What am I? I'm answering in, first in a little Greek for you: *Cogito ergo sum*. We'll get to that in just a second. That's a statement of existent association. I'm not going to prolong this. You don't know how to respond to me because you are not accustomed to it. You are not accustomed to what? The *Course In Miracles*. You are not accustomed to the *Workbook* of the *Course In Miracles* which continually offers you an ultimate solution, within your own mind, to the question: What am I? It doesn't solve it for you, but I'll tell you this, the reasoning process of *A Course In Miracles* is so beyond anything! I'm going to use the word "integration." The integration of *A Course In Miracles* — and I'm talking about philosophy and psychology, is so extraordinary that there's nothing even remotely that compares with it. And I'm talking as a Greek. I'm talking as a mind that knows that.

So here we have a great philosophy of "I can come to know who I am." That's great. Not to decree there's a God — that may be all right, not that I've got to kill my partner which may or may not be true, now that I've got to exist. Those are definitions of the meaning of life in the existent association with yourself. Suddenly emerging in the human condition — somewhere it has to be termed "objective," because philosophy is finally objective — it says by the discernment or reasoning process of our own mind we can arrive at a conclusion of a shared reality. This is an admission of that possibility. Let's use the term "singularity" for a minute. It says that somewhere — I knew this by the time I was 6 or 7 — if there was anything, it would be everything. Everything there could possibly be would be included in. Yet I was using my existent association to justify the religion of the nature of my conceptual self identity. Say to me "I don't know what I am." That's what philosophy is. That's what religion is. And that's what psychology is.

Questioner: "That doesn't help me know what I am." You don't know what you are, and stop trying to ask the question. But you refuse to do that. Shut up. I'm going to take it one step further. Listen to me. I'm going to take the step for you. I already gave you all that, and the answer is, it doesn't. But you won't let me get to that. You are very legitimately sitting here saying "What the hell is this? What is that tree? What is this house? What am I doing here? What is this stuff? What is this Universe? Who am I? Who is Jesus Christ?" You're asking those questions. Not only are you asking it, but you are answering it. The terms for your existence have been set in this association. They include the philosophy of Plato. Basically, all civilizations use the Greek philosophy. Do you understand? Even if it only leads to Aristotelian utopia, which is where he got to. It is possible for us to find peace and harmony in our existent association based on the realization that we have a common denominator at the minimum, and a common Creator of singular association at the maximum.

I was aware by the time I was 10 years old — this is the way my mind works, and most of you work this way — that the idea of dualism, or separation in what you call Platoistic philosophy, to determine the answer had to include the singularity of my mind. The question I always had was: Why can't I be singular? Not that I could figure it out, but I was aware that an association with complete separation was impossible. Now, the reduction to what you call Aristotle says, no, very simply, that it is possible for you to exist separately from each other and still reach an ultimate conclusion. That's not what

Socrates said, and it's not what Plato said. But it's the conclusion that you would have to reach because you have been given value — and apparently the Greek philosophy has given value — to the reasoning process of your mind. Now we have the dilemma of *A Course In Miracles*, or the dilemma of all human associations. What is the solution to Platoism in the idea that through a reasoning process — this is not complicated, guys — that a conclusion of the purpose in life can be reached? You can't reach it. No matter what you do, based on the reasoning process of your mind, you can't reach it. So you get old and you die and you struggle. Or you simply accept it; somewhere, you accept your existent association. Now obviously you are involved in the reasoning process, aren't you? And you have been told that you ought to be able, reasonably, to figure out an answer if you have the question. That's Plato. If you can ask the question, you must have the answer. And if you must have the answer, it must be in your own mind. I know this smacks of the *Course In Miracles* because it is *A Course In Miracles.*

I used to have a little meeting with what I call "bright guys." Guys who used to listen to jazz and drink Jack Daniels with me. You guys don't really get this. These guys understand perfectly well what *A Course In Miracles* is. These guys understand very well what the *Course In Miracles* says. The reason that it is not acceptable to them is because it is not necessary for them. This is just the fact of the matter, because those are the kind of minds I hook with. That's the whole fun of getting together and asking: What is the meaning of life? I know perfectly well that I have always been a searcher of the meaning of life. They love that. They say, "I see you solved your problem through Jesus Christ." And I say, "Amen." It's senseless to try to give them an answer, because they are determined in the dualistic possibility of philosophical associations — oh, poop, I'm into the real answer. Incidentally, this is the entire civilization of man. I'm encompassing about 6,500 years in about an hour. Yesterday we covered about 2000 years.

So here we have a dilemma. We've got a great reasoning Greek philosophy that spills over to the conquest of Rome. It gives it justification for the adopting of self identity for unity purpose. Don't think that this is not Platoism, because it is. It continues to cause a lot of conflict, and what you say is that war is reasonable. That's Platoism. We will find a peace, and I will set the terms for that peace within my own mind to justify the gratificational need for the purpose of what I need. Never avoid this. You are going to sit with me and talk *Course In Miracles*, you admit to the fundamental question: What am I? I'm not saying that you don't know who you are, I'm saying that's the question that you continue to ask. What am I? Who am I? What am I doing here? What is the meaning of this? We agree that that is the human condition.

So here suddenly we have a philosophy that says that answer is contained not only in me, but very possibly in my creative, objective associations. I can set terms in the consciousness of me, I can justify my existence not only reasonably but I would add passion to it. That was very fearful to Plato. He didn't want to get too passionate about it, because it would begin to involve a process of reasoning that could not be recognized within the reasoning process. What he actually said was that while there may be another power that we are all using, we cannot employ that passion to determine it because somewhere it may not be reasonable within our process of reasoning. You guys think that Plato didn't know about that; he knew about it, but he said that's not what we want.

I'm not going to give you the whole story of Plato. Out of this springs what we call the philosophy of rationalism which says very simply that I'm in the process of existence, I admit to that, and the problem is solved by my existence itself and is not open to interpretation. So we have the rationalists. They didn't last too long. They might satisfy the guy individually, but they didn't satisfy the group in association. The other 400-year solution to the idea of Platoism, the idea of the reasoning process, is called Skepticism. Most human beings who have reasoning processes become skeptics. I was the greatest skeptic in the world; so are you. Your mind is fundamentally skeptical. But to arrive at a religion on skepticism really doesn't make too much sense. The inevitable conclusion of Platoism is Skepticism, because you can see very plainly that no matter how you organize the associations of your own mind, the conclusion that you reach is still what? Skeptical. The idea of not knowing who you are is what Skepticism is! You are skeptical about your own existence. So you sit around maybe drinking with a group and philosophizing, and that's where Skepticism turns into Nihilism, where Nihilism may provide another solution. That's the conclusion of acquiring the evidence of the psychology of your own mind.

There is one other alternative to Platoism, or the idea that you can reason to an existent association, if it's not Skepticism, through the determination that first it's not basically reasonable — it wasn't to my mind — because dualism is not reasonable to me in association with an entirety. The conclusion that must be reached, and is reached in *A Course In Miracles* in terms of philosophy, is called Neo-Platoism. When a philosopher asks you, "Well, what are the fundamental tenets of *A Course In Miracles*," you say Neo-Platoism, everyone knows that. All Neo-Platoism says is that no matter how much knowledge I have in my association, that since you have already told me there is power that transcends my association with myself, or if not transcending, certainly I am using, that logically what? That power must be available to me! This isn't hard. Why is that called Neo-Platoism? Because it's an indication of an experience ("Neo") that transcends or offers another — divine if you want to call it that — a wider alternative to the conclusions that you have so valiantly reached in your Platoism. Let's go to Plotinus, about 200 A.D. If you read Plotinus it's all *Course In Miracles*. Some of the conclusions that he reaches become Aristotelian. I'm not concerned about that.

That's the end of the philosophical discussion. Here's the fundamental premise that I've given you: You are in a process of determining through the psychology of Plato — that is, I have a process of thinking and that I'm using a power that we all, the Universe, uses a power of that mind. If you would like to read about this in the little book, *All About God,* that's pure Neo-Platoism. It says that I may have an experience through a reasoning process that includes a moment of entire synthesis that I know fricking well that I'm just fooling myself. Somewhere there has to be another alternative because I feel the frustration of my process. The difficulty with that obviously is it transcends the Neo-Platoism association in regard to how you can then correspond with the process of your own mind.

So the *Course In Miracles* is a reasoning process that involves the entirety of Universal Mind. That's all. It admits to your dualistic association, it admits to your consciousness existence, it admits that you are a problem-solver in the fundamental question: What am I? And it offers you an entire solution based on what you must know is true since you are employing the process of your own mind. You say, "Well, I'm very skeptical about that." The reason you are very skeptical about that is that you have not admitted, apparently, to the possibility of an experience within your own reasoning mind, that will give you a broader range of reasoning process. It doesn't take your reasoning away from you. I'm trying to be reasonable with you without having you go to Light and disappear on me. My answer is so obvious in my reasoning process! This is the *Course In Miracles.* Please don't let it be reduced to attitudinal healing, or let it be reduced to some sort of Foundation for Inner Peace. That's all just crap. My assignment with this incredible mind who calls Himself Jesus, He's laughing — what a great guy He was to talk to. You want to sit over a jug of wine and talk to someone! He'd tell you a parable that you didn't understand until three days later. He is always offering you a transcendental association with the correspondence of your own mind by including the power of your mind — *A Course In Miracles!* Of course it appears as a miracle because it apparently is "Neo." It apparently comes from outside of your association, and that's called Neo-Platoism.

The alternative to that will be that when the reduction occurs, or the necessity — have you all read the *Journal* of Endeavor Academy? The first page says that we reach knowledge by a transcendental association. All we teach, the *Course In Miracles* would say, is that the manner in which you come to know you who you are includes all of the things that you think you are, using the power of what you're not sure about. Knowledge can be gained through Neo-Platoism or by that application based on it. It doesn't involve what God is, or a doctrine in association with your mind. It has nothing to do with that. It simply says that you know perfectly well that you are utilizing the universal power of your mind. You say, "Well, I think I've got what you're talking about. I think that you mean that I am in my own association with myself, and that's what life is. I've certainly heard something like that." This is what people do to reduce *A Course In Miracles* when this occurs.

Say to me: *Cogito ergo sum.* Is that so? That's the conclusion that all human beings actually arrive at. *Cogito ergo sum* means *I think therefore I am.* I think therefore I am. The term for that, so that you won't have to go out and look it up in the library, is Existentialism. Can you get that? It means that I admit that I think and that I exist. *Cogito ergo sum,* I think therefore I am. What's the problem with declaring the *Course In Miracles* to be Existentialism? The question What is the meaning of your existence? is not answered. Actually it's a form of Skepticism. Sartre could not, he wanted to say *cogito ergo sum* — I think therefore I am — that's very true. The problem with the philosophy of Existentialism is *ergo.* It's the problem of perceptual mind in association with itself: I think *therefore* I am. What did that do? That didn't do anything! I just associated with what I previously thought I must be, and I existed within that association. Existentialism seemed to reasonable; it just doesn't work. The reason that it doesn't work is you think because you are, but it doesn't answer the question of who you are. It just adds to the problem of your thinking and you end up with yourself! Say "Amen." If you don't understand me, enjoy my process! That's what it says in the *Course*— don't try to understand it. But if you want to take the *Text* sometime and watch His process of this and that and time in association with eternity. It's absolutely extraordinary. Every time you think you understand it, you'll get hooked. The whole process will go around and hit you; take another look. He always says that: Take a look again. By that process, while you may exist in your Plato association with yourself, you are always asked only to look again. Never be gratified by the limitations of the answer to "What am I?" that are given you, because what you are is a reasoning process to arrive at a conclusion of existence which you have already admitted is separate from reality. But there is no question that you are in the admission of that Existentialism.

It's very difficult to formulate a philosophy that says there is a transcendent association, another form of totality of reality, that does not include the doctrine of dualism, or the doctrine of individual separate associations. Isn't that so? Very simply because you, as bodies or separate human minds, are separate from each other. Aren't you? You admit that you are separate. You are a separate human being, you're a human being. You are arriving at conclusions within your own mind and then you are sharing them objectively with the world. That's a not-too-subtle admission of an alternative. It's an admission of religion. It's an admission that you have a common denominator, all religion admits to a common denominator. I don't care if it's light; I don't care if it's truth; I don't care if it's the sun. I worship the sun, and we worship the sun together. We use the power of the sun to establish our existence separate from each other and live in harmony based on quotients of codes that we can set up through existent separation. That's religion.

The opposite of what you call Existentialism is a very popular philosophy called Transcendentalism. While it reduces to God-In-Nature — say Walden Pond, say Longfellow, Emerson are great Transcendentalists — they say that my reality is finally based on the transcendental association that I have with everything. It was so obvious to me that Transcendentalism does not involve a specific god. Transcendentalism involves the entirety of the admission that God is in everything. Most of the people who come up here to Byron Bay, to this beach, are what you would term Transcendentalists. That probably reduces itself to planting gourds, and that's perfectly all right because it says God is in everything and I am enjoying my transcendental association with nature. Have you got that? I'm enjoying going out and being — God is everything! In that sense, God is not specific at all. I'm going to share my transcendental experience with my present dualistic mind. Wonderful. Except it didn't satisfy me. It did not answer my fundamental question. If, indeed, life is transcendental, what is the connection between the entirety of life and my need to exist in my own association? That's called *A Course In Miracles*. So I can exist over here; I can transcend over here.

If anyone ever asks you — I'm giving you this as a fact — the best definition you can give for what *A Course In Miracles* is in regard to philosophical connotation is Transcendental Existentialism. I'll do it once more for you: *A Course In Miracles* is nothing but the philosophies of Transcendentalism with what you call Existentialism: I exist, therefore I am — but if I am, so is God. If God is, God is everything. There's a manner by which, through transcendence, I can come to know the entirety of my own existence.

Here's the problem: That finally cannot be understood in the philosophy of it, but in the application of Transcendentalism. This is the whole *Course In Miracles!* It says that no matter how you look at anything, available to you in your entirety of association is a continuing Transcendentalism. It's not at all concerned about whether you find God in the plant or God in that tree or God in that person, only that you don't give that objective identification the deity of your God objective association. You have a tendency to set up an idol that has justified the beautiful Transcendentalism that you just experienced. This is one of the great chapters of *A Course In Miracles.* And you begin to objectify it, this is Christianity, because it gives you — let's just say we're going to change the bread and wine to the body and blood of Jesus. That, folks, is a transcendental experience. Agreed? The idea that there would be a place where you could go and drink the blood of Jesus and have that bread transformed into His body, is a ritual of transcendence. I understand that it has been reduced to drinking a little wine and having a little cracker. But that's beside the point. That's the whole problem. What Jesus says is stop objectifying the symbols in your own mind because you are living by the symbols that can only be verified in a continuing reassociation of yourself in the ritual being performed. Otherwise you'd tell me, "This is the altar of the truth, and you're all full of crap." You cannot *not* do it because you have arrived at a reasonable conclusion through what? The experience of your own objective mind. Don't you let anybody tell you that all religions are not experiencing the existent mind, because they are. Why you are with me, hopefully, is you are finally not gratified with the answer to the question "What am I?" The question "What am I?" has not been sufficiently answered in your own mind.

It's possible, even though you may have answered it, for you to re-examine it based on the evidence I am offering you, because of my positive assurance that you must share with me the frustration of your own existence. Tell me you hear this. Come on. You want to be sharing with me the unanswerable question "What am I?" If you'll share that with me, you can begin to arrive at the reasonable conclusion that the question "What am I?" is senseless. That's what Socrates did. Certainly my mind did it immediately. The question "What am I?" must involve my knowledge of the solution. Say you understood that.

It's impossible that you would ask the question "What am I?" and not know the answer. You might not know where it is; it would be somewhere. So you are searching for the answer to "What am I?" You must believe that it is contained in your reasoning process because you are a construction of consciousness that lives in a cause-and-effect relationship that justifies your temporal location. I'm doing *Course In Miracles* now.

Questioner: Is "Who am I?" synonymous with "What am I?" Jesus likes "what" because "who" has a tendency to personalize itself. He uses the word "thing" in Chapter 31; He doesn't say "Who am I?" He says "I do not know the *thing* that I am." That's actually what He says. It's a lovely thing. "I do not know the *thing* that I am." It's not that I'm not a *thing*, but I don't know what that *thing* is. Obviously the question "Who am I?" is immediately answered by your "you." And you immediately turn that into an existent association with yourself and become Existential.

Here's the solution if you want to hear it. It's impossible the solution not be contained within your own mind because it is reasonably impossible that you could ask a question for which there is not an answer. Your admission that you do not know the answer did not gratify me. If it gratifies you, the answer to your question "What am I?" is "I'm a lawyer." The answer to your question is: I am in the occupation of the existence within this little ball of crap. And the reason, or purpose" — Jesus uses purpose – "the purpose for my life is to exist." That's what we do. We all exist here in this association. What have you done? You've given purpose to your existence, ignoring the fundamental question "What am I?" Do you hear me? I can read this right out of the *Course* for you.

Since you are busy existing, you don't allow yourself to examine the alternative because you know perfectly well that there is an alternative, but damn if you're not too wrapped up in everything that you're doing. That's why you need *A Course In Miracles*. The *Course In Miracles* says that no matter what you're doing, the answer is always right there. And not only is that true, but since your conceptual associations are only justifying your temporal existence, each moment that you don't justify them you will experience a transcendental moment. It's Neo-Platoism. It's a chair. Questions? Come on, guys, this isn't all that hard.

Obviously it's going to require the experience of your own mind, isn't it? You're in an experience of your own mind anyway. Everything you do is an experience, justified by the association of your necessity for existence. Obviously, the idea that life is nothing but existence is abominable to you. Why wouldn't it be? It doesn't make any sense. So somewhere in the association of the occupation of living and dying, you afford all of yourselves the creative purpose of your own mind to continue to justify your existence. And you're very successful at doing it. What you're saying is, "I can remain separate from everything and be happy." This is the *Course* now. "I can use the power of that mind and find happiness in my existence. I can be happy that I must accept that my grandma just died. I can be happy in fact that a drunk ran over my friend." Come on. I'll get you to the psychology. I must be happy in that because my Platoistic mind, my Aristotelian mind, is a reasoning process that will not allow for a transcendental location. If you don't start to hear this, I'll be ashamed of you.

All the *Course In Miracles* is, is the admission that knowledge of reality can be gained through the expansion of your consciousness association with yourself. Do you hear me? It's nothing but that. It's not concerned about what your concepts are. In effect, it says to you that while you may exist — this is the early lessons — my existence depends on me sitting in this chair and putting my stuff on that table. Now, that does not answer "What am I?" But it answers it for me because I'm the carcass that sits in this chair and looks at that table. If you're happy with that, what the hell are you doing here? Why are you here?

Jesus says you're not a body at all. All that stuff can come later. But there's no sense in looking at that stuff if you're going to insist that I should recognize your contentment with your own existence. The reason that I applied and was able to undergo a transcendental association of my own mind is because I was never gratified by the answer that I got to "What am I?" You nodded your head on that, but I mean that literally. I'm trying to get your head open so you say: "There's something wrong with this. I don't know what the answer is but I know it's not this."

How have I arrived at that? Reasonably! Everything turns to crap. I get everything in order. I'm working my mind real good. Boom! I'm existing in happiness and it turns to crap. It's not fair. I've existed. I've done all of the things in my association I'm supposed to do. I'm searching for happiness. I have apparently found it. I am aware that I think. I'm applying that process. And yet I get old and continue to get old and die. There must be something fundamentally wrong with the idea that I could really be separate from God. There must be something fundamentally wrong with the idea of dualism, the idea that minds could be separate — the First Law of Chaos, that minds are actually separate from each other. That's absurd. Do you know why that's absurd to me? It's not reasonable. It doesn't solve the problem of my own existence even if I admit my mind is separate. I'm still trapped and listening to a train at four a.m. That doesn't solve my problem. I'm still aware that people are murderers and are slaughtered. I'm trapped in my own human mind.

The alternative I'm offering you has nothing at all to do with what you define as God in the sense that your problems can be answered by the associations of your own mind. That's absurd. If they are, why don't you answer them? This is Chapter 31, first page. You keep searching for the solution in your own mind about who you are, thinking you're going to find it. You say, "I can." I say that's nuts. Then you must be asking the wrong questions. Instead of asking me in your own association of cause and effect what you are, why don't you say: "There must be something outside that I've already admitted to that's not a part of this cause and effect?" You already told me there was. So your condition of consciousness is nothing but a conscious entirety of God in a consciousness form of reality, based on a combination of the thought forms of your own mind in a previous, separate, historic existence. That's what you do. You organize it in your own mind.

Are you happy with the organizations of your historic reference? This must have to do with you individually. It is the only question that finally can be asked. And you say: "Well, I'm pretty happy. I know that there's no alternative to that." And I say: "Screw you." I'll tell you frankly: "The hell with you." Most of my friends are getting old and dying, and I'm not getting old and dying because I said: "Screw you." I'm talking right to you. I said: "Screw you." I don't know what the alternative is, but I am not going to exist in the crap of my own association. It doesn't make any sense to me. Go ahead, make sense out of it. It couldn't possibly make any sense. The conclusion is that everybody gets old and dies. That's not difficult. Don't they? Everybody gets old and dies, including you. Screw you. There has to be another answer. I don't have to know what the answer is, but I sure as hell can know that the condition I am in is not the answer, not for me. If it's the answer for you, why are you coming to me? You're still going to try to justify your own existent association, which is what? Separation of cause and effect — dualism, which is one thing or another in my association of "other" contained within my own mind. And don't tell me that you're not that solution because you are. It's what a human being is. See, you like the idea that somehow you should analyze your own consciousness association. That's not possible. You are that consciousness association. *Cogito ergo sum*: I think, therefore I am.

Questioner: Is it delusion to say that life can't be reduced to meaning? Am I in delusion in saying that?

Why would meaning be a reduction? Come on, you're talking to the Old Man here. Of course. Life is meaning. Why would life have to be reduced to meaning, except that you've reduced yourself to your own meaning. No, come on. This is a good demonstration.

Questioner: What I'm saying is I'm reducing life to mentality, to the mental process.

Sure. What's wrong with that?

Questioner: It's not a reduction. Okay.

Well, not knowing who you are would be a form of reduction because you're basing your reality on not knowing who you are.

Questioner: But if I say that... I've sort of copped out. You see, I've said that life... I can't get the meaning of life. I can't get it, you see?

I know.

Questioner: Is this delusion? Or is it a cop-out?

No, it's real. Your demanding: "I can't get the meaning of the world" is very real. That's exactly what the world is. The world is not an illusion to you. That's camel dung. The guy that tells you that the world is an illusion except in its entirety is absurd. It's not illusion to you or you wouldn't need the Atonement. Do you see? You are in time. You do exist in time.

Questioner: Delusion. I said, the mind deluded.

Delusion is having an illusion. I understood what you said. One is concept, and the other is precept. Precept, concept. But whatever, however you combine them, you still are in your own association. "Well, there's nothing I can do about that. I'm just going to be happy. I'm going to the doctor this afternoon. I've got cancer." Screw you! You can do that if you want to, but I'm not going to do that. "Yes, you are." No, I'm not. "Yes, you are. I have you trapped in my own mind. We exist together in the separation and there's nothing you can do about it." The hell with you! "We've invented a God that solves our problem by letting us get sick and die and justifies ourselves in our own mind." The hell with you. It's not reasonable to me. It is not reasonable to me that if there is a totally loving, eternal God that this world exists. Explain it to me. Explain to me why I should get old and suffer and die if there's an eternally loving and creating God.

Questioner: Why would I?

That's what I want to know.

Questioner: Well, I can't do it.

There is no explanation.

Questioner: That's right.

That's it. That's the beginning of salvation. I don't know who I am or how to look at this, and I'll stop trying to explain this crap within the parameters of my own mind.

Questioner: It's the freedom from my mind that you're speaking of.

Freedom from what?

Questioner: Freedom from the mind which you're speaking of.

Well, it's freedom expressed in a reassociation of yourself. See, the wonderful thing about it is that it's not really an explanation of your self at all. It's the emergence of yourself as you are created in the Universe. That's the fun part about it. You already told me that it's there. You already said to me that there's a power of Universal Mind where I am eternal in Heaven. I agree with you. Why would you attempt to associate it then with the separation of your own mind? Say to me, "I have no alternative." You don't, either. You're trapped in your own mind. That's why you need what? Me. You wouldn't need the *Course In Miracles* — if you admitted that, you'd have no problem. It's nothing but your mind, and understand, this is from that mind! Hold it down! I haven't finished my philosophical talk yet.

I used to love to do this. The reason I got this job was the *Course In Miracles* is a course in reason. Let's not crap each other that the *Course* is some sort of course in faith. The entire *Text* is nothing but the reasonableness of your mind. All reason requires is the admission of the possibility. Without getting into the statistical evidence of it, all it admits is the possibility of your communication with reality. So contained in that possibility must be a method by which it can come about. The method by which it comes about is obviously the release of your own historic reference with the existent association that you're in. That's a lovely, lovely philosophy.

I wouldn't care where I was in my own determination of my mind in regard to what a human being is. I would love the *Course In Miracles*. The problem we've had with the *Course* is the refusal to expose it, the refusal to expose the *Course*. The Foundation for Inner Peace refuses to expose the *Course*. Do you hear me? Any interpretation of the *Course* is a denial of it. You understand? That isn't even open to discussion. Any foundation that would attempt to interpret what the *Course* says is denying the *Course* very simply because the *Course* teaches that Life is not interpretation. Say you heard that. The *Course* has nothing to do with your interpretation of it. Does the *Course* mean what it says? It means what it says. Where's your problem? It says that you're perfect and loving as God created you. That does not require your analyzation of it. Because to analyze it would actually be a denial of what it says.

The first time I looked at the *Course*, I was well into my illumination. That's why I got it. And I looked at what the foundations were doing, and I said: Why do they form groups to study the *Course In Miracles?* How do they study it? Do they study it in association with other philosophies like I just offered you? Or would you admit that the *Course In Miracles* is a way of Life. The *Course In Miracles* is a way by which you can come to know who you are with God. It doesn't involve an interpretation of it since the philosophy of it is that your interpretation of yourself is not true. The reason that Ken Wapnick cannot talk about the *Course In Miracles* is very simply because there's no such thing as Ken Wapnick. The whole basis of the teaching is that your persona, the association of yourself, is not what you really are because it's not what Life is, amazingly enough — I'm going to share this with you — if you can get past the interpreters, who somehow insist they're supposed to be a student of the *Course*. They don't make any sense. How could you be a student of your own limitation? You'd probably then study yourself in association with yourself. You could do it, but only after a reduction of the *Course* into some sort of philosophical jargon that retains your own egotistical identity. I'm giving you the fact of the matter. It doesn't have anything to do with Wapnick. Without getting into the idea that you're fearful of the *Course* — you ignore the certainty that you must be fearful of the *Course* because it's a threat to your existent association. That's the psychology.

I'm going to share something with you. And I understand that the *Course* had to be crucified in the beginning. But there would be no excuse, no excuse for any philosophy department that would begin to teach the *Course In Miracles* not to teach what the *Course In Miracles* is. That's a philosophy. If you're going to analyze the *Course*, analyze it by the philosophy of your own mind. If you're going to look at the *Course*, look at the *Course* as an integrating process of your self identity. Are you able to do that?

A Course In Miracles didn't come from time. It came from out of time. Now we're into a discussion of the *Course*. I want to finish this. I promise and guarantee you that I can take the *Course In Miracles* to anyone —and please, not connected to a *Course* group; I mean, not connected to someone who's taken it and reduced it to interpretation. That has nothing to do with it. I can take it up to any philosophy department, including here, if you want me to do it. I can sit down with them and say: "This is what this says." I can turn the pages, and they'll say: "Boy, what an interesting philosophy." Now, that doesn't mean that they accept it. That doesn't mean they're going to practice. But there's no excuse for you not being able to say what *A Course In Miracles* says so that you open it to a meaningless interpretation of your egotistical nonsense. That doesn't make any sense. Did you hear what I said? Why would you interpret the *Course?* You already told me it came from a divine source out of time. The philosophy is so beautiful if you don't begin to discuss it in your own association with yourself. Very simply because if you discuss it in your own association, you can't hear it. I just did Neo-Platoism for you.

Now, fortunately, what I loved about it is, no matter how much I — we used to call it "chomped at the bit" — there's no compromise in it. And that's what pisses you. You demand an answer to it, but you won't accept that there's no compromise in the relationship of entirety with your egoism. Why? You're dualistic. That doesn't mean you have to solve it in dualism, but you have to admit there's no compromise. Did you get it? That's the whole *Course.* Come on. It says: "Either this or this is true. Not both." You keep trying to integrate it, even including, "I'm in the process of transformation."

I'm feeling a lot of energy. I love it. I saw the reports. You saved yourself about 2200 years. You are outstandingly beautiful, incidentally. Some of you, when you begin to hear this, begin to radiate a lot of inner beauty. All it is, is an integration of who you are. It doesn't have anything to do with how you look. You still think it does, but it doesn't. It has to do with only the certainty or security you have found in the love of God, for goodness sake. And you can't share it with anybody, but you can sure as hell share it with yourself. And that's the joy of it. That's why you call it transcendental.

Questioner: It's catching. Some of it's catching.

Well, that disturbs the Plato mind because it involves the passion of Transcendentalism. In other words, what will occur is that your reasoning process becomes more passionate because it becomes more creative. That's pure *Course.* Do you see? Your mind, all mind, is designed to give an association of itself even with what appears to be out there. It's a process of self-recognition based on the reasoning process for the purpose of your existence. Obviously you have a problem with that in your own mind. The *Course In Miracles* offers you no solution to your problem at all except a continuing reassociation of yourself with the objective reality that's apparently around you. You got that? Talk to me. Questions? This is what *A Course In Miracles* is — in that sense, it's mind training, isn't it? If you are existing in the association that previously made you unhappy but justified your existence and have found a new means through this *Course* to eternity, when you begin to exist, when you come back into that existent association, you will immediately begin to feel the frustration of *cogito ergo sum.* It's inevitable because you have seen an alternative. That's called the mind training of *A Course In Miracles.*

Now, somebody here yesterday said, "I have been studying the *Course In Miracles* for ten years and I don't know what the hell you're talking about." I have no way of knowing how to respond to that. *A Course In Miracles* is not a course in study. I would look at it and say: It's hard for me to believe that you could open it, in the process of the *Workbook* of turning your will over to God, enjoying the freedom of your own mind, and tell me that for ten years you're sitting there, being what you are. Something must be escaping you in regard to what the *Course In Miracles* is. "Well, do you know Kenneth Wapnick?" And I said, "No, I've heard of him." And I said, "Do you know Sam Lupitas?" He said: "No, I don't know Sam Lupitas." And I said, "Well, then I won't tell you what he said about you." Those are the kind of retorts that you enjoy. "You should hear what Wapnick said about you." "I'm not going to tell you what Sam Lupitas said about you."

I'm going to give you the answer to the Foundation just real quick here, and then we'll pass it by. Most of you know there is a law suit against us for maintaining that we're going to dispense the *Course In Miracles* to the world based on Jesus Christ. It's very simple. We have the freedom, they can have all the copyrights they want, it really doesn't concern us, but that we be allowed to give it away free. Where the position is now, this is for all *Course* groups in the world, is as follows:

In order for the Foundation to verify the copyright they had to maintain that Helen Schucman wrote *A Course In Miracles*. That's the fact of the matter. I want you to understand this. That's perfectly all right with us, except that Helen Schucman didn't write *A Course In Miracles*. But if Helen Schucman did not write the *Course In Miracles*, it is not copyrightable. So that you understand, I want to get all of that out of the way. Obviously poor Judy is caught with having to say that Helen Schucman wrote the *Course*. That's not true. That should be unreasonable to you, because it is unreasonable to her. I'm not answering that for you, but I want you to know that's the position that had to be taken to collect $2.5 million. There's no way that you could say that *A Course In Miracles* came from Jesus and copyright it. In that sense, you can't copyright the Ten Commandments — unless Moses says: "I wrote them." But as soon as he says: "They come from another source not of this world" it can't be copyrighted. I'm just giving you the legal thing — it's just the fact. You can copyright the scribe, you can copyright interpretations, but nobody can stop you from declaring that Jesus, your savior, resurrected, is talking to you. That's the freedom of your mind. So, in the suit, I think we owe them $1 billion from these little books, and they stopped us. We're not even allowed to say: "This is what it says." It doesn't have anything to do with money. We're not collecting money, we just want to give them away free and they won't let us. That's the internal difficulty.

The other foundation, what Kenny is involved in, obviously is not *A Course In Miracles* group, it's a philosophical association of the study of the relationship of the philosophy of *A Course In Miracles* with other associations. If you want an answer to the position of Kenny, when we finally went through this last association with Kenny, he said very emphatically that the author of the *Course In Miracles* is a fraud. This comes from Kenny Wapnick. He says, and will maintain right now — it's a position that he would finally have to take in his own mind if he were going to continue to analyze the *Course In Miracles* — but the absurdity of saying that the *Course In Miracles* is not the work of Jesus Christ of Nazareth, that He is not who He says He is, is crazy. It doesn't make any sense. That's just not *Course In Miracles* — not because of the containment in it, but because He says He is. I mean, to open up the book and read the first three chapters of *A Course In Miracles* where Jesus talks about His own crucifixion and resurrection. He talks about being that man, doesn't He? Does He or not? He says in it: "My disciples didn't understand me." He talks about Himself. So Wapnick, who many of you know, says emphatically that He's a fraud; that the mind that maintains that it is Jesus of Nazareth and wrote the *Course* is a liar. How a mind like that could arrive at that conclusion I don't know.

Questioner: In what sense is He a liar?

He says that the *Course In Miracles* is not written by the historic Jesus.

Questioner: Who's it written by?

The historic Jesus, it says so. Wapnick says it's not — he's a liar.

Questioner: What does it matter?

It has no divinity if doesn't come from outside of time. He's reduced it to nothing.

Questioner: But if it gives the answer and gives the beauty and the teaching, what does it matter if somebody says something about it? That's their concept.

I agree with you. All I'm saying is that Ken Wapnick said the historic Jesus did not write the *Course In Miracles*.

Questioner: That's just his business.

No it's not. He called himself the Foundation for Inner Peace and he's denying the authorship of *A Course In Miracles*. I say the *Course In Miracles* is nothing but Christianity; it's nothing but pure Jesus' Sermon on the Mount. I have no objection to Ken Wapnick saying: "I question it" what I object to is him denying who the author says He is. That doesn't make any sense to me. On what basis does he deny that the author who says He's *A Course In Miracles* is a fraud? Shall I answer it? He denies it because it's not what established Christianity says. And obviously established Christianity is not the teachings of Jesus of Nazareth. But to say that since established Christianity in not what the *Course In Miracles* says, that therefore Jesus of Nazareth is not the author of the *Course*, is crazy — if only because He says He is. Jesus says very explicitly, you know it and I know it and when you open it up you can see it, that "I am the man that was crucified and was resurrected and am talking to you." Ken Wapnick says: "Camel dung, He's not. He's not who He claims to be." I want that to settle it with me, and I don't want to have somebody else ask me what Wapnick says.

Wapnick denies that the historic Jesus is the author of the *Course*. I don't know what you do with the *Course In Miracles* then. I don't know what you would possibly do with it except continue to interpret it. But you are going to have to form a philosophy outside the basic tenets of resurrection. Certainly you can't deal with tenets of Christianity; the necessity for your mind to have an experience of transcendence through a process of forgiveness, which is the teaching of Jesus. In other words, I could take the book to anyone, it wouldn't matter who it was — I'd say "Read what that says." "Well, it says that I'm Jesus resurrected teaching the *Course*." Is that what it says? Yes! Do you believe it? "I don't know whether I believe it or not, but that's certainly what it says." Wapnick says that the guy that says it is a liar, that it's not the same Jesus. I don't know how he gets that. That there's another Jesus that wrote it. Maybe his Jesus?!

Questioner: How can you possibly understand eternity if someone from eternity couldn't come back and tell us about it?

Sure, not only that, but it's impossible that we also don't know about it. That's the talk I just gave. It's impossible that you sit here, in your own existent association and ask me the question "What am I?" not knowing the answer. And I know that you say: "Well, I can never know" or "Screw you, I found an answer." It has nothing to do with me. If you want to share my mind with me, which is an illumination to the certainty of eternal life, I will share it with you because I believe that minds communicate. I believe they communicate because there's only one mind. I say that there's only one mind; I can open the channel wherewith you then can communicate without previous separation through the use of the divine love of Jesus Christ resurrected. If that's not Christianity... I could have said that in any pulpit in Christendom and they would have said "Amen." They would have. They would have said, "Boy, isn't that lovely? Jesus taught me to love my brother, and give and that's the answer to my problem."

Questioner: So this man Wapnick?

He formulated the *Course* philosophically.

Questioner: Right, so is he saying that the man accessing Christ consciousness, or who's realized Christ consciousness, wrote it?

He's saying He is not. He says that Jesus — somewhere if you admit to the source of Jesus, you don't have to accept the idea that Jesus Christ who wrote the *Course In Miracles* says "I am the Jesus that walked the earth 2000 years ago." You don't have to accept it. But you can't deny that He says it. Wapnick says that He's a liar for saying it because his philosophy of the *Course* does not agree with the historic references of Christianity. It makes the author of the *Course* a fraud.

Questioner: I can't believe anybody that hasn't been there.

You can't even believe anybody that's been there. You just have to accept it. Like Paul says, where I am you can only come through experience. That's *A Course In Miracles*, that knowledge can be gained through the transformation of your mind. Neo-Platoism, flat out. The dilemma of the admission of what you term the *Philosophia Perennis*, the ancient wisdom — that somewhere we all know the answer through a transcendent reassociation; that there's a manner by which we can come to know who we are — is actually the predicate of the entire association of civilization. Without that, there would be no civilization. I'm not concerned about how that finally comes about, but the worship of a God, an accessibility to the admission of a common cause, is what civilization is. Otherwise, we'd just kill each other. In other words, the human being is a religious animal. He's constructed a consciousness. He is a consciousness in his own mind in relationship to the Universe. These are the teachings of the *Course.*

If you can see with me that that is what you are, your progress can be very rapid, because you will be allowed to admit the frustration you are feeling about not being able to gratify your own consciousness existence. Do you see?

Say to me "Faith." It's not faith in something because my faith in something failed me. It has to be faith in something other than this. That's called Transcendental philosophy.

Questioner: Is that all I have to do?

That and shave your beard and cut your hair. (He did it a week later!) So after the long episode yesterday, most of you have some sort of admission that the continuity of conceptual existent association has undergone some sort of change, that has given you — at least hopefully — some joy. Now if it hasn't given you peace, maybe it's given you some agitation; a determination to continue to examine it, which is finally the same thing. I don't

41

teach peace of mind. I teach a reasoning process to determine it, and that's what my peace is. Jesus calls it function. If you really like the *Course*, and I just love it, Jesus says the function of your perceptual association is to discover through continuing temporal observations, Universal Mind — or who you really are with God. Did you understand me? Now the idea that Wapnick takes that and reduces it down doesn't make any sense. All you'd have to do is open it up, and you can see it's an offering of the transformation of your own mind.

We're going to distribute 10 million copies of the first fifty lesson books in the next year in all languages. You listen very carefully, if you handed me the *Workbook*, I don't care what philosophy I was in — I don't care if I was praying to some sort of gong god — I would understand that *A Course In Miracles* is a mind-training device to get me to an alternative association with myself. Is there a question on this? By denying what I am in association is what reality is. Have you looked at the *Workbook* at all? Be sure to look at copies of it here. It's against the law, but we're giving them away. We're not allowed to do that. We're not even not concerned about your appeal to astrology. I love it. Because if your mind is maturing in the nature of your transcendental correspondence with yourself, you will take the symbols that have been presented to you throughout all of man and give them a new meaning and purpose based on your new creative mind. Isn't that so? So that suddenly being a Capricorn makes more sense to you. Being an imperfect perfectionist makes a lot of sense to you. Capricorn is an imperfect perfectionist. And this is the dawning of the age of Aquarius; she'll have a water jug. So all of the so-called esoteric, revealing associations are actually a part of the continuity of your own passion of creative mind. That's why it's so much fun!

I know some of you are sitting there saying, "Oh, I'm really going to have to examine it." No, no. My philosophy is that you can experience the joy of God or reality and find a solution to you in the entirety of Eternal Life! Say: "Who are you talking about?" Who has the problem? If you don't have the problem, you won't need a solution. If you continue to examine me based on your cancer, what do you expect me to do about it? Cure you from cancer so you die of something else? There, I just took care of that little node you got there. In fact, you guys depend on your own little nodes, and then you fret about whether it's real or not without getting an examination, because you're both afraid that it will be and that it won't be. If it is, at least you have a fatalism with me; if it's not, you have to look for some other thing. Life is a sacrifice. Isn't that amazing? It's nice to be able to be heard! Your dependence on that is extraordinary because it's part of the justification and insistence of yourself. So your reason for being is an existent association trapped in such a limited formulation of itself that nothing has any meaning. If you refuse to accept the possibility that there is a manner through salvation, through Jesus Christ, through me, through anybody, or reassociating your own mind, you don't need me. Certainly I'm not going to deny you what you are within your own association.

If there's enough forbearance in you, based on my certainty to continue to examine perceptually Aristotle, I'd appreciate it. The conclusions that you will reach within you must be more than Aristotelian; they must involve the emergence of the passion of your mind in recognition that you are the creating forces of the Universe. If that comes down to "the salvation of the world depends on you" or "you have all power in the Universe" there's no requirement that you understand it, because you don't understand anything. The requirement is first that you can't understand it because you don't understand anything which is reasonable; and that since you don't understand it, there must be an alternative that you can't understand. However you arrive at that, you can say to me, "Well, I'm going to die before I find it out." That's what you still think. You still think time passes. You think thousands of years are passing and maybe I can never figure it out; but if I don't figure it out this time, I'll figure it out next time. What the hell does that mean? Well it means that next time — I didn't mean to do your reincarnation. This is called Pharisaical.

The Pharisees were the leaders in reincarnation, if you are familiar with that. Jesus never denied the Pharisees. All He said was when you come back, how is it going to be different? And the answer is: the place that I will come back to will be different. And I said: How will that solve my problem? How do I know how it's going to be? My teaching says that you're going to bring the world with you when you come. Do you understand? You brought this world with you when you came. And it's an entirety of your association. At least that gives you the solution. Otherwise, you'll separate the cause and effect; you'll come into this place, you're born, and you'll let this place tell you what you are. That's what the human condition is. And it will, and it does, and you do accept it. That's the process you've got to go through in your mind to determine what? The meaninglessness of this place. Somewhere you've got to say, "Yes, I know that's true, but how can I find the solution later on?" You have a right to know why you can't find the solution now, and why you must depend on your own termination to find the solution because it doesn't make any sense to me.

Now it may make sense to you; you want to make sense out of it because you are suffering from the Third Obstacle to Peace: The attraction of death. Since you can't solve the problem, you are attracted to death in the existent association that you are in in order to solve the problem for you. But to my mind, how is death going to solve my problem? If death will solve my problem, what is it? If death, if termination of myself will solve the problem, what is death? And you say, "I don't know." How does that solve my problem? "You'll know when you die." That doesn't make sense. It doesn't make sense to me that I would have to get old and suffer pain in order to know eternal happiness. It may not be senseless to you, but it is senseless to me. It would be senseless to anybody with a reasoning mind, if you'd look at it. Sacrifice doesn't make any sense to me. It makes sense to you because you are in the sacrifice of the exchange of the purpose for your life. The purpose for your life is to exist in a body and get old and die. What can I do for you? Then you say, "Help me exist better to die. *A Course In Miracles* teaches me that I can find happier ways to get sick and that I can improve my separate relationships to the point where they become whole." Never! Your associations are whole. Your concepts are what are keeping them from being what they are. You can't bring separation to truth. Do you hear that? Separate minds cannot communicate.

Are some of you experiencing new forms of communication? Do you find that you are better able to associate yourself with yourself? Why are you laughing? Since there is relief from the crap that you were in, you seem to have found something. This is just the fact of the matter. I'm offering you the entirety of the solution and you have to reject it somewhere because it's not justified in your conceptual association. That's why it's a miracle. You don't have cancer anymore because you don't have cancer anymore. There's no reason for it. You just don't have it. There was no reason for you to have it in the first place. Now I'm just teaching the *Course*. Having cancer was a decision you had made to justify your existent association with yourself and die. The purpose for which you came here was to exist in that association and die. What's wrong with that? Nothing. I hate it.

Questioner: Isn't sickness a justification for the performance of it?

How do you know that you are? I don't get that. Why don't you try to re-perform so you won't be sick? I discovered that all performance here is an indication of the existent association that justifies the aging process. All of your performance is justified, then, based on the previous historic reference. That's what life is. I exist within an association of a maximum potential and then I die. Now, within that association, I can perform any way that I want and attempt to find objective happiness.

45

That's the condition of the human being. That frustrated me. You told me that I could perform acts of charity or giving that would alleviate the problem. And I couldn't. No matter how much I attempted to alleviate the problem — as a doctor no matter how much I attempted to aid the suffering, no matter what I did (most of you are pretty much like this) other people continued to suffer and die. It was just a process in my own mind of what I wanted to serve, and was frustrated by my inability to render the entirety of the faith in God that I had in my own mind. The answer to it is the acceptance for the responsibility of the causation. This is *A Course In Miracles.* There is no other answer to it except that if I am the cause of this, because my mind is associated with God in it's entirety, if I can change my objective association with myself, that will heal — that's called healing. That's the power of my mind to heal you. Is it a power? Of course. Does it come from Universal Mind? Sure. Sickness is just justification for bodies.

Has everybody got Neo-Platoism? Existentialism? Remember the Skepticism? Remember the idolization — Jesus calls it: "Do you think you know what an idol is." He says an idol is any thought you have about yourself in association with someone else. He doesn't even hesitate. He says that. He says an idol is any thought you have where you prefer one over another. At that time you idolize it. Did everybody bring lunch today?

I would think at the very minimum that you would enjoy your participating in *A Course In Miracles.* That's why when you say, "I've been studying the *Course* for ten years. I'm a student of the *Course.*" I really don't understand that. A teacher and a student are the same thing. You are only teaching yourself. *A Course In Miracles* does not require a group of any kind. You could take *A Course In Miracles* and open it up and spring into Heaven. Some of you here when you listen to what I say immediately said "That's the guy I was looking for because he's teaching what it says" if you were *A Course In Miracles* student. Or "He's teaching what I want to hear

— that this is crap and that there's another way that can't be found in my own addiction to the world."

Wherever you are in your association with what appears to be conscious contact with God — is it okay if I call it that? — the basis of this program is to evolve in you continuing conscious contact with a happy harmony of reality that transcends your situation. Say to me, "That's not practical." Yes it is. It just offers you a continuing solution in a broader range of possibilities of the solution to your problem that you've locked yourself into. Can you hear this? The miracle of your mind is nothing but another way to solve the cause-and-effect problem that you think that you are in. Do you see? The frustration of not solving the problem based on the terms of the problem are what you experience as a human being. Say you heard me somewhere! If the problem is not immediately solvable, it must be that the application of the attempt to solve it is faulty somewhere in the relationship. This is the separation of cause and effect.

So you look for ingenuity — an invention — to solve the problem of how to get the stones up to build the pyramids, since they didn't have wheels. You would think that someone would have thought of the wheel. Instead of having to put rocks so they could roll these giant slabs up and then grab the rocks from the back and put them up front, that it would have occurred to somebody that a wheel would serve the same purpose. Can you hear me? Is the wheel an invention? It has to be an invention. I'm not sure I know how the wheel works. In my mind, if I take a slab, and I put the wheels underneath it, when I roll it, the wheels will still be there. You're saying that I can put things on and move and the wheels will turn along with me? Wow! How does a wheel work? You know how it works — what is it friction or what? Why is it that the vehicle moves — the axle doesn't move, does it? But there must be enough friction on the wheel — I'm beginning to get it. Does it involve grease? It probably needs some grease because if the axle is tight to the wheel, the wheel won't turn. You're very inventive. All I'm showing you is that you have an inventive mind. And the ingenuity that I'm offering you — I'm talking individually —will cause you a great deal of happiness because it's a happy feeling of having a justification for your own existence. I have a purpose!

When I give a good philosophical talk, I like to know whether you are understanding basically that you don't have to go six years to the philosophy department; I can give it to you in a couple hours. That's why they kicked me out of the philosophy department. I could never go to school. I had a problem with going to school. I always wanted one subject that incorporated all of the other subjects. There are some of those, and I looked at them, and all they do is retain the separation to justify their own associations rather than including them. Is *A Course In Miracles* a required course? It is a required course!

The idea that it is possible to accord instantaneous communication is already in the works. Do you understand quantum? It's already been determined that there will be methods of communication that are actually simultaneous, not in relationship with the speed of light. The reason it will come about is because it is reasonable. If the separation of cause and effect is reasonable at the speed of light, then communication is reasonable. It also becomes reasonable that the more rapid the communication, the closer the evidence will be to the truth of it. Do you understand? Time does not pass. If no time passes, the evidence will be immediately available to you. That would be what you would term very complete and true communication. At least it would be true and complete in the association to which it's directed. Boy, that's a hell of a step! That's what you're trying to do in your various images. It's like instantaneous communication that's a long way away: "Oh, that just happened this instant." Too late, it's gone because somewhere it involved the association of the cause and effect at the speed of light, so that it's always over.

The only real frustration that I ever felt as a human being was being unable to communicate what I was because I didn't know. Attempting to communicate with the knowledge that I didn't know what I was caused me to see a world in which everybody attempted to define their own limitations of what they thought they were. And it didn't make any sense to me. When I asked you the question of the meaning of life, you gave me an answer that was contained within the existent association of my own mind. You said the meaning of life is to be a householder for fifty years and then come to the temple with me and we'll study God together. I said screw you, I want to know now what the purpose of my being here is.

There is no such thing as meaning without purpose. Since you don't know the meaning of life, you give it a purpose of existence. The purpose then, which is the meaning of you, is to exist, and to get old as a body and to try to be happy, and to watch things that go on around you. So what can I do for you? How may I serve you? And you say, "Tell me what the solution is." There's no solution here because you can't be separate from everything. If you were separate from everything, there would be no solution. Now that made perfect sense to me. Did that not make sense to you? If you don't know who you are, how are you ever going to find out? I don't say I don't know who I am. You say, "I don't know who I am." Are you going to try to find out? You're going to try to find out, aren't you?

Response: "I've thought about it."

You're always trying to find out who you are. Not only are you trying to find out who you are, you are justifying your own existence. It doesn't take any thinking about it. You are always what you are in that association all the time. I just got through saying that. Your purpose, who you think you are, is to exist in that association. And that has begun to frustrate most of you, and I would think that it would. I would think that you would say: "What's the meaning of this? Why do I exist here? What is that out in the Universe? What do you mean a billion stars? What do you mean a trillion miles away? What do you mean a million years ago? How does that satisfy me in my association with my own mind?" And you say, "Well, it satisfies me." You don't need me. What do you need me for? I'm only interested in those who are saying, that's the basis of this whole talk, that there's got to be another solution beside this.

Those of you who have begun to have an experience — *have* in the sense that you recognize the crap of your conceptual association with yourself — that's what *A Course In Miracles* is. The philosophy that I am offering you is a continual change in the present condition in which you find yourself. I have no concern whatsoever about the conclusions that you have reached in regard to what you are. This is *Course* for a minute. All I want you to know about mind is that it thinks. You don't have to know anything else. There is no *ergo* in it. Your mind will *ergo* it sufficiently to reach conclusions of your consciousness condition; it's what you are. You cannot *not* reasonably reach the conclusions of the evidence of your own mind. Now, when I tell you that your evidence must be false because you don't know who you are, you are disturbed by that. But to my mind, an association that does not know what it is can only ask questions about not knowing what it is. It cannot accept the answer that very simply it is whole in everything that it is because it is, as Jesus calls it, the questioning aspect of separation. This is right out of the *Course*. It's the question that all human beings ask: "How did I get here?" "How did this happen?" "Who am I?" That's the condition that you are in. That's an indication of separation, isn't it? I am an indication of separation? Positively! I see it as a Universe out there; I'm separate from it. Otherwise I wouldn't be searching for myself.

The idea of "What am I?" is an indication that I am separate from what I am. Yes or no? It would have to be. All I'm telling you is to stop searching in your "I don't know what I am" because it's not in there. If I taught this in mathematics for a minute, if I separate myself from the entirety, the solution cannot be in the parts of the separation. It's impossible. So there must be an intervening association between the objective associations that are apparently in my mind that will integrate me to the reality of what I am. Einstein calls that a Unifying Force Field, a unifying energy of reality. We call it the Holy Spirit. Do you hear that? In other words, we say that there is a Holy Spirit or a wholeness of the unifying field of energy that will take the particles or wave association and convert them to an entirety of the particle/wave where you cannot distinguish between the potential, which is the particle, and the wave of continuing creative mind. Tell me you understood that.

I'm breaking up your particles! I'm showing you that in between all of the particles in your conception is the totality of an answer. All new physics teaches this. So don't tell me that there's not going to be a point of instantaneous communication, because I'm telling you that's exactly what I'm doing right now. If you'll admit to it, you won't be trapped in the old continuum of time that you're in. You will be in a different continuum. But you cannot express a different continuum without remaining in the one you are in. Do you understand? Your attempts to express it will confine you to the slow, laborious time of your need to examine all of the alternatives within your own mind, which I did. You know, Jesus says, "quit doing it, it won't work." But you go on examining the alternatives in your own mind. Let them go for a minute and, holy mackerel, the problem will be solved! "I tried it and it didn't work." Camel dung. It worked perfectly. You are already in a unifying association. All it means is that you refuse to accept an alternative that was not contained within the function of your own cause and effect.

Cause and effect are never separate. And I know that doesn't solve it for you. They are actually the same. Since that doesn't solve it for you, I'll give you a guarantee that any ideas you have never leave the source of your mind. That's reasonable to me. I mean, I use them all the time, but if I have an idea, when I think of it, it's certainly in my mind. I'm telling you that it never leaves your mind; that you have accessibility to every decision that you have ever made in regard to the conclusion you want to arrive at within your own mind. Got it?

51

You have a grid of intelligence. This is the first page of Chapter 31. We're going to read it to you. Is that reasonable? It's so reasonable that it's scary. I'll tell you, working with Jesus in the *Course* is so reasonable that you don't know what to do.

I remember, I was in my illumination, I picked it up and I started to read it. I had never seen this. It was delivered to me. I started to read it. "What is this?" And you know the first thought that came to me? "The world won't need me." I was aware that I was in illumination. I said: "Well, they already got it." It's already here, isn't it? All we'll have to do is open this up, and they'll see everything that I am because that's exactly it. Imagine, ten years later, fifteen years later, there's no admission of what it says because there's no admission of what you must say. The requirement is that you declare it. See, I'm offering you the solution in your own mind. You see? The solution is not in my mind. If you recognized it was in my mind, it would be your mind in the solution.

The reason that I haven't been allowed to communicate, I have a — what we call it in reality, I have terms for what my mind is — they are what they call eight gates. I've never been able to express this very much. Obviously my illumination did not come about by an historic factor. That is, it was not religious. Most of you know my story: I couldn't stand the world, I couldn't solve the problem, and God solved it. And I was certain in order to do that. It doesn't involve any doctrines except maybe the religious elements to the recognition that we discovered the truth in love of God by transformation. That's all it is. But I also discovered that I was emanating a power. I never even talk about this. See, I didn't know anything about this stuff. I didn't know anything about the *shaktipat*. I knew that people communicated emotionally with each other because I communicated. I know that when you want to buy encyclopedias, I knew there's an exchange. But I didn't know that I actually, in the certainty of who I was, actually generated a catalyst — I'm teaching this at a high level — of energy, where there would be a communication, or a joy expressed in what I am. I couldn't believe the crap I went through. I would go into the banker, and he'd try to give me money. Fact. That's just a fact of the matter. I was always a very gregarious guy, anyway, as much struggling as I did. I mean I communicated real well. And suddenly I saw that everything that I did — Phew! — I could do anything that I wanted. It didn't matter how meaningless it was. So that's called temptation. You be a little careful with that. Because I saw immediately I was going to get the result of that, and I didn't want it. It'll cause you a little travail. But that's a fact of the matter. I'll share this with you now because most of you are operating on a frequency of correspondence; this is called the keynoting. I'm actually giving you a keynote address. This is the beginning. There's a key or a note that sounds in our relationship with each other where we begin to communicate with energy. Do you understand me? It doesn't have to do with concepts at all. Certainly it has to do with the utilization of concepts so that when I say something to you, and you go: "Wow!" Why? We communicated based on a mutual recognition of a moment of correspondence of the love of God, or reality. That's simple. Remember that your individual association is literally a break in communication, and that while you have strived in any way possible to communicate — Jesus calls it devious associations— that you have still been using the power of your own mind in an attempt to express yourself.

So this teaching is the power of mind is available to you, with the admonition that if you misuse it in the corruption of your determination to accumulate, you'll get the result of that misuse. Why? There is only your mind. Class, did you hear me? You cannot, *not* get the result of the exchange that benefits you and deprives someone else because in effect you're depriving yourself. You're sharing the limitation of your own mind. Okay? The difficulty heretofore that you have had with this is there has been no one within the correspondence of you individually, in your own world, that gave you this continuing method of communication. Maybe you found it in the admission that Jesus Christ was resurrected, and it didn't do you any good. Maybe you found it in going to a temple, in Buddha, where you had a transcendental experience and went out into the world. What I am offering you is an entire new association of temporal identity, based on a propinquity of our association. Quite literally, you don't have to do anything around me. The difficulty that I have with that is you take the idea that you don't have to do anything around me and attempt to find a pacification justified by the belief that you can somehow avoid your own mind. You don't have to do that any more. What does Jesus say? *I need do nothing.* Say that to me.

The explanation has nothing to do with whether you do nothing or not. I just thought I would tell you that. You might well whisper that to yourself at the time the problem is not surmountable. "I'm going to stop trying to solve this. I'm going to let that solution come in." It never worked for me to tell me that the solution would come in. I would always try to solve it. But I would just broaden out all of the solution possibilities. So that's a transcendent experience for you. And it's true because it's contained within our communicative purposes of mind. The Universe is mind, single mind, and we are a total part of it.

Do you understand it would be impossible for you to want the solution that I am offering you and not have it immediately available to you? One or the other is not true. Now, how you examine that in your own mind is at least the correspondence of the admission that the problem can be solved in your own mind. So you won't confront somebody else to solve your problem. That's the beginning of it. The evidence that increases in your existentialism that the problem cannot be solved causes you to release it through the frustration of solving the problem. That's the whole teaching. Do you teach *A Course In Miracles?* If that's true, all communication is a miracle. That's a sentence in the *Course.* A miracle is nothing but a moment of identification of what you really are. Of course it's a miracle because it had nothing to do with what you thought you were. It didn't have to do with what you thought you were. If you don't hear that, it's because you don't want to. Why don't you want to? You've solved your problem. Do you hear me? I'm talking to you. I mean, I'm not trying to solve your problem for you. I'm telling you, it can't be solved. You say, "You're full of crap. I can too." I say, well, I couldn't. So you say to me, "Well, I can." Say to me, "I can solve my problem." Go ahead. I don't know. How do I know?

I can't help you with the process of solving your problem because I never was happy with the solution. Either that or I couldn't solve it and had to pretend I did. Or fake it and put the ego out in front of me and crouch down behind in the certainty that I had presented the camel dung out in front of me without being willing to examine what I really am behind me. I'm teaching the *Course* here now. As long as I had it out in front of me, as long as I've got my own stuff sticking out in front, I can use it as a protection against the admission of my helplessness. That's a fact for those of you who are really beginning to look at this. Are you helpless? How could something that doesn't know who he is not be helpless? It doesn't know where to turn in its own association to discover what it is. It finds itself confronted by all of these things to which there are apparently no answers. It's chaotic.

Those of you who believe you have some specific assignments in this association are very right. I wish I could teach this. All I'm doing is offering you the entirety of your mind. Stay with me in this. This will be real simple for you. I'm not offering you any identification of myself in a correspondence with you that is not transcendent. I'm not at all concerned about what you think you are. I'm only concerned that contained in what you think you are must be the ultimate happiness that you're seeking because it cannot *not* be a part of you. If I can get your attention to the fact that the problem can be solved in you, but not by your objective associations because they don't make any sense, the quantum of reality in you will come to your memory. That's a fact.

The difficulty and the frustration that you feel in this is that you're teaching the experience without the experience.

You are literally teaching the experience to the denier of the experience. Do you hear me? Now I'm teaching *Course In Miracles*. The last thing that the association wants to hear from you. — and I'm telling you this is a fact — the reason you never came to me before, was you didn't want to believe that no matter what you do in your own association, you cannot solve the problem of what you are, that all of your values are based only on getting sick and dying, and that there is no solution. Yet that's the only message that I can give you because as you are contained within your own mind, there is no solution. You cannot in reality be separate. Do you understand? But the entire structure of your human condition is to justify the separation. And you are extremely energetic and have a great deal of ingenuity in the power of your mind to justify your own existence. Because that's what your value system is.

When I tell you that you love murder, it's very difficult for you. But obviously, you must love death or why do you die? The things that you love die. Don't tell me you can disconnect the things that you love from death because you can't. And that pisses you, but you can't. Therefore you must love death. It must attract you. You must be a part of that association in your own mind. I know you're going to end up saying, "there's nothing I can do about it" and that's the way it is with you. But I couldn't stand that. I couldn't stand the idea that the things I loved all rotted and died. Can you hear me? I'm telling you the frustration that caused me to have the experience. This is an unjust, unfair place that pissed me off. It's simpler than that: Why do the good die young? And the murderers live on for fifty years? It's not fair. You're talking to a guy who saw his best friends killed right next to him. And damn it, it's not fair. There has to be something else besides it. That's a fact of the matter. You can tell me all you want that it's got to rain on the good guys and the bad guys. My answer is, then how in the hell do you tell the difference? You say, "Well, we'll find the answer later on." The hell with you. I don't know if I can understand "I'm under no laws but God's" but I can understand the futility of the laws of man. It's very understandable that the only outcome to the laws of existent civilization are to exist and die. Yes or no?

Am I all right? I've got a tremendous amount of energy that I'm retaining. The reason I'm retaining it is that I want somewhere for the Pentecost to find reason in you, through you. It would be almost impossible to come into this accumulative association and not begin to have experiences. I want you to have the joy of the freedom of your heart in your love for the moment of this expression. I teach physical resurrection. I teach you "Yes, that's true" and the entirety of your mind association is a body identity. I'm actually teaching resurrection in its entirety. That requires your mind as well as what you call your heart. Finally, you will listen to me because my process has become reasonable to you. I'm not concerned about the manner in which it becomes reasonable. The reason you are sitting with me now is that what I'm saying is reasonable to you. "Well, I'm just going to have to accept it." Camel dung! That may be good initially, but you're going to have to evolve.

You asked me about discipline yesterday. You only accept it to the part where you realize that you can come and take this seat any time you want to. I'm giving you the fact of the matter. I'm not offering you anything but what everything in the Universe knows. Everyone in the Universe knows there's no such thing as this. How would you be separate from everything that is? I'm sorry for the mistake.

Questioner: Sorry for what?

I'm sorry that I screwed it up for you; that you're sitting there in that piece of crap you're in. That's a fact of the matter. It was a screw up. I got the body to tell you it's not true. That's called resurrection. My mind is resurrected. This is Jesus Christ of Nazareth. I'm offering you the solution. I'm actually appearing momentarily in resurrection. You can't hear me. I'm a resurrected body. I'm not from here. I came to take you home. You couldn't possibly be able to understand that unless you wanted to. If you give my body your identity, you'll be locked in the association. If you don't, you'll see it as an image of transformation. Obviously you can't teach it because those who saw Jesus — obviously Jesus came back from the dead and He stood around like this — went: "Wow! It's really Him." But when they went out into the world, what good did that do them? They said, "We know a guy that was a carpenter, and He died and He resurrected." They said, "Yeah, camel dung. Show me. Where is He?"

It's an amazing idea, and the problem is that you think that spirit is not solid. Somehow you have an idea that there's physicality and there's spirit. I've never been able to tell the difference, anyway. I'm going to be what I am in my entirety. That's the freedom of your mind to recognize me and not identify the continuing crap of your own mind. That's nothing but a process of your own revelation, isn't it? And obviously you are a process of the denier of God. You are totally a denial of eternal life. Now, if you want to read the *Course*, please get a copy and read it. There's no in between in it. Time is nothing but a denial of eternal life. Do you understand? Time is nothing but the idea that life begins and ends.

Questioner: The misunderstanding was you said I'm practicing something all the time. And I asked you just to explain to me what you meant by practicing something.

You're practicing being something on the planet, something within your own containment. You're practicing and justifying being a body. You're practicing and justifying murder and death and loneliness. You practice it in everything you do, and you justify it in your own association, and it's not true. You've been a liar from the moment you came into this association. There's no truth in you at all, none, zero. Anything true would know what it was because truth is knowing what you are. If you don't know who you are, you're a liar. I just turned that around a little. What it really means is that you don't want to know who you are.

Questioner: I'm telling you that I do.

Okay, then you will. And the process of knowing that is an admission that you don't know. But each time that you think you know, you cannot learn. Because as soon as you think you know, you have justified the association. Give him a copy of the *Workbook*. In ten days he'll be gone and he won't even come back and give me a hand. Can you hear this? He already has and did and I already know what he is doing. It's impossible that I'm not instructing him in exactly what he wants to hear. He's going to say exactly the same things he's always said to me. This is a very personal reference for you. It's impossible literally that I am not offering you what you asked me to offer you if you are trapped in time, because obviously I'm offering you the solution to the problem that you're having. And obviously you must know what the solution is even though you refuse to accept it. Jesus really talks about this. He says that all we're really doing is setting up memory continuums to remember this together. And you assume the role of that time association and bring with you all of the identifications of the continuance of your own mind, based on a perfect reference you have of what you really are. That's what you're doing with me right now.

Jesus says, "Bring yourself and all of the people that are with you." And you're saying, "Who are you?" And I'm saying, "I'm the guy you know from out of time who sent you here, and you forgot the instructions that I gave you." So I come down into this crap and give you the instructions, and you say, "Who the hell are you?" And I say, "Don't you remember? I sent you here." Like Jesus said, everybody who is here came from Heaven. That's a lovely sentence. He says you know perfectly well that you came from heaven and you're going back. You just forgot. Is the word "amnesia" in the *Course?* The great amnesia. You can't remember who you are. I'm reminding you that you came into this journey and got screwed up. I'm telling you literally. That's why you don't know who you are. I'm here to tell you you're not from here. There's no such place as this. The expedition already left. We're not here anymore. They left you behind. No wonder you're pissed. Can you hear it? I'm sorry. I already apologized to you. You say, "Why should I trust you now? You screwed me up before." Then don't. Stay where you are. See how valuable forgiveness is? You cannot know it is not real until you forgive it. Once more. You cannot know it is not real until you forgive it. The moment you forgive it, it will not be real to you because you're the cause of the conflict. Am I doing all right? You laugh now.

Questioner: I am that.

I bet you are, too. I have no reason to doubt you. I have no reason to doubt any of your associations with yourself.

Questioner: What's the association in hell?

I have no idea.

Questioner: Nor have I.

Okay, if you have no idea who you are, then why do you...

Questioner: But I say "I am that," the inexpressible. It doesn't mean that I don't know who I am. But I acknowledge I can't say who I am.

Who does?

Questioner: The "I" that is all.

Camel dung. The "I" that is all knows what it is. Don't crap me. If you're going to look at it with me, look at it. You know perfectly well who you are.

Questioner: I say it knows what it is, but this, this apparent separateness, can't say. He's unable to say.

Why? All he has to say is "I am what I am through the Universe."

Questioner: I am.

Okay. Then why aren't you eternally happy? You told me that there was eternal happiness and joy.

Questioner: And why not?

I don't know. It hasn't anything to do with me. I see this world is very painful and death. I see slaughter and pain going on here.

Questioner: It is not.

Not what?

Questioner: It is not. It is not painful. It is. It is not painful.

Well, it was painful for me.

Questioner: If it's painful, I'm in ignorance. It is.

No, I suffered crap here. You go ahead.

Questioner: I'm not denying that.

Yes, you are. You said it's not painful.

Questioner: Right, it's not painful. There's no solving people. It's all imagination. Right now, this is what we've got. This is very, very beautiful. It is. It's not even beautiful. It just is. There's no answer to thought. It is what is without characteristic. So what I am is what is without characteristic. Please shoot me down, but that's all I can see.

That's just Muktananda camel dung.

Questioner: It's not Muktananda. It has nothing to do with...

I don't know, but it's just camel dung. You're presenting me with the condition of your own mind. I'm not questioning it. I'm in a world where I see a lot of pain and loneliness and death, and it's real to me. You don't need me. You've solved your problem. Each time I look around, I see what's going on, and I'm in a service of the power of my mind to relieve it. I don't need a flipping definition of myself. My definition of myself is to be that, to be — this is Christianity — to be a servant of God in the realization that the power of my mind to bring about peace and happiness.

Questioner: I heard you just say it, to be that. This is what I'm saying. I'm here to just say. You mirrored it back to me. If there's any truth in what I said, I'm wanting to hear it back.

Okay.

Questioner: What am I missing?

Nothing. You're just saying *cogito ergo sum.* I'm just going to go back into Existentialism. The hell with it. I'm not going to do it again. "I think; therefore I am." I have no doubt about that.

Questioner: No, but while I think, I don't know who I am.

What nonsense is that? While you think, you know exactly who you are. You know who you are that you think you are.

Questioner: Why have a quantitative process?

Do you know why it's hard to teach this? I'm teaching that duality and singularity are the same thing. It's hard for him to see that his self is all that there is. In fact, he can be as corrupt or as unreal as he wanted to be, he's only his own self, and that separation is just exactly as real as unity. It's the fact of the matter. Boy, that's a hell of a step. Is that in my Prayer talk? Be sure you get my Prayer talk.

Questioner: The separation is real as unity?

Of course.

Questioner: It is?

It would have to be. At the moment that it's real. Fortunately there's no such thing as time. That's the difference between separation, which is time, and reality. They're both real within their own worlds. Holy mackerel. This is the whole teaching.

Questioner: If I say, "I am thou..."

What do you mean, "I am thou?" Who would say that? Why would you have to say it? I don't get what the hell you're talking about. Everything that knows what it is doesn't say, "I'm the only living Son of God."

Questioner: Am I saying that?

I don't know. You're saying: "I am thou" or "I am that." I have no...

Questioner: I'm saying, if I separate, I'm just expressing ignorance, aren't I?

No, you're expressing knowledge. You're acknowledging the separation. That's not ignorance. That's knowledge.

Questioner: That's what the separation is. From existentialism: "I think I am," yes. But you're not saying that that is true. That was your frustration.

And you are, so there's nothing I can do about it. That's true. Because my alternative has nothing to do with your expression. And that's why we teach transformation. This is the confrontation, incidentally, that you can get over a bottle of Jack Daniels. Anybody can do it. You're not telling me anything that I didn't realize. You're not telling me that I didn't feel anything but the total frustration —telling me that pain is imaginary was always crap to me. That's crap. That hurts. And there's no way that I can subtract that from my arm.

Questioner: But those starving millions are pure imagination...

Camel dung. Those starving millions are very real. And I'm a part of that in this body.

Questioner: Where are they?

You want to take a drive with me and...

Questioner: No, that's imagination. Right now, I have no back, I have no heart, I have no organs, I have no back of the head, I have nothing. It's imagination. Those starving millions are imagination.

Whose? Whose imagination? Whose are they? Whose imagination?

Questioner: Well, I don't have them. You tell me.

You don't recognize the world as a place of suffering at all?

Questioner: If I go out in the world and I see what I perceive as suffering, yes, I do. I'm saying right here, now...

What do you do then? Avoid going out or what?

Questioner: No, not at all.

Well, why don't you go out and see it? Why don't you go out and see them suffer?

Questioner: Well, why not? I don't deny that...

Well, come on. You don't answer my question. Why don't you go out and see that they're all...

Questioner: No, that's all right. I'm talking there's only now. Now there's no suffering in this room that I can see.

Only because you've isolated yourself from it. You've isolated yourself in your own mind from it. You don't want to hear me. I'm teaching you are the cause of your suffering.

Questioner: Yeah, I can hear that.

No, well, then hear it. Don't try to isolate yourself from it. What he misses entirely is that if his brother's in pain, so is he. He's already rejected it. It's very valuable for you to hear this. The more you feel your brother's pain, the more you'll attempt to relieve it. When you discover you can't relieve it, you'll stop trying to share the pain and share the solution given you by God.

Questioner: Well, if I've given you something I don't know to be true, Chuck, I apologize. I've given you a teaching. It's untrue.

Of course. All teaching is untrue. It has nothing to do with what reality is at all. My whole first hour was a discussion of what I was trying to get you to look at. How he constructs Chuck in his own mind, I have absolutely no idea. All I can guarantee you is when he said "Chuck" he was constructing himself. I guarantee you that whatever he thinks I am in my entirety is nothing but his own hate, whatever that is, is an association that has given me an identity separate from himself. It's not true. The more we correspond with each other, the happier we will be in our separation. But our correspondence in entirety will transcend the necessity for separate identification and does.

Boy, what a strange idea. I was looking at having a name. I just looked at that for a minute. This is why I've avoided this. You think that somehow the experiences that I underwent justify my awakening. It's really not true. It's not true. It's just an observation of the futility of this, contained within this association. Otherwise, you'll say, "Well, if I had had your experiences, I'd feel the way you do." I am those experiences, and you are having them. That's nice.

Where the dilemma is, for those of you who want to share the difficulty of teaching miracle mindedness, is that I am only teaching Transcendentalism. See, I'm in a continuing condition of offering you reality. See? That association says I am here and I'm not. There's a lot more to the Universe than what you see out there, a billion stars and a crappy little body and the crappy associations of yourself. That is not what Life is. If this existence within this basis of time, of cause and effect, examination of your consciousness in regard to the denial or assertion of it are what life is to you, that will be what life is. I'll do it once more for you; stay with me because I'm leaving. There's nothing I can do about your determination to be what you are, except to offer you a continuing alternative to it if you are examining alternatives.

I'll give this talk from the *Course*. Would you like it out of the *Course?* Since you believe you are separate, the solution has to be change. In reality nothing changes, but that's a complete abstraction. Nothing has to change because there's nothing for it to change to. The solution to separation has to be change. You have to be searching for a choice in your own mind. This is actually a sentence out of the *Course*.

Now, the admission that each moment that it is changing and that you cannot solve the problem in a manner of identification with the change will afford you a very rapid reassociation of your own mind, and should cause you to become fairly happy and creative without the necessity to define happiness. That is, happiness may well be a definition in your own mind; but if it is, it will be limited to the definition you have given yourself in regard to the possessions of having thoughts in association with yourself. And you believe me, brother, when you have thoughts in association with yourself, they are very real. They are real because you possess them in your own mind. It's the difference between having and being. Having and being are actually the same thing. You can't *have* thoughts about anything. It's impossible. It is impossible. You can possess thoughts of your association with yourself. But what is it that possesses them, and why? Why need you be a formulation of conceptual association that possesses an identity? Reality is not a possession of any kind. It's a creative giving of yourself in your mind. Any possession of a correspondence of objective reality is simply not eternal. And if it is not eternal, it is not life.

Actually most of you are at the point where you see that the requirement is for a little Neo-Platoism, isn't it? You're going to have to take the process of your mind and admit that you are in a transient solution to an impossible problem. That is, the species of man, if you want to do it that way, is emerging from the chaos of an association with time and eternity to the realization that he's eternal. He suffers from split mind. He doesn't know whether he comes from here; but he knows about out there. Wow. So you're either from here or there, but you can't be from both. You're either in time, destined to correspond to a beginning or an end, or you're out of time and before and after time was. That's how simple this is.

One of the first questions I asked in my mind, for those of you share my dilemma, was "What was there before time began?" That's a very legitimate 7-, 8-year-old question. "Well, nobody knows that. More time." So then I'd say, "Yeah, but before time began and after it's over, what is it?" "We don't consider that." "Why not?" "That's not in our consideration. We don't know what we were before that." "Oh." You don't know who you are, where you came from, or how you got here. You're living in an illusion, locked in a little bubble, spinning around a little hot thing that you identify as a gas. There's billions of them, and you're trapped in a cigar box. You have no idea what you are in your own mind.

One thing I know for sure: It seemed little to me. The human condition finally seemed little to me. The ego, the justification for all things human, didn't finally make any sense to me. They all resulted in the same thing, anyway. I was not happy with that. So when I was not happy, I was in pain. And when I was in pain, I said: "There's got to be another solution to this." So I attempted to find another solution by reordering my life. Most of you have been through this for the last forty thousand years. You just keep ordering and reordering: There's another way, I can find the solution. And at the time you discover it, it seems very reasonable to you because you're addicted to the idea of death and that the solution to the problem can be found within the beginning and the end. And it can't. It can't. Not only is that true, but the invention of time is an indication that you know it's true. Wouldn't it be? In other words, if you know you're in time, you must know of something before time was and after time ended.

You know the other thing I couldn't stand? That eternity was a long time. I didn't like that. I hated it. I was unhappy with my existence. And you said: "When you get to Heaven, you'll be happy." And I said, Why? How does longevity solve my problem? "Well, you get to eat all the watermelon you want." Yeah, but I ate all I wanted here and I got tired of it. This is Ecclesiastes. If you haven't read Ecclesiastes, read it. That's your assignment. Ecclesiastes is 3000 years old and expresses exactly the frustration of any human being: "Vanity, vanity, all is vanity." Two words that are used in Ecclesiastes are "vanity" and "vexation." Life is a vanity and it vexes me that no matter what I do, everybody finally gets the same end, anyway. That's a fact of the matter.

I'll share this with you because you know the answer perfectly well. All you said to me is: "I'm not in pain." In case you want to know. That's it. That's just it. So it means "Somebody may be, but..." I couldn't accept the Eastern tradition, that this is an illusion except that I would be a total part of it. That's Christianity. It just moves from Buddha to Christianity.

Questioner: I want to wrap this imagination up, then. You know, that's what I'm trying to do, wrap it up.

You can't because the entirety of imagination is what truth is. Anything that you can picture in your imagination is true.

Questioner: But it's always partial.

First because you think some things are real and some imaginary. I guarantee you, you can't tell the difference. You can't. It's impossible. You just can't. It's impossible. You try to control it, whether it's imaginary. Generally speaking, if it's imaginary you dream it within your own association and keep your own self separate from it. So you set up storybook characters that you can imagine. Now, you allow yourself to participate in them to the extent that you're the good guy and not the bad guy. Although some of you may want to be the bad guy. But you're always playing a part in your own association of mind. Boy, this is nice. This is called *The Dreamer of the Dream* in the *Course*, if you haven't read it.

Questioner: What is the difference between illusion and real?

Not any. The question is not a valid question. Not because you do not think there is, but there is no such thing as differences in reality. There can be differences in apparent reality, but the "sourcefulness" of them will cause no conflict in your mind. The only reason there could be a difference is if you're in conflict. If you're in no conflict about what you are, there is no difference. This is all *Course*, isn't it? That does not mean that we would not observe differences in our own mind. I'm not trying to teach you that we do not see differences. I'm showing that you see them in the unity, first of all, in the purpose of why we're here — that's to get the hell out of here; and second, that the certainty that if we apply the power of our determination to get out of here, we will join in that unanimous effort. Because it's impossible to have a common goal without joining the effort. You cannot say, "I'm going to share this with you" and have us not have the power of one mind. Separate things may be separate, but a common goal leads unto God because God is a common goal. It's not defined by the separation but by the admission of a common goal that transcends the association of our minds.

So I'm asking you to come on a goal with me of something that you can't know about. I'm asking you to take a leap of faith. I'm asking you to look at the frustrations that you are experiencing within your own mind. I am offering you an alternative that is not of this world and that you cannot know about until you take the first step. Once you take the first step, which is what I'm teaching, you will immediately be able to make legitimate choices in regard to whether you prefer that or this. This is one of the principles of miracles. Until that time, there's no possibility of the transformation. The idea that you could choose between what is nothing and what is also nothing is the condition you're in. The entire purpose of the *Course In Miracles* is the sentence that told you that if one thing is not real, another cannot be more real. None of this is so. Obviously that's an experience, isn't it?

Questioner: I don't know.

What do you mean, you don't know? It would have to be an experience because you think that this is real.

Questioner: Someday I will know what's real.

And you never will, either. No, you can't.

Questioner: Someday...

No, you can't. There's no way that you can because you don't want to. You'd rather just examine it in your own association, which is another way of saying that you haven't had enough pain. You have to feel the frustration of the ego with your experience. Until then, you'll be on that treadmill to oblivion. You'll just keep repeating it in your own mind. Not only is that true, but you will believe that the solution is evident to you. The more rapidly that you are disillusioned by the solution, the closer you will be to the truth. When you no longer can find any solution, you might just ask for help, which you never intended to do. So the whole teaching is nothing but: Ask for help and mean it, not based on the terms for the solution you want, but on the determination that you can't solve the problem. That's an experience. You bet your boots that's an experience. That's why we get together to share the experience of God that we gain by the surrender of our own associations. For goodness sake! That's fairly simple.

Then you say to me, "I'm never going to do that." And I'll say, of course not, you're not in enough crap yet. But as Jesus says, everybody has to come to this point eventually — it's called a bottom. Finally everybody has to come to a point where they say, "I can't stand this." It's not an identification; it's a realization. It's Gethsemane. What's Jesus call it? The last useless journey. Christianity is an incredible thing, isn't it? The admission of the fallibility of Jesus Christ, the savior, is the greatest thing that ever happened to any philosophy because it is the admission of the ultimate inability of conceptual mind to discover God. It's been denied for 2000 years. In 2000 years nobody wants to admit to the fallibility of Jesus Christ. But that's not so, finally; in His own association, how in the frick is He going to save you? It's impossible for Him to save you unless He felt the ultimate frustration of the realization that there was no justification for what He was doing at all. Have you got that, class? That's an experience. Jesus talks about this. He calls it a useless journey. That doesn't mean that He didn't make it. He's all set to be the savior of the world, and who better qualifies? He's been baptized, receives the dove, seen the dove, He's been tempted by the devil, everything that could possibly happen. He's healing — literally, He's actually raising the dead and He's got all sorts of power, and they obviously are going to attack Him and kill Him for no reason — except that He's offering them the truth of what He is. It's an amazing idea. In His Gethsemane, He goes out and He says to God, "They're doing this to me, and all I did was tell them I love them. All I did was to try to show them how wonderful I am. All I did was to take their mind through these works." His mistake was raising Lazarus. He was okay until He raised Lazarus. He turned out to be a good buddy. Jesus knows perfectly well that body is not real; yet He felt the pain of the body of Lazarus, he was still stunned. When they said to Lazarus, "How was it when you were dead." He said, "Very much the same as it is here." He was utilizing the power of His mind in the demonstration of His body, which is what the human condition is. Here He is, all alone in the garden, and He's sitting there. All the wonderful things that were going to happen to Him, all of the determinations that He had with the power of God to work miracles — His disciples are what? Asleep. His disciples are asleep; He didn't bother to wake them up. They've already resigned themselves to the fact that He's going to get it. So He goes out alone and He says, "Father, God (like many of us) I'd appreciate it if you'd give me a little hand. Father, help me with this. I'm having a problem." What does God do? Nothing! Nothing! God does not know of sacrifice. God does not understand the relationship of your mind presented with the truth.

That's pretty tough. "God, I've done everything you told me to do." It's like the rich man parable a little bit. (Matt.19:16-22) "How come I can't get this?" That's His dilemma. Isn't that incredible? Do you know what I love about it? It's an incredible religion. The last thing — the second to last thing that your savior says is "my God, my God, why hast thou forsaken me?" (Matthew 27:46) What the hell kind of a savior is this? He's the savior that you need to admit that the solution cannot be solved by the separation. This is very advanced theological Christianity. What does He decide to do? "Father, into thy hands I commend my spirit." (Luke 23:46) It reduces to: I can't; He will if I let Him. That's the 12 Step program. The problem is always being solved if you let it be solved. He also threw in "it is finished." (John 19:30) He actually didn't say that; but it sounds good.

So we'll end this with a little Greek philosophy. And in the association of your conceptual mind, you might want to look at *A Course In Miracles* again. It will tell you that all of your self-conceptions, justified by the reasonableness of your existence, can be enhanced and increased immeasurably by the continuing admission of a solution that transcends your association. It's basic Neo-Platoism, not reduced to Existentialism — that I can solve the problem within my own mind — because that denies the admission that I'm using a power to solve the problem. That's the fundamental admission that there is an entirety of reality of which I am an association. All power is given unto you in Heaven and earth. If you construct it in the association of your own mind, you will get the derivation of the antecedental causation of your existence.

In my writing of this, I would write down this whole long association. The difference between the scribe and that is that I knew exactly what I was saying. I'm just trying to express it. When we try to express our relationships with each other, in separation compared to knowing we're from Heaven — or certainly knowing somewhere else, for all I know it's the Pleiades, but I know it's not here, I know this is just a temporary place; it's minuscule, this has a beginning and an end. We inevitably tell stories. You are a story about how you got here, what happened, all of the so-called imagination that you use are descriptions of our relationship with the Universe. What an extraordinary place to be in, to be able to construct in your own mind associations.

Your stories usually have beginnings and ends, don't they? "And they lived happily ever after." You tell that story within the association. The more you are able to enter into the parable of your own association with yourself, the more you will be willing to see that you are playing a part in a scenario of a scene of a cause-and-effect relationship. This is the old Flat Earth talk. You are actually playing a part within this association, as Shakespeare would say. You come onto the scene and you play that part in your own mind. Is that a part you were designated to play? When you came here, you were pretty much locked into the part that somebody told you that you had to play. Yes or no? Certainly you had limitations as to the part you were expected to play in the association. Most of you in this room rebelled against it. You said, "Screw you, I don't like the part that you gave me. I'm going to find another part." So you fought a revolution and killed me, or did something. You played another part. But you weren't entirely satisfied with the part you got. Finally, the most you could do was fiddle while Rome burned. I guess the idea that you've assigned yourself your own part has value, doesn't it? The question is not that, the question is, are you happy with the part you've given yourself? Inevitably you're not really happy with the part because you've given yourself a part that you're not at all certain or secure in the knowledge of what you are. So you play out the part as it seems to be the best you can do under the circumstances — which is nothing but an admission that the circumstances were here when you came, and that somehow you had to adhere to them in the principle of the separation of cause and effect. What a place to be!

Questioner: You've used the word "ascension." Could you say something about that?

Ascension? Look at it as maybe a black hole explosion. Ascension is any motion from any aggregation of point, which couldn't be real. An ascension, in the sense of moving out, is the idea of a space/time location that contains a potential of energy association that can ascend using the power of itself. Let's say that ascension would be burning coal. In that sense, you are increasing the temperature. It's an ascension of the molecular association using energy based on fission. Does that help? I'm trying to give you an answer. Ascension doesn't have any meaning, except it must be an ascension from something to something. If you are coming from something, it must be a location of where you think you are in that association. I have to do something with that leg, or I'll just ascend out of here. Do you see that? You love the idea of ascension, the idea that you can find a bright reality. The problem is not that, the problem is where you base your assumption of the necessity is limited to the correspondence you have allowed yourself in the use of the material of your own potential. Who heard that? That's nothing but the use of the energy that is carbon-based to demonstrate the power of the expansion. Do you see that? That's exactly what we do. In fact, it's what the condition of space/time is, isn't it?

A star is nothing but the ascension from the coal of the relationship with the helium and the oxygen, out into the power of that. The idea of ascension, or coming from something below to something above, could not be true in reality. But that didn't solve my problem. My problem was I knew there was something out there and I couldn't get to it. I discovered I couldn't get to it using the potential that I had been given by the world, because the world was a demonstration of the limitation of potential, rather than the admission of the entirety of the black hole, which would get me out. There was nothing outside of me that would prevent me from having a body resurrection.

So I teach the potential of your DNA, which you call your memory association. It contains a factor that involves not only what you call fission, or use of the material within your own body, but what you would call fusion, or the entrance of the hydrogen molecular association to the entirety of the power of your mind. In other words, reality is not "using up." Class? In space/time, reality is using up. God does not use things up. This is the whole quantum theory, for goodness sake! Why am I talking to you about quantum? The whole idea is that the whole Universe contains all of the energy of the entirety of the association. The most incredible energetic association in slow time is water. That's a fact. I mean water in the intimacy of its relationship with itself. H_2O, hydrogen and oxygen are exploding at a rate — that's why we're here in this illusion. We come from the water. We come from hydrogen and oxygen. But the power contained within water would instantly destroy us, so we walk on top of it or swim in it. But the fact of the matter is that we're 98 percent water anyway. But we're afraid to utilize the power of the association, except in the limitation of the combination of other elements. You get a little helium and a little barium; we have to end up with carbon. And nitrogen. Phew! Right after carbon comes nitrogen. Can you get that? We have to burn that crap, and it doesn't smell too good. We're in compounds of associations of energy.

You can have carbon-based life, but you can't make it real because life is eternal; and if it's based on carbon, it sure as hell is going to get used up. That's the futility of the second law of thermodynamics. I hate it. I couldn't understand thermodynamics because it says that whatever the potential is, I could be used up. And I'd say, "And then what?" Where did the potential come from? "We don't worry about that; let's just depend on the potential that we have." So by evolving our potential, we could use more and more in our own association with each other. And that's what establishes time because you were told you had a great deal of potential to be a great classic pianist. Now you feel the frustration of not fulfilling your potential. Why don't you fulfill the potential of being what you are — an entire, beautiful, loving creation of God, eternal in the love of yourself and your brother. For goodness sake. Nobody felt the frustration of not being a classic pianist more than I did. Why weren't you one? I didn't have the discipline to be one. I saw that if I was the greatest pianist in the world, I would only be the greatest pianist in the world. It wouldn't gratify me. Most of you in this room are not satisfied by the credential of your limited potential correspondence. You see that no matter what the potential is here, it all ends up in the same crap.

The only real question that we ever come together to ask, if you really want this in the vernacular, is "What the frick am I?" "What is this?" "What am I doing here."

Questioner: What can we do, then?

There's nothing you can do. That's my answer. Now what? Just be you, and die. There has to be a solution outside of your own association. The "we" is obviously some sort of generic association of separate minds. I'm demanding it to the attention of it's individual capacity to experience this. It has nothing to do with the other associations at all. If you can hear this, it will really help you. Obviously that will get up and walk out because it would be the admission of the causation within your own mind, that you are causing the pain of your brother. It's not true because I say it is; it's true because the power of your mind is what this situation is. You got it? That can cause you a great deal of pain and unhappiness; and it can also cause you a great deal of pleasure. All I'm really trying to get you to look with me at what Jesus said: There is no world. The entire purpose of *A Course In Miracles* and my offer to you in the transition of your conceptual association is to promise you that if life is eternal, there is no such thing as the existent association in which you find yourself. Your continuing need to discuss it with me is only your justification in the very limited form of your self identity. Obviously you are not using a million degrees. Obviously you're not using 1000 below. You're not using any part of the Universe. You're limited to this carbon-based nothing, you breathe poison (oxygen), you live within this body, and you call it yourself. To hell with you. This is *A Course In Miracles*.

So the sign says "I am not a body, I am free. I am still as God created me." It means that. It doesn't mean that you nod your head. It means that you are reality. It means that this was a dream. It means that you are waking up from that. Who do you think I'm talking about? Your own self-conceptions justify the existence of yourself. If you couldn't be in pain, you couldn't be here. If you didn't lose the things you love, you couldn't be here. If you couldn't get cancer, suffer pain, you couldn't be here. That's what the earth is; so that's what you are because you are a part of it. Then you say, "Well, I've got to look around in my mind to find out what he's talking about."

I'm talking about eternal life. I'm talking about God. And you say, "Well, I've just got to have faith." Why? God's going to be God whether you have faith or not. Your faith has nothing to do with God. If you think it does, then I'd suggest you have it. You must be admitting that you don't have faith in Him, or why would you require faith? Faith is the reality of the certainty of what you are. If I were going to have it, I'd sure have it in something I didn't understand, because faith in something I understood always frustrated me because I knew it had to be crap, because I was crap. We can all present our own crap to each other and then hide behind the fact, except after three or four drinks, that we didn't know who the hell we were — but then it didn't matter.

So, there's nothing new under the sun. Your new minds are beginning to be exposed to reality. This is the great cover-up, your minds are so thick, you are in such deep poop here, there's no excuse for this at all. Do you understand? This is deep crap. You're just examining yourself in slow time. Come on, put your toys away. Paul would say come up with me — when I was a child, I thought as a child; but I've grown up. At least come up and take a look at where you are; you might prefer to be up here. Nobody who uses more than 4% of his mind is going to be here. Come on up and see — Jesus calls it the real world. For a minute come up and take a look at the crap that you've been in. You say, "Can I do that?" Yes. But you can't go on being in the crap. It requires that you get out of it!

Isn't it amazing that the step that you take out of time is the only step you really take. All of your other steps are just repetitions of putting forward where you intend to go. As long as you can sequence that, as long as I know what's there, I can take the step. I'm sure as hell not going to take the step into something I don't know. I'll crawl off. As long as I have a previous construction in my mind, I can project that from my own memory in my mind and have a place that I can step based on where I was. So I become a relationship of where I was with what? Where I was. This is the *Workbook*. I'm a relationship of where I was before projected into where I was before, or where I intend to be. But as soon as I take the step, it only can be where I intended to go.

Do you mean that if I come to a place and have no intentions, I won't have to take the step or I will? Yes? The answer is yes?! You involve time and space at the same time. You mean if I took the step in time, I would also take it in space? I bet you can't prove that. You know what you'd have to have? You'd have to have an image of an association who took the step and one who didn't. There's a great deal of conflict in that. This is an image, this is an illusion. If I'm about to take a step in an illusion, it's impossible that if I have the idea in my mind that I did not take the step. Somewhere in the old association I must have taken it. Or how do I know about the step I'm going to take? Somewhere I've got to refuse to take the step that my image intends to take. Jesus calls this your body. That's kind of frightening because I'll get left behind. For just a moment, I'm going to lose my own association with where I was and where I intend to go. Does anybody hear me? Tell me if you hear me just a little bit. This is *A Course In Miracles*. But if I stand up and take the image step, I will have to, for just a moment, leave myself behind. And I will be abandoned by the image of my previous association and my future association. You know what that's called? NOW! That's called now. It's impossible for me not to be in motion in my mind if that's what I am. I don't have to take the physical step. I have the security of my previous association. I can take it whenever I want to in perfect trust that based on my old crap, I can have an association that justifies where I was and where I'm going. If I teach you: Don't make that decision! Suddenly you will see yourself begin to step forward. So the you that's going to step forward will be the justification in the ego — at no time does it really exist, it's always either before or after, which are really the same thing. For just a moment if you don't take that step, you will be abandoned by your ego. Or better, you will abandon the ego from your old association into your new one. What will you be? The Christ! At that moment, you will be the entirety of the image of your location in all of space/time.

In the *Course*, Jesus calls that: Don't destroy the continuity of thought that is a process of the entirety of you. If you break up the continuity into sequential time, you will combine what you were before with what you intend to be after, and you will avoid the moment of your own realization of yourself. I'm standing as a resurrected body in front of you with no reference at all to my past and future associations, and am offering you an entirety of the congruity of my mind association with what we are. It does not involve the process that's going on in your mind at all. It can also be demonstrated in physicality by healing. Since what you brought into the association was sick, if you don't take the step forward in time that justifies the aging process of your own mind, you will be eternal at that moment; and at that moment you could not possibly be sick. It's called a holy instant. There is an old Buddhist tradition, an old Hindu tradition, that says that Brahma does nothing. He is aware of the entirety of association. To break that down into caste systems is pitiful, but that's what you do to justify the Brahmaness of your own association. I can't do anything about that. But I can guarantee you this, whole mind is what you are somewhere, because you know about it. While you can sequence it in time, you cannot *not* get the results of your previous sequentiality. Okay. That's it.

But that's physical. What will you say? I'll be abandoned. Look at where I've brought myself, guys. I'm here, undergoing all of these experiences, and God doesn't hear you. If He hears you, He says, "Why are you basing Me on your experiences? What do I have to do with you? I'm your Father. I'm Creator. I'm eternal. What do I have to do with your mind? What do I have to do with an association that has condemned himself to his own crap?" I don't have anything to do with that, except to recognize his unreality. My denial of his reality is what causes him to leave. Did I get it simple enough for you? Do you understand me? You're not real. Now, since you believe that you are, you will get the result of that. Time is not real. Time is an invention of the separation of the human mind, isn't it? Boy, what an astonishing place to be. So that's the argument.

The reason that the world does not hear this is that the world will never hear it. Why would it? If it heard it, it wouldn't be here. Come on. That's the solution. There is no world. All you would have to do is stand up with me — this is the whole *Course* — and say, "The hell with this. I'm not going to die any more. I'm just sick and tired." This is the whole *Course In Miracles: Swear not to die, you Holy Son of God. You made a bargain you cannot keep.* Do you ever read that? Well, read it! It's in the *Course In Miracles*. It says that you have an agreement to die. You've sworn to die together. Can you hear me? You have an agreement that you're honoring that's called temporal association. Everywhere you look, you have that agreement. No matter what you share together, you have an agreement that you're separate. *Swear not to die, you Holy Son of God* means that you have sworn in the imagery of yourself to justify your separation from true love, or wholeness. Wherever you hear it I'm not concerned about because it's what you honor. What a sad thing. What a sad thing I discovered to have my honor based on death.

Let's see if I can do this with you. It is not that dying was not honorable to me in the sense that I have one life to give for my country and/or the greatest honor I can do is to die for my brother. It's just that I was never dead. I saw guys die for their honor of themselves, and I was still alive. I said, "Well, why can't I die for the honor of my country?" When I tried it I was still alive. This is the fact of the matter. So the honor that I found in death turned into the admission that to die did not really — while it was honorable — solve my problem. I did not deny the honor of it. I was in a very close association after the war with a guy who taught me a lot. That's the sword — will you see if you can get my sword back? I got a sword that would solve all of the problems of our credentials. The guy that wounded me, I got his sword. I love stories. I have great stories. So it turns out that the sword that I got when I went to Japan is a very, very valuable, real old Japanese sword. I don't know why I'm telling you this. Who knows? But it's the same sword that he wounded me with. And he was dead and I was alive. And all the lovely stuff that goes with my feeling of: "How come he's dead?" Because to the Japanese there's a great deal of honor in death. And I could see that the toughest guy I was ever going to oppose was the guy that was willing to die for a cause. And so I had to evolve in my mind a willingness to die for my cause. We called it *semper fidelis*. It didn't matter what we called it, but somehow we had to honor the commitment that we had made in the defense of our self and our honor and our — can I say God? — God, in the defense of our God in that association.

But there was a lovely consciousness who was expressing with me the advantages — and suddenly I was in Japan, suddenly, after all this crap, and I loved it immediately. For me, the idea that he had been that — I loved the culture. I began to — *Watashi wa nohomo nigato gozaimas* — I loved the Japanese language. So I'm not very sushi. I met just a lovely guy, Shinto, just beautiful. And he defended *hari-kiri*. He absolutely defended death in order to retain honor. And his justification for it was impeccable. The only thing that I discovered was every time I ran the sword through me I had the same crap and problem I always had. I couldn't solve it through death, no matter how honorable or dishonorable it appeared to be.

You listen to me. A god of death can never finally be the answer to your problem! I don't care if you serve him under any name, because life is not the termination of yourself in your own association. But notice how careful I am with this. I'm not saying that it was not honorable in his own mind. And I'm not saying it was not honorable to its fullest intent, because it was. This is what I tried to say to you. Death serves no purpose because it's impossible to die. The admission of the impossibility of death through continuing experiences of death, I suppose, will finally set your mind to say, "Screw you, world. I'm not going to die. It doesn't do me any good." God bless me! I went through all that crap and everybody's dead all around me and I'm alive. And I felt guilty about being alive. Try that one on. You know that one? "I must be a coward. I'm not dead." Pinning a medal on me could not solve that. I felt the pain of: "How come I survived?" I was not entitled to survivorship.

Very early, I became aware that all situations dictate terms for all future references. This was why I got this job. I was aware when I read about the history of the world that that's not really how it was. Can you hear me? It's always written by the generals or the political associations, and it's really not the way that it was. Not only is it not the way that it was — let's see if I can do this for you — the Second World War was won because a guy named Corporal Kleek stood up on Saipan with a .45 — he was not even supposed to have it — and said: "Follow me." That's how the war was won. It's not open to discussion. It was won at that moment. It's in the entirety of the dedication of his mind. All of the events that happened after that were associated with the entirety of that commitment. Quit examining it. All of the sequentialities can only be based on that moment of your determination. Do you hear me? When I read about the history, it's funny. And I can share with guys that have been there that it's not like that. It's all messed up. And it's always someone who says "No, let's do this. Not the plan. Not what we decided was going to work. That's nonsense." I'm giving you the fact of the matter. So when I came out I was very much aware that none of the plans really work. They just set them up in order that they can be changed or thrown out. Why am I getting into some of this stuff? Who knows? I'm leaving here very soon, so I'm able to tell you my story.

Now, if you want to evolve this into 1000 years of: "There was an old man who came here and told me all about it," what do I care? They've been around since the beginning of time. They're always telling you exactly the same story. The guy that walked out of here heard the same story 1000 years ago. He's listening to the same crap in his own mind. All they could possibly be telling him, all Buddha could possibly be telling him is he's not from here. He's very determined he's going to be a part of the organization that denies the entire simplicity of the problem. The simplicity of the problem is this ain't and God is; that there's a universal mind in its entirety.

It couldn't be three hours. Could it? Is that so? Three hours. Is that gone? It is true that the time passes faster when you're having fun, or when you're expressing yourself. So a lot of you occupy yourselves in order not to look at yourselves. And that's okay. Thank God it's Saturday. This moment will inevitably be all that there ever is, and if you'll let yourself enjoy it through the auspices of the certainty of your ultimate reclamation and the inevitability that you will be whole and perfect and eternal without the necessity to define it through your own consciousness, it will be true. If you want to believe what I tell you, it will be valuable to you. I am telling you as a fact of the matter that this is not Life. I'll do it once more for you. I don't know what you think Life is. This is not Life. You may say to me, "What is it, then?" And I'll say, "It is not sickness, pain and death." This isn't life. Life is eternal happiness. Life is what you are.

You might start to hear this! Life is all that you could ever be. And that recognition is the illumination of your mind. That recognition is letting that Light of energy, of consciousness, enter the darkness of the cause and effect relationship or the chaos contained in that moment of separation. Each moment you but relive the single incident that has been going on. If you let that be so, you will never spend more than an instant here. And if that reassociates into other instances, it will not concern you because you have accumulated a haven or a safety of love in the admission of a reality, a holy instant, that transcends your association. You literally use up all your time. The quicker that you use up all your time, the sooner you will be out of here.

You listen to me, some of you guys in the back. If I am here, telling you that your time is up, I mean it. If you'll stop examining why that's so and accept it as a fact, you'll be out of here in just a minute. Whatever you have done in this association to demonstrate what you thought you were, you are no longer able to die. I have taken away from you all the references that guaranteed your death. Now you're trapped. I've taken death away from you. What is the sense in being on earth if you can't die? Answer me. None! Can you hear it? There's no sense in participating in existence if I can't die. That's called the end of time. That's also the beginning of time and the end of time. Boy, is that ever lovely.

So I know that's frightening to you because you depended on death to escape from fear. Can you hear that? All you really do is suffer, get sick and die. That's crazy! You had no alternative but to exist until you die?! To hell with you. I'm offering you an alternative, and you must want it because life as you construct it doesn't make any sense. It's senseless. You know, what is the meaning of Life? "To exist, suffer, be in conflict, get old, lose the things I love and die." That's the meaning of Life? "Well, what is it, then?" I don't know, but I know it's not that. And so do you. Otherwise, how the hell am I telling you?

You say, "Well, are you sure it's time that you tell me this now? It doesn't seem like the right time." Brother, if this isn't the right time, there's never going to be a right time. I just got through telling you that there is only this time. Got it? Putting the right time in the future will just be a dependence on your old time. If you didn't get it last week, how in the hell are you going to get it next week? You say, "I can't, but I'll die even though I can get out of it." You can't. "Yes, I can." No, you can't. "I'll kill myself to prove you're wrong." You don't do that. You kill me to prove I'm wrong. That's what you're doing to me right now, because if you heard me, I'd become you.

Do you understand you're always crucifying the savior? You're always killing the guy that's offering you a total relief. He's been sneaking up on you, tracking you, chasing you. No wonder you're paranoid. You think that you're guilty and the guy that's pursuing you is going to capture you and punish you for what you did to him. He's not. He's trying to catch up to you to tell you it's not true. That's paranoia! Is everybody here familiar with that feeling that "someone's after me"? That's the Christ! That's the one guy you're going to try to crucify because you're afraid he's going to tell you, "Ah ha! I finally got you. You killed God and you caused all the chaos." This is all right out of the *Course.* You really believe that you've done something in reality. So you get a messenger, and you listen to him for a moment and he says: "Hey, I'm glad I caught up with you. Everybody else is gone." You say: "No, really?" He says: "It really didn't happen." This is John the Baptist. He says: "Really?" He says: "Didn't you get the word?" He said, "No." "We were pardoned! We're all back in the good graces." He says, "I can't trust you. Can I trust you?"

So you'll kill the messenger. That's important. Because the messenger may be bringing you news that you don't want to hear. So like the king, you kill him. So if you're a messenger, you'd much rather bring the good news than the bad. The worst thing you can finally give him is: "All you're doing is futile. You've been hiding in the caves for 30 years now, and the war's over." It irritates you. It's the grievance of not being told the solution. I'm here now, telling you that it was a mistake. I finally caught up to you. The Hounds of Heaven have been pursuing you. We finally got you cornered, and you don't have any way to turn. That's the *Course In Miracles.* Somehow you're going to have to look at it for a minute. We've trapped you. You can't escape. You're going to escape by killing us or killing yourself, and finally you say: "Wait a minute. That's enough. I'm going to..." What? "Stay here and listen; confront my fear." The *Course In Miracles*, in the first chapter, says this is leading you directly into fear. For just a moment you're going to have let that boogie man catch up with you. You can't get out of here without letting that happen. Who is he? He's the evil you. He's the association that is justifying all the things, the devil, if you want to know. Of course he's the devil. He's the great deceiver. When you approach him he always justifies what you are. He suffers just as much fear as you do. Together you use your power through the fear of God.

There's a sentence in the *Course* that asks Jesus, "Is the devil real?" He says, "Are you kidding? Of course he is." You think that the construction of an objective association of evilness is not a part of your mind? If it were not, you would have to admit that you are not only the advocate but the causation. You could then do an entire concentration of separation in your mind with God, which is exactly what I offer you. But you can only be one or the other.

So all of this paranoia can be released. Stand there for a moment. Let the fear enter in and say: "God help me. There's a solution to this not of me. I can't get out of this. I can't find the solution." Ask for help and mean it, not under the terms where you were able to escape it before because I cut those off. Once more: Not under the terms through which you tried to escape it before, because for most of you in this room, I've cut that off from you. I'm allowing you to admit that you feel the futility of the solution that you formerly had. I've literally taken it away from you. This is how I overcame my addiction to alcohol. Do you see that? But that did not solve my problem. I saw that my problem was that: "I don't do that any more." That's it. Whatever else I do, I had one problem, and one solution. I'm telling you, in your mind you have one problem and one solution. The problem is you in this association. The solution is eternal life. So you won't try to solve the problem any more.

Is that fearful? Is that frightening? You are frightened. You are fearful. What are you afraid of most? Are you ready? God. Fourth Obstacle to Peace in the *Course In Miracles*, as strange and ridiculous and insane and incredible as it seems, is that you are afraid of your Creator. Not only are you afraid of your Creator, you justify His creation by your fear. Who heard that? Say to me, "He's a good, God-fearing man." Say that. I didn't mind being God-fearing. All I wanted God to tell me to do was what He really wanted me to do. Every time I did what He wanted me to do, it didn't seem to work. He gave me a standard within my own association. I was afraid of Him because obviously He was going to punish me. Why not? Everything punished me. I had been bad.

The basis of this world, and the basis of the First Covenant, the basis of all religions, is fear of God. Questions? But the idea of fear of God or something outside of you is what the human condition is. Consciousness of a fox is not afraid of something outside of him. He's in a total identity of his own foxhood. You have established space/time fearfully and literally everything. There's not one single objective thing that you identify that cannot cause you pain or pleasure. Including the little ball that you give to the baby which he chokes to death on? I hated it. I hate this place. I hate it. I hate the idea that air bags are killing more little kids than they're saving. Do you hear me? It's just not fair. You see what happens in your own mind, that you've objectified death. But you die anyway, don't you? You think: "I can live an extra ten years if I take care, if I do this, if I do that." All you are is an existent fear association of yourself.

I've got you trapped. I've shown you the futility of your existence. You don't know what else to do. I'm not offering you an alternative. The alternative I'm offering you is not contained within your own association. I'm offering you that moment when you say: "I can't. God will." Or better: "I can't and God will." Not because of your determination. Is that a physical, mental and emotional happening in the human condition? Yes. You want to talk to me about this? I'm saying that the whole *Course* requires you to come to that moment when you experience the ultimate fear of being separate from God. That's all. Until you do that, there is no hope for you. The one thing that you must avoid in your ego or conceptual mind is not the peace of God but the fear of God. This is right out of the *Course.* If you knew that God was loving and peaceful, why wouldn't you just decide to do that? Even if you knew that God was separate from you, why couldn't you just say: "He's a loving, good God." Notice that you can't. If He's separate from you, He must be fearful because separation is what fear is, because fear is not knowing who you are. And if you do not know who you are, you must be fearful because you must establish a reality in your own mind without a true causation. I'm going to give this to you and then we'll end this and have lunch.

The reason that the world is not real is that there is no cause for it. It is the effect of a cause that is gone. All relationships must have a cause to have an effect. The cause of God is the effect of His son. The effect of the Son is the cause of God. Two effects are totally meaningless. Jesus teaches it this way, if you'd like to hear it. He says that the thought of separation, the cause of separation, immediately returned to Heaven, and that the effect of that is where you find yourself. Or that the expedition that sent you out deserted you and went home. So when you came back to the place where you're supposed to get out, you couldn't get out. So that your grievance is against God. And you have every right to. And I apologize for that. I'm directly apologizing to you for the mistake of the condition in which you find yourself. But you must understand that you cannot be sinful or guilty because there isn't any such thing as that. You may believe that you are separate from eternal life, but you cannot actually be because there is only eternal life. These are sentences that you should begin to read in the *Course In Miracles.* What a divine book.

I want to say welcome to some of you new minds. Those of you who heard this for the first time and said: "Oh, that's it" are the way it will be any minute now. Some of you are a little early in this practice. You know that's true. I mean, some of you, you listen to me and think: "What kind of a weird guy is this?" But there's a certain certainty about me that, at the minimum, you're attracted to. But mostly, you simply said, "Hey, that's what I've been looking for." Because it is what you're looking for. I'm offering you eternal peace and happiness based on your own mind. If you're not looking for that, what the hell are you looking for? But it's too sensible to be true. So you need someone to justify it. I'm doing that for you.

Now, it doesn't mean that I could not be wrong, but wouldn't you rather that I be right? Everything considered, wouldn't you rather what I'm telling you be right? That you really don't have to suffer sickness and pain any longer? Wouldn't you rather that that be true? That's the way the *Course* reasons with you. It says: "Everything else considered, why wouldn't you be happy to learn that you are actually eternally happy; that a mistake was made, and that I have come to tell you, 'I'm sorry you didn't get the word. We're leaving here at four o'clock this afternoon, would you like to go?'" Without the necessity of saying, "Where are you going?" Your salvation is: "Boy, am I glad to see you. I didn't know what it was, but I knew it wasn't this." So my solution is not of this world, is it? Boy, how did I get from Neo-Platoism to this?

I'm a positive example of what many of you will do, at least as well or better than I'm doing. The reason that is so is I have a very broad field of associations with you because you can't hear me. See, you can only hear me circumscribed within your own mind because there's too much chaos going on, too much separation. So you needed a mind, or a catalyst of Light, that was able to deal with you under any circumstances. The reason that is true is because the circumstances by which I came to know this had nothing to do with the specific instances in my own life.

I had nothing to do with my own awakening. You hear that? But I assure you that it began to happen to me. What's that? Are most of you having experiences? I hope so. You should begin to have an experience. Scary? How the hell do you think I got it? I'm glad I don't have to have that one again.

See, the trick in what you call the metamorphosis, the awakening, the hatching out, I knew the fear coming out of my room for a second. I remember, "What the hell is this?" That's very fearful to you, and you protect yourself. I guarantee you, when it's time to hatch, you're going to hatch. There's a period in Homo Sapiens, in the species, when it emerges from this split association to reality. It has nothing to do with your determination at all. You will be included in because you're part of that batch. You can be a little early or late in time, but you cannot *not* do it. Obviously you're early. But you can't turn back. Your shell is broken. There's nowhere for you to go. Jesus teaches, "Don't go back to the room that you were in." It's been clean swept. If you go back there, you go back to your old neighborhood. You've lost that reference. Good! Just stand there for a minute. It's going to be okay. As long as you could keep that one, you didn't have to look at another one. Now you have no alternative but to look at it because we've burned down your house. Jesus says to you in a beautiful parable: "Don't try to go back into your house to get another possession." He says, "Don't do it!" (Luke 11:24-46) Everything goes. It'll be okay. It's going to be with you when you get out. It's already there, waiting for you. That's lovely. What a great teaching. You're not going to go anywhere where you won't find all of your loved ones waiting. Don't go back in there. Let it go. Can you hear me? Just let it go. It was a grievance, anyway. Be glad to be rid of death. Tell them: "Screw you, death." If death comes to get you and he's blood-red and all that, say: "What the crap! Take your mask off." This is the *Course.* Don't let the Grim Reaper tell you to follow him, in mourning and in chains. "What a beautiful life. What a great life. How beautifully you died." The hell with you. You can't sell me on that. I've seen too much pain and crap. You want to have some more in honoring death, wait until you get into some. Wow. What a place to be!

I'll talk to some of you this afternoon. I have to give that philosophy talk. This is a philosophy that tells you that you, as a human being, can reason to the truth to the admission that the truth can be discovered in the entirety of the universe, not in your own dualistic association. Does that involve God? What the hell's wrong with that? Certainly it's going to involve the admission of an eternal Creator, if that's what power you are using. We'll have lunch here. What time is it? 12:30? Response: 12:45. I could stay a couple more minutes and we could have an early snack for supper. Stay kind of loose on your food; don't eat a lot of stuff. There is a lot going on physically in your body reassociations. Sometimes when you feel the joy, it expresses itself in consumption — everything you taste is going to taste real good. And that's perfectly okay. But be sure to burn it up in happiness. Otherwise the calories will pile up on you. Does cholesterol make you happy? Just use up all the clogging and be happy! The admission that the occurrence is physical is a necessary part of it, because you think you're a body. The idea that your glands are responding with enzymes and endorphins and all the other stuff that goes with your ductless glands is true. But so what? It will be as true as you let it be true in your own mind. The Light is going to come on. It's all just in your own mind. Is it an ordeal? You bet! But you're in an ordeal anyway. It's your ordeal. Just turn it around for a minute to that solution, and from then on, that will be the solution that you enter into in everything that happens to you. While it may appear to be momentarily sacrificial, it won't bother you at all because you will simply include it in with the inevitable metamorphosis process that you must undergo.

Say to me: "This is a required course." There's no way that if you are separate from God you will not have a course to get home. The question is not that, the question is when it begins to happen to you, will you let it happen or not? Or will you deny it and therefore deny yourself access to Heaven? Got it? Do you hear me? It's important that you even sort of hear me, because my mind training is to reasonable conception. I can put up with you. I don't have to listen to that. I'm offering you salvation. There's been so much broad awakening in what you call relational- ship identity that I'm being allowed to present my relationship to you. That's the end of time. Jesus teaches that you actually aggregate in what Jesus terms the borderland. You come to the borderland together with every purpose of sharing momentarily where you were with the certainty that you are no longer there. In the 12 Step Program, that's like telling your inventory. You tell everybody about how you were, and how happy you are that you discovered God getting out. In that sense, there's a great deal of value in *A Course In Miracles.* The problem we've had with *A Course In Miracles* is that they come together to study the conceptual association. That's just absurd.

Can I tell you one other thing? As we're presenting the *Course* to the world, we are astonished by how much of it is immediately being admitted. It's not in the structure of so- called *Course* groups. They look at it and say: "Oh, you teach mind training and transformation." We say: YES! Is that what *A Course In Miracles* is? YES! It's a mind-training process where we can come to discover love and happiness through the process of the forgiving of our grievances. That's all there is to it? That's all there is to it!

I'm looking for a minute to see how you let this in. It's here. The statement that "the world is not real" is here? Good! Did some of you have some lovely experiences last night? Was anybody afraid? Raise your hand if you were afraid. The anticipation is both fearful and joyful. Can you see that? Because you don't know what it is!

Let's have the Mormon Tabernacle. We'll probably all leave about 4 o'clock if that's okay with you. If that's not convenient, try to rearrange your time. Then you say to me: "Well, 4 o'clock came and is gone, and I'm still here." And

I said: "No you're not." "I am too." "No you're not!" The inclusion of space and time is quite an event. Space and time are actually simultaneous; they're going on all the time. We teach this and we teach it and we teach it. Jesus says we just keep teaching the same thing over and over again. That's all we do. The same thing, over and over again: You are perfect as God created you. It's going on in your own mind; it's not true. You're in a dream. Pain and death are not so. The fun part about it, when you hear it, and it's really fun — there's a Socratic notation of being heard. (I think, isn't there?) I have a tremendous amount of energy. I've been doing this for 18 years. Suddenly they begin to look younger and younger. Isn't that fun? It's just the joy of self!

The Call to The Quest

O Force-compelled, Fate-driven earth-born race,
O petty adventurers in an infinite world
And prisoners of a dwarf humanity,
How long will you tread the circling tracks of mind
Around your little self and petty things?
But not for a changeless littleness were you meant,
Not for vain repetition were you built;
Out of the Immortal's substance you were made;
Your actions can be swift revealing steps,
Your life a changeful mould for growing gods.
A Seer, a strong Creator, is within,
The immaculate Grandeur broods upon your days,
Almighty powers are shut in Nature's cells.
A greater destiny waits you in your front:
This transient earthly being if he wills
Can fit his acts to a transcendent scheme.
He who now stares at the world with ignorant eyes
Hardly from the Inconscient's night aroused,
That look at images and not at Truth
Can fill those orbs with an immortal's sight.
Yet shall the godhead grow within your hearts,
You shall awake into the spirit's air
And feel the breaking walls of mortal mind
And hear the message which left life's heart dumb
And look through Nature with sun-gazing lids
And blow your conch-shells at the Eternal's gate.
Authors of earth's high change, to you it is given
To cross the dangerous spaces of the soul
And touch the mighty Mother stark awake
And meet the Omnipotent in this house of flesh
And make of life the million-bodied One.
The earth you tread is a border screened from heaven,
The life you lead conceals the light you are.

- Sri Aurobindo

The Substitute Reality
A Quasar of Light
In An Eternal Moment of Love

Bonsoir. Comment allez vous? Fermez la porte. And welcome. We're going to share today the readings of the Master of the universal association, Jesus of Nazareth, along with the mastership of the totality of our association with each other, in regard to the certainty that by our expressions with each other, we can share immaculate re-associations of light that define our true reality. Opening sentences were contained in the incomparable Sri Master Aurobindo, in the *quest* that he made within the determination that standing with us, right now... Shall we teach a little French here? I am Master Teacher, I am an illuminate, trying to express to you my certainty of the correspondence we have found with each other, represented by figures, who appear to be historic references, within our individual minds. Who joined me this morning was Sri Aurobindo, along with another great French contemporary, Teilhard de Chardin, the incredible French anthropologist, along with a very special guest, Sai Ma -- Master Sai Ma. So together I have some very broad French ideas about the teaching. In order to formulate it within my own mind as Master Teacher, I should tell you that I flunked French sixty years ago, in my own determination of my self in body form. So I will not attempt to speak to you in the French association of our mind, without the inevitable certainty that the communication of our vocabularies, in

THE PARADOX OF ETERNAL LIFE: Discourses With Master Teacher

regard to the manner by which we will represent our selves as
the equality of instant mind conversion that's going on, can be
as well represented by you, at this moment, as it can by Master
Teilhard, or Sai Ba, or Sai Ma, or Jesus of Nazareth.

Look with me: This is our Course In Miracles, this is an
attempt to find the immediacy of a correspondence of light
associations of body form, (remember from this satellite now
that's broadcasting the reflections of light), so that there is no
reason, in all the universe, why, as you read the lovely message
that we just shared today, or from our Course In Miracles,
which we intend to do today, we cannot see the immediacy,
not only of our mental correspondence in the idea that minds
can communicate; not only with the emotional involvement of
our minds, in the certainty that a new light correspondence that
transcends the necessity for the physicality of the light images
that we represent, can be a whole part of what we are...

The moments of quiet we're going to have for the next
seven minutes, are going to be indications that within that
fabric, these two lovely gentlemen who are with me along with
this Sai Ma, are only finding instant correspondence with each
other in what may, at any moment, appear to be body forms.
Can you see this? My body forms of association, in the *quest*
that we have with Sri Aurobindo, are just determinations that
I just recognized him. Practice: "all recognition, in universal
associations of correspondence of light, is in my mind." "My
mind", in my determination to offer you that instant solution,
with no concern about the identity that you have given that
factor of memory, within your own mind (you listen to me now,
I am teaching now at a very high level), except to tell you that
within the memory fabric that you have about your self, can
be a continuing description of continuing alterations of mind
factors of association of the illusion of light correspondence,
in which we attempt to communicate with each other, through
ideas pertaining to, let's use, "universal associations of light",
that, just for a moment, were condensed into limited light
reflections, and refractions, that don't, at that moment, give us

a true image of the reflection of the correspondence of our body form. Now, in that regard, say that I were to teach for a moment the idea of Teilhard de Chardin: He is an anthropologist, he was obviously shut up by the church, and, without getting into the details, he dared to make an assumption, within Christianity, within the life of Jesus, that it was possible for any individual, within an environmental association, what we would call a revolution of ideas, a correspondence of body alternatives, based on a process of evolution, (are you listening? This is his exact teaching), that you could reach other conclusions about separate bodies (this is the teaching of the Holy Spirit) that would represent what Teilhard calls a *noosphere* of light energy.

I love to teach. Shall I tell you why? You're hearing that. Now, was he told to be quiet? Of course! Because he, inevitably, through my savior Jesus Christ, would begin to teach the inevitability of the transfiguration of the body, and that a transfiguration would lead to the *noosphere*, what we call the parameter of light consciousness that surrounds the idea that we are contained within this time frame reference. Can you hear this with me? What I am going to try to teach today... Shall I tell you? Somehow I got involved in (I love the idea of teaching) "evolution". Revolution of the mind is possible, very simply because it's true. Can you hear this with me? Now, the immediate confession that this has nothing to do, within it's entirety, with the idea of revolution, or evolution of the mind, does not deny the particulars of the body function, which appears to represent you, and has been demonstrated as a moment of transition of your body in a new light form, beginning with the resurrection of Jesus and culminating in his return with the revelation of the light forms that we now represent to each other in self realization. That was very, very lovely. Remember I said, "Fermez la porte", in French, close the door... That's Sai Ma. "Close the door." Let's enclose our self with pictures of light.

I am going to teach. Are you familiar with the Text of A Course In Miracles? I think I'll address my self directly to the idea of replication. Shall I? Say to me, "I am replicating my self." What a great definition of the revolutionary process of alterations in multiplicity of the idea of evolution, which is nothing but a continuing inevitable multiple replication of itself, over and over and over again until we're ending up with an infinite number of species. Finally we end up with an infinite number of species that are representing the entirety, not of a body form, but of the transition into light that utilizes an instant of body form, in the term that we employ as resurrection. So that the idea that you can learn from me, now I am teaching the Course In Miracles, that in the repetition in the meditation of our association of mind, we will continue to discover new goals, in the direction in which we want to be led, in our certainty of the increase of the light procedure. OK?

Now, we're going to begin. For those of you who are not familiar with the Course In Miracles, this is a mind training to bring about the immediacy of the possibility of a light revealing to you, in which this little enclosure of light, will simply disappear. We inevitably begin with the idea of the basic acknowledgement that you would like to hear this. And that admission cannot not include the idea of the confession that in truth you actually have no idea who you are, or what you're doing, because the reflection of light that you're getting back to your self, has no meaning whatsoever. So, shall we begin the learning process of the discovery of the light that you just made, in the great opening of the quest for the transformation of the human condition?

Listen: *There is no statement that the world is more afraid to hear than this: I do not know the thing I am, and therefore do not know what I am doing, where I am, or how to look upon the world or on myself. Yet in this learning is salvation born. And What you are will tell you of Itself.*

This is the only thing that you need do for vision, happiness, release from pain and the complete escape from sin, all to be given you, say only this but mean it with no reservation, for here the power of salvation lies. Ready?

I am responsible for what I see. I choose the feelings I experience, and I decide upon the goal I would achieve. And everything that seems to happen to me I ask for, and receive as I have asked. (Chap 21:II)

Here it is: *The secret of salvation is but this: That you are doing this unto yourself. No matter what the form of the attack, this still is true. Whoever takes the role of enemy and of attacker, still is this the truth. Whatever seems to be the cause of any pain and suffering you feel, this is still true. Here it is. This single lesson learned will set you free from suffering, whatever form it takes. 'I have done this thing, and it is this I would undo."* (Chap 27:VIII)

There, that was an exciting presentation of a reading, wasn't it? Have you done this thing to yourself? Practice: are you being undone? Yes. Chapter 18 of the Text of Jesus of Nazareth is a direct revealing of the idea that you are continuing to replicate yourself, within space/time.

Teilhard, fundamentally, taught, obviously, that as he began to communicate with other human beings, he was very much aware, as you may be within your own definition of yourself, that somewhere, within the entirety of the universe, we could not not be sharing the totality of a single reality of mind, very simply because, in a reasonable process, in consciousness association of our self, all of us are perfectly aware that somewhere, out in the universe, we are sharing moments of the entirety of our self, in relationship with what everything is. There maybe some value to you, in the idea that when I teach this to you, if you'll look at me in a formulation of body form, I could tell you that you're a substitute for who you really are. The problem that will arise in the teaching of substitution is that once the idea of the wholeness of your body, in the moment that you have spent in the entirety of space/time occurs — the substitution occurs from that moment on, in the reflection of light correspondence, even out into the universe, — all of the details that appear to represent correspondences of light (are you going to hear this?), will be an illusion. And they'll be an illusion! Very simply, there's nowhere in the formulation of your body form that you're not getting, from your own memories about yourself, ideas about the solution that you seek within the patterns of memory that represent our attempts to communicate with each other in consciousness, in an infinite number of ideas about ourselves, in which we complicate the simplicity of the admission, — listen to me, this is the resurrection — that if there is a true form of a single reality in the idea of reflected light, it is impossible that somewhere within that arrangement of the expansion of the universe, we are not a whole part of what we're searching for.

Now, I am going to take just a moment to introduce you to Chapter 18, with just an opening paragraph that's going to define what you have been doing in your substitution of conceptual ideas about yourself. Listen:

To substitute is to accept instead. If you would but consider exactly what this entails, you would perceive at once how much at variance this is with the goal the Holy Spirit has given you, and would accomplish for you. Why? To substitute is to choose between, renouncing one aspect of the Sonship in favor of the other. For this special purpose, one is judged more valuable and the other is replaced by him. The relationship in which the substitution occurred is thus fragmented, and its purpose split accordingly. To fragment is to exclude, and substitution is the strongest defense the ego, the human condition, has for separation. (Chap 18:I)

Could you see that with me? I am going to continue to read you just a little bit. We've only got a few minutes left in that first twenty seven minutes. That's unbelievable! But what I want to involve you in is the idea of that moment of substitution, when we thought our bodies were separate, we can merge into an idea of light and love. This is the teaching of our Course In Miracles. Listen: *The one emotion in which substitution is impossible is love. Fear involves substitution by definition, for it is love's replacement. Now. Fear is both a fragmented and fragmenting emotion. What a lovely idea. It seems to take many forms, and each one seems to require a different form of acting out for satisfaction. While this appears to introduce quite variable behavior, a far more serious effect lies in the fragmented perception from which the behavior stems. No one is seen complete. The body is emphasized, with special emphasis on certain parts, and used as the standard for comparison of acceptance or rejection for acting out a special form of fear.* (Chap 18:I)

In this first twenty seven minutes of correspondence of the idea of teaching union of our mind, hopefully you've been introduced to a very fundamental idea that decisions about how you want to look at yourself, in your body formulation, are being made by you, and that the idea of the reflection of light (now I am speaking of the whole universe out there), can be increased in intensity of love, by the relinquishment of the fractured-ism of your mind, in the idea that holding a particular association of the formulation of your location in time, cannot give you a true reflection, because you have particle-ized your body formulation into an infinite number of possibilities that are all in fact only self contained, within the idea of an illusionary moment in all of space/time that lasted just for that moment and was immediately extended outward in a power of light that we are deciding to share in this Course In Miracles.

Thank you for that miracle. I'll be back with you in just a moment. That miracle of light had nothing at all to do with the fractured-ism of your mind or body. It was a simple admission of the power to unite in the natural uniting of the universal mind of God that is a part of what we are.

I'll be right back. Remember, God goes with you and me, wherever we go, because God is the mind with which we're thinking. Say it, "God bless us, each and everyone."

* * * * * * *

Here we are. Could you see in that two minute interval, in the light reflection, in refraction of our self? I am going to teach for just a moment. It's so good to see you here. Practice: "I remember you." This is the entirety of my teaching. Teilhard... Master Teilhard de Chardin, Sri Aurobindo, Sai Ma... Listen, they appear to be separate body forms. The simple idea, the truth of the matter, and this is Master Teacher, is that we communicate with our minds, since fragmented communication of body form is impossible. Humans, billions of people inhabiting this earth, all we're really getting, within the stricture of the idea of light form energy, is the darkness of the idea of the necessity for activation of the conversion of mass that represents what the universe is, in its relationship with itself.

I am going to stay with this, just for a moment, because I can see that you're hearing this reference of my mind to yours. Minds communicate. Practice: "you're not a body." Now, it would appear that Teilhard, or Sai Ma, or anyone you can name, Jesus of Nazareth certainly who just came into this perspective, is standing somewhere in a physical body of association of the correspondence of the light ideas of reflections we give ourselves in an attempt to identify our individual identity in a consciousness state that cannot not include the entirety of the universe. Now, the idea that you're going to say to me that association is over and dead in his body, listen, could not possibly mean anything. If the formulation of the idea of body form, I am going to teach it just for a minute to you over here, were a continuing replication of the idea of variant ideas of separate body, it is impossible they will not include exposé's, openings, of ideas that were previously substitution of body form replications. Can you see this with me? The idea that we're going to fax to each other, facsimiles of light ideas about our minds that find fractured correspondences in definition of our minds. You're hearing this with me? OK, this is from Master Jesus, who says to you, the place that you now occupy, this is our New Testament, that you now occupy, within this little arrangement of time, is not where you're from. Let's simplify it for human beings: Are you ready? You're from Heaven! Now, the recognition that you're from Heaven is actually not necessary in the mind of the totality of universal mind, but just as certainly, if you have in your mind an idea of fractured-ism that causes you to search and search for new ideas about your body formulation (listen) in which you always appear to fail, we can teach you (this from Jesus, from our illuminate mind) that, almost immediately, there will now be a sufficient light reflection of your self, which first will give you a great deal of joy and happiness. That's inevitable, because happiness is what you've been searching for. And while you have found joy and peace in sharing of your human condition, in innumerable ideas of attempts to communicate within the illusion of the moment of separation, the inevitable result was the loss of the mass of energy in light that you previously sustained yourself in, in order to formulate an event horizon, an event circular association of yourself, an advent of a circle of energy that has held you in the bondage of a reflection of light. And at that moment, you forgot who you were.

Now, we're holding each other in the perspective of the possibility of a continuing illumination of your body, in the fundamental certainty that once the substitution occurs, once you formulated within time, the idea of the instant of separation, it multiplied itself in an infinite number of possibilities of space/time in the idea of light formulation that could have represented the entirety of the power of the universe and reduced you to this, we often term your black hole reference of yourself, in which your emotion of searching for love and finding it, constantly suffered the conflict of the projection of your own mind that gave you a false correspondence (are you listening?) in the belief that there was actually a separate body out there, giving you a replication of an illusion within your own mind.

I don't know whether you object to the idea that Teilhard is standing with you, I assure you that there is no reason why he would not be standing next to you, since anybody standing next to you, in your body correspondence, can only tell you what you want to hear, in the ideas that you have about your self, concerning decisions that you continually make, in order to retain the idea of the limitation of the formulation of your self that you hold (ready?) as a substitute for what you really are. This is the entire teaching of Jesus (you want to hear it?): you're not who you're pretending to be. The place that you're in is wrong. Your right place is in Heaven. This Chapter 18 of our Text of A Course In Miracles says it so beautifully that I hope, along with Jesus, that you'll go out and obtain a copy of it.

Let's listen to the description of a physical association, of what occurs in the idea of separation, in a moment of the schism of light. Listen:

You who believe that God is fear made but one substitution. It has taken many forms, because it was the substitution of illusion for truth; of fragmentation for wholeness. It has become so splintered and subdivided and divided again, over and over, that it is now almost impossible to perceive it once was one, and still is what it was. Listen to me. That one error, which brought truth to illusion, infinity to time, and life to death, was all you ever made. Your whole world rests upon it. Everything you see reflects it, and every special relationship that you have ever made is part of it. (Chap 18:I)

And I am back for just a moment. I am excited. I saw you within your own "fracturedization" of conceptual observation of your self, begin to entertain from my mind – and now I am teaching along with Teilhard de Chardin, Jesus Christ, Sai Ma, and (say to me your name) you, – because in the recognition of you will be a continuing re-definition of your self that is giving you glimpses' of reality that are not within the fragmentation of your mind. I think I'll get into the idea that I can teach you physical transformation within the physicality of the body, we call that transfiguration of your body, so that even though you have been substituting ideas about yourself, in images of yourself, somewhere with you, out in the universe, you're going to recognize the entire wholeness of who you really are. Let's just read a little more of this.

You may be surprised to hear how very different is reality from what you see. You do not realize the magnitude of that one error. It was so vast and so completely incredible that from it a world of total unreality had to emerge. What else could come of it? Its fragmented aspects are fearful enough, as you begin to look at them. But nothing you have seen begins to show you the enormity of the original error, which seemed to cast you out of Heaven, to shatter knowledge into meaningless bits of disunited perceptions, and to force you to make further substitutions. Just a little bit more:

That was the first projection of error outward. Now, the world arose to hide it, and became the screen on which it was projected and drawn between you and the truth. Why? For truth extends inward, where the idea of loss is meaningless and only increase is conceivable. Do you really think it strange that a world in which everything is backwards and upside down arose from this projection of error? It was inevitable. For truth brought to this could only remain within in quiet, and take no part in all the mad projection by which this world was made. Listen. Call it not sin but madness, craziness for such it was and so it still remains. Invest it not with guilt, for guilt implies it was accomplished in reality. And above all, be not afraid of it. (Chap 18:I)

And above all else, (look) don't be afraid of the idea that there's a new image of light that I can show you, in correspondence with a continuing conversion of your body form. The description that Jesus used in Chapter 18, in the idea (I am going to teach just for a minute, I love to teach)of the description that you heard, in regard to backwards and upside down, in the illusionary nature of the correspondence of the reflection of holograms of ideas of your self are my exact teaching within my own mind. I was glancing together this morning at the idea, (let's use the idea) I used of parallel universes: a parallel universe – that you're meeting your self in fracturedism? – Precisely what I teach! The reflection I am getting is multiplied in parallel universes, in an infinite number of definitions of correspondences that can only reflect back to me ideas out in the universe about a refraction of light that is not my true self. But as science has pointed out, somewhere out there, in all of the light formulation, you're going to meet your self. This is the whole idea of the teaching of A Course In Miracles. As you see yourself now, there's no manner in which you can get a true view of what you are. I remember when I tried to teach you (here... look...) quantum teleportation, I tried to show you that as long as you... This is quantum – the idea of instantaneous communication. I can teach this in the direction of all attempts you have to teleport to ideas of your body association, within yourself, very simply because that's the condition that you're in. You see that, can you hear this with me? You have a movement of ideas of yourself, in body form, in which you make decisions to move in location, at the speed of light, from this object to this object, in attempt to teleport the ideas of your mind, physically, to other associations. Listen, the problem you have in fracturedism (can you hear this?) is that, contained within your mind of body formulation, is a previous association of body that you had about your self. This is the entirety of the teaching of the science idea that you can only meet yourself, because the image that you now utilize in time to identify your old association, within your mind, holds you in a future idea that continues to fragment you, within your own mind, very simply because you haven't located your self in the only moment of truth that could possibly represent you – that is going to be when? – Now, here! So, the idea (and this is going to be Chapter 18) that there is a moment of revealing of light form that's available to you at this instant, as a designation of a continuing new location of your body form, is what, along with the ones that I represented, this old man, (and I am called the old man) Master Teacher, is trying to represent to you. You're going to hear this, very simply because I am just an image of light formulation, attempting to give you, (you're going to hear this?) a better reflection of who you think you are. How many of these associations are necessary to give us moments of true reflection? Why would I be concerned about that? Your body formulation is not going to be true in any regard. It's the same fundamental idea that as long as you have an idea you're a body form in time, you cannot not suffer the consequences of an aging process in body form. I am representing to you now Master Teacher.

Here's the solution of the healing that just occurred. (Thank you.) In that healing that just happened with your body formulation, the reflections of light of your body are changing all the time anyway. At no single moment does the actual formulation of the illusion of your body exist. What you've accepted in this Course In Miracles is a light reflection of you that, just for a moment (ready?) if you would let it, would represent a whole body – a better illusion. But what a better illusion of sharing from my mind to yours, the certainty that we could find that correspondence in light that would reverse the procedure of the energy formulation of our mind that has held us in an illusion of a reflection of light! Let's look at it this way, just for a moment. This is Chapter 18. It expresses itself in a particular way. This is *Scientific American*: *"Are You a Hologram?"* *"Information in the Holographic Universe"*. I'd like to read you a little bit about it, and if you get a chance, get the article. I'll tell you in essence what it's going to say. The idea of mass or density, in the necessity of the conversion of light, that is the idea that the universe, in entropy, is undergoing loss of energy and is going to be reduced to nothing, is not possible, simply by the continuing examination about the formulation of time. Now the idea of a holograph universe, is the simple application of the idea that all of the reflections, going on in all of the galactic associations of definition, are finally only continuing replication of the ideas of that formulation that I am attempting to teach you in Chapter 18 of the Course In Miracles. I am going to try just a little bit. Listen:

*The **World As A Hologram:** An astonishing theory, called the holographic principle, holds that the universe is like a hologram, just as a trick of light allows a fully three dimensional image to be recorded on a flat piece of film, our seemingly three dimensional universe, could be completely equivalent to alternative quantum fields and physical laws painted on a distant and current vast surface.*

*The **Physics of Black Holes:** Immensely dense concentrations of mass, provides a hint that the principle might be true, because studies of black holes show that although it defies common sense, the maximum entropy, or information content of any region of space, is defined not by its volume but by its surface area. Physicists hope that this surprising finding is a clue to the ultimate theory of reality* and can represent its truth to us just as I can "represent my truth to you", in Chapter 18 of our Course In Miracles, where I would acknowledge to you, in the entirety of the light of the unlimited power of what we associate within our own mind as creative reality, that the moment in which we were confined in the complete density of a billion trillion forms of impacted light, only lasted for that moment in representation of black hole ideas, from which we emerged and expanded instantly out into the universe and are continually formulating holographs of what we really are in our light. What does Jesus call this, "The dark night of the soul?" He says to you, boy you look good to me in the physicality of the mind of your body association. You have finally reached, within the idea of the mass density, the idea that you are contained in attacking and defending yourself from your own projections of the images of your reality, conflict, war, loneliness, pain, death, which are only structures of your own mind, that at any moment can give you a much better reflection of who you are in reality. This is Master Jesus' Sermon on the Mount. The reflections you get back from your enemy out there could not be more than ideas you have about yourself, because in a literal sense, there isn't anything outside of you.

Thank you and thank you for the associations we've had with the divine brothers that came with us in this first hour of the idea of an evolutionary process of light that's available to us at this instant. I am going to come back because I want to show you the light factoring of the recognition of love that we recognize in our association with what previously defined to our pitiful little self, what we're not. That, very simply because in that new light, God is going with us, wherever we go, and suddenly we're beginning to recognize each other in true reflections of who we really are. Will you say it with me? "God bless us, each and everyone." Because that truth will be with us in this little interval between this idea of a chapter of a solution in the divine admission of our Course In Miracles.

* * * * * * *

This about Beyond the Body: *There is nothing outside you. That is what you must ultimately learn, for it is the realization that the Kingdom of Heaven is restored to you. For God created only this, and He did not depart from it nor leave it separate from Himself. The Kingdom of Heaven is the dwelling place of the Son of God, who left not his Father and dwells not apart from Him. Listen. Heaven is not a place nor a condition. It is merely an awareness of perfect oneness, and the knowledge that there is nothing else; nothing outside this oneness, and nothing else within.*

What could God give but knowledge of Himself? What else is there to give? The belief that you could give and get something else, something outside yourself, has cost you the awareness of Heaven and of your own Identity. And you have done a stranger thing than you yet realize. You have displaced your guilt to your body from your mind. Yet a body cannot be guilty, for it can do nothing of itself. You who think you hate your body deceive yourself. You

109

hate your mind, for guilt has entered into it, and it would remain separate from (you and) *your brother's, which it cannot do.*

Just one more idea, listen: *Minds are joined; bodies are not. Only by assigning to the mind the properties of the body does separation seem to be possible. And it is mind that seems to be fragmented and private and alone. Its guilt, which keeps it separate, is projected to the body, which suffers and dies because it is attacked to hold the separation in the mind, and let it not know its Identity. Listen. Mind cannot attack, but it can make fantasies and direct the body to act them out. Yet it is never what the body does that seems to satisfy. Unless the mind believes the body is actually acting out its fantasies, it will attack the body by increasing the projection of its guilt upon it.* (Chap 18:VI)

You're here with me. Now, these are what we call episodes. This is our Course In Miracles – the requirement of the possibility that you can engender, within your own perspective, a self, a new arrangement about what you want to be, in the perspectives of the illusion of body form.

They call me the Master Teacher, and if you remember on that first hour, we began to give other mind identities to other bodies. I believe we spoke of Teilhard de Chardin (the great anthropologist, who represents the certainty of this communication from the idea of body formulation to the truth) or Sri Aurobindo, who is with us or Sai Ma, the lovely current teacher of the idea of the inevitability of the power of our minds to communicate. Obviously the only reason that I use them is because, as you read with me in this idea of correspondences of our mind, our body functions of definitions of our self have precisely nothing whatsoever to do with the discovery that our minds are not communicating.

We're using Chapter 18 of the Text of the Course In Miracles, from Jesus of Nazareth, who has returned, within a fabric of the conversion of our mind, to show us in the mind training of our self, a procedure of the re-vision of the light that I am attempting to represent to you in the illusion that we are a body form. You remember in the first hour I taught you, in the Science American, are you a Hologram, and I began to demonstrate to you that, so evident in Chapter 18, the reflections of light that you're getting in your determination of the incredible limitation you place on yourself, in correspondence with your body form, are, in actuality, entirely meaningless.

So, the Workbook of A Course In Miracles is training us, in a systematic way, to continually recognize new situations of consciousness stories that we tell our self, within frames of time that seem to represent (shall we use the word, "dream") dreams about our self, in our identity.

How full we are with ideas of the stories that are being projected onto the screen, beginning with very fundamental ideas of consciousness association that we could communicate in descriptions of ideas we shared in separation, and projected onto screens of other identities, being represented by thought forms we had about our self, that then organized into an illusion (say to me, "fractured") of fractured lights about our own minds, in the projection of the idea that we are actually representing our self in this little infinite maze of containment where, number one, we stood together as we're doing now in this world, and just for a moment began to share, deep within us, the idea, as we stood there, of the love that we knew had to be somewhere, yet we were unable to find, because of (I am going to teach science for a minute) an event horizon of energy that surrounded us in dark light form in the galaxy, that, in a literal sense, prevented us from seeing the light. Into this situation came a single light mind of eternal life, from outside the parameter –and thus not operating at the speed of light, (which would be a mass determination of light association) – with the certainty that the fundamental difficulty of the containment of the human condition is, in a particular sense, the totality of his inability to get a true reflection of who he is, within his own mind. Emotionally, (practice, from the Old Man, "I am afraid".) What? Of course, why wouldn't you be afraid? The objective association of light you're getting back within your own mind, (you listen!) cannot not be memories, contained within you, of all the fear and all the loneliness and all of the death that you experience.

I love to teach revelation, from the idea that I could share (shall I use you?) with you as a Master Teacher, (I am talking to you now) Teilhard, that I spoke of, Sai Ma, who we know, Aurobindo, all of the ideas that their new minds have shown them the solution. I was talking to Sri Aurobindo this morning, and he told me the story, (and I remember it very well, and it's written up in the scriptures) about how, typically, he was in jail. I might share that with you, dear ones. All of us, somewhere in time, have found our selves incarcerated for ideas of... So was Aurobindo incidentally, so was I, but this was a particular story, because Aurobindo was in despondency, he had attempted to teach the whole idea of Yoga, the whole idea of light, the whole idea of everything he knew to be true. And, let's face it, dear friends, the totality of light is not acceptable to any representation that is determined to be separate. But right at that moment of that devastation, a beautiful, (here it is) light occasion came into his mind (and he was in jail, oK?) and it was a moment of devastation. Do you see this with me?

Would you like to hear this with me? I'll speak to you directly. Do you want to hear? If you're in a human condition of your self, it's impossible you are not living in memories of your idea that you're a body. Say to me, "I am a body." Yes. Why? At this time and place you appear to be a body, yet it's impossible that contained and not contained, within your formulation of memories about your self, are not (say to me,) "moments of light." Shall I teach you about some experiences that I know you're having in your mind, within the relationship of the entirety idea you have about your self in, (sometimes Jesus calls it) Gethsemane? He says you find your self looking for the solution, you go out and you love, you share, you give and all of a sudden that wasn't it! It didn't work! It's dark! "I am going to die." "I can't find the answer." "There is no solution." At that moment the answer will be there, because the power you can utilize, at the entirety of the idea you're separate in all of space/ time, lasted just for a moment and had absolutely no effect on reality, yet it seems to be a memory within your own mind

And Aurobindo shared with me the joy of that light, because, there's a little story (that goes with this) that he was teleported to another association of time. Listen: this is a much commoner procedure than you're willing to admit with me. As we just told you in Chapter 18, if everything is backwards and upside down in light, any moment of the truth of you, in any correspondence, can actually place you in an entirely different situation, in the longevity of time, than you previously represented. The problem with it is you're going to bring your memories with you, but that does not belie the possibility of the regeneration of your body, based on the conversion of memories that you hold, concerning the fabric of the history of your body that's actually contained within your own mind.

One of the original light episodes that Master Teacher had, (and I am teaching just for a moment,) occurred almost sixty years ago. I found myself in an impossible situation of a devastation that occurred: (I believe the anniversary is today, of the explosion of an atomic bomb) that was one of the most devastating ideas that could ever be experienced in the mind. I have in my mind the memory of sharing (can you hear me?) with a brother, Japanese, the certainty that, in any event, the war was going to be over. But it did not subtract all of the conflict of memory that I held in my mind, with a determination that in sharing the innocence of our self, in moments of peace, we found a new correspondence that has been available to us since the beginning of time. Now, do I have a memory of the death of a hundred and fifty thousand incidences? Yes. What happens in the particulars of the human condition, is that the devastation of it is so immense, (are you listening?) that you project it. I can share this with virtually everyone who's ever been in combat, or anyone who has ever suffered the conflict of the occasion of the illusion of conflict in the projection of self identity of our minds, because these are moments of terror and they can be points within your own mind that show you the inevitability that all of this containment of time (are you hearing?) is nothing but a single memory of a moment of disaster that will represent to you the entirety of the possibility that there's a new you available to you, in the idea of what we just shared there.

What occurred? I had in my mind a projection of hate and pain, and defense, because of what had been done to me, or what I have done. The teaching of this Course In Miracles is inevitably one of forgiveness, very simply because the projection of your mind, in ideas of who you are, in the conflict of images that you maintain, cannot give you a true picture of who you really are. This was in this idea of the hologram. This was in this idea that in the mass or density, contained within galactic association, your reflection is so limited that while you attempt to escape out into the universe, there's no where that there is a guiding principle in it's entirety that can show you the individual solution, because that light, right there, has been buried deep within you. Now, you're at this point with me, aren't you? And this is the sharing of all of the ideas of all of the history of man that has been written, in which they have been given body identities. You listen with me: My concern about your body identity of the illusion of you is zero! My concern is that there is a new bright way that we can accumulate ideas of new association of light that then become a part of our history of sixty years ago, when this body formulation had to undergo the experience that everyone, who is in body form, is continually undergoing, in the laws of density of body association that is the loneliness and pain and death that now appears to be part of what you are in your own mind, that can't be escaped. Are you with me in this? We are memories that need to be changed within our memories of our self. Look with me. Here's a new bright light reflection of "I know who you are", and this is Sri Aurobindo, and this is Sai Ma, and this is reflection of light (are you listening to me?) Teilhard de Chardin, who says that this is a noosphere of light (and the Pope told him to shut up). I am not picking on anybody, but there is no way that you really want to admit that, through my savior Jesus Christ, the salvation of the world not only depends on your mind, but it depends on the conversion of the formulation of your body form, which has held you in the illusion of objective associations of form. OK?

What's been revealed to us from our satellite now, with this Course In Miracles (are you going to hear it?) is nothing but a new continuum of time. You are so long accustomed to the necessity of taking all of the old references (what is it, forty thousand years?), taking all of them and projecting them into the future, in order to protect yourself from the instant of devastation that I am offering you, (which you refuse and subsequently suffer a moment of the loss of consciousness of your body). Practice: "I am going to heal you in light recognition of your mind." You will be delighted, now I am teaching new correspondence of mind, with my determination of what you think must be this Advent of a... (I must be seventy seven years old, ha, ha...) ...or the idea of my memories of Waterloo, or the ideas of my memory of anything: Moses, my ideas of Mohammed... My ideas of all the energies of association in my own mind, are only defining what I want to believe within the prospect of what appears to be the illusion of my body formulation. The result of the idea that we are bodies cannot not be death and termination. You going to look with me? Whatever you think you're doing with your body, at that moment right now, the light that we just found, perfectly healed this old seventy seven year old guy.

Now, the idea that you are going to maintain the body, rather than declare with me, (This from Jesus. Say to me:) "I am not a body". There! "I am free." Now, at that moment, within the aggregation of light, where our minds communicate, it had absolutely nothing to do with my body formulation. It's changing all the time in the light reflections of my self anyway.

The moment I saw my mind as whole, the illusion of my body immediately assumed the love and forgiveness that I felt in my association with my self, by laying down my defenses, (this is called Sermon on the Mount) of my determination not to turn the other cheek when you attack me. Ha, ha! I taught a little Jesus!

My time is up, in this first idea of the second hour of Hologram. What I wanted you to see with me, from personal experience, is that you don't have to project out from you the guy who you're going to have to forgive. You recognize this new light image within your own mind, and he will take on new aspects, degrees of power of light, intervals where our separations collapse into black holes of ideas about our self, and convert agencies of who we are. Shall I teach just for a moment? I am going to be back to describe this, in which we come out of the black hole, at the speed of light, before we went in, because the pertainments of the enclosure of the idea of a hologram cannot exclude the possibility of the using up of the black hole in it's entirety. Yet obviously, as a human being, if you're trapped in your Gethsemane, the request for aid, even in the idea that God has forsaken you, is necessary within the logistics of the possibility of mind conversion that I just gave to you.

So, all of your future was based on your past. Now, all of your future is on the certainty that your past has been brought into a present condition and somewhere in time cannot not include the next fourteen thousand million years. So we'll recognize each other in this moment of love, before we came into this procedure and after we left. And we'll say together, "God has gone with us wherever we went, in this pain. And we're going to share together now this moment of love, within the dream, where we escape from the mere idea that this would be what life is." Shall we say it together? "God bless us, each and everyone."

* * * * * * *

I am very excited to see you, in the perspective of being allowed to view the video that you're watching now. Shall I tell you that? Will you share with me the idea, in it's most basic sense, that everything, in space/time, all memories, all ideas of consciousness associations, at or beyond the speed of light, are actually going on within your own mind, at this moment, and that this is what you have been afraid of? Will you let the Old Man practice with you for a moment, along with anyone else that you'd like to hear, including the guy that's next to you? Say to me, "I have been doing this to my self, I don't want to do it anymore, I am tired of blaming my brother. Yet when I accepted the problem my self, I also didn't seem to be able to find the solution. I need some help." To you there, as a human being, I am here to help you, because I can share with you, in my mind, the devastation that we are undergoing in the idea that we are a body form. Yet at any moment, we can escape in the simple recognition that we are not only not bodies, but actually are not in the location that has given us this identity that somehow we're separate.

We are in a dream of separation that lasted just a moment in our mind and is now over and gone. Now, the particulars by which you become willing to accept, within your own individual mind, do not in any sense require what has been projected outside of your mind (that is inevitably going to return) in order to justify a parameter of consciousness, where you appear to be trapped (this is the teaching of Jesus) in the idea of a *causal loop*. In Sermon on the Mount, he says that every time you look out there, the image of pain, loneliness and death that you get back, is nothing but a projection of your own mind. Now, that conversion of love that I just felt for you was a moment that is eternal, in the inevitability that we share together a single whole Mind of God. Was forgiveness in there? Certainly. Was there really something to forgive? Only yourself, and since your self could not possibly be guilty of anything, if you are indeed the living Son of God, I do not hesitate at this time to stand in the light of my own revelation and declare to you, as you now stand with me, in the ideas of what previously separated us in body form, that available to us, in space/time, is a new continuum of time that transcends the necessity to remain buried down into this black hole of devastation.

He is risen, he is risen indeed. Good. We just saw your body transfigure. It's a very common procedure in this teaching to suddenly feel a healing of light that was actually all around you. Practice: "I am the light of the world." Say it. No matter who you are, no matter who you thought your procedure of your self was, that light, albeit deep within you, is available to you, because as you relax your defenses of objective association, you will collapse down into where that moment of terror occurred, and then expand out into the universe. Here's why Master Jesus talks about it:

A little bit about Light in the Dream: *You who have spent your life in bringing truth to illusion, reality to fantasy, have walked the way of dreams. For you have gone from waking to sleeping, and on and on to a yet deeper sleep. Each dream has led to other dreams, and every fantasy that seemed to bring a light into the darkness but made the darkness deeper. Why? Your goal was darkness, in which no ray of light could enter. And you sought a blackness so complete that you could hide from truth forever, in complete insanity. You listen. What you forgot was simply that God cannot destroy Himself. Why? The light is in you. Darkness can cover it, but cannot put it out.*

Here's what happens to you, you listen now: *As the light comes nearer you will rush to darkness, shrinking from the truth, sometimes retreating to the lesser forms of fear, and sometimes to stark terror. You're going to hear this? But you will advance, because your goal is the advance from fear to truth. The goal you accepted is the goal of knowledge, for which you signified your willingness. Fear seems to live in darkness, and when you are afraid you have stepped back. Here. Let us then join quickly in an instant of light, and it will be enough to remind you that your goal is light.* (Chap 18:III)

And it will be enough to remind you that our goal of finding correspondence in the light that is being reflected from the intensity of a predetermination that it's available to us, is what we're sharing together. I am going to take just a moment as Master Teacher, who has been through all of the devastations that I am sharing with you, in the recognition that we're actually sharing the devastation of what's going on in this world today. All I want to help you with is my certainty that it's not out there.

Here's a problem: as long as you believe that in the projection of your own mind, there's a light formulation that can, at the speed of light, hold you in the bondage of light separation, you cannot not believe that it is true. Look with me: you will use, within your conceptual formulation of yourself, every device that you can employ to keep from the complete resurrection. I am going to use the word "repair": The repair of the instant of the schism, of the idea of separation, within universal mind, has been accomplished, and you're actually back in a new parameter of time, in which we share. We'll call it Heaven. Certainly you're at the gate of Heaven (can you see that with me?). Because every time you now begin (it's time for you!) to get a reflection of the pain and death, you have located (this is our Course In Miracles) in recognition of self responsibility, your determination – that you have been causing, out in this world, in a false refraction that is the illusion of the "particlization" of light form – that has not allowed you to see this instant of joy that we're sharing.

Now, from our satellite broadcasting down into the light, there's a great deal of chaos going on in the world. Come on, you can hear me! I saw what's going on in your world. Do you think, for one moment, that I would actually participate in the idea of blowing yourself up in body form, the idea of protecting yourself, within your own body, the idea of declaring a martyrdom about your self in your determination to die, the idea that love is necessary within the containment of your own mind, when the simple truth of the matter is that love is what you are? Now, your need to experience that (that just occurred to you) in the idea of the dream, will change the illusion of your self and will formulate a hologram of light association, in which the energy conversion of the power of the mass of light, has been converted. This from our science magazine – remember how I described about the hologram? This will only take a few minutes. I want to include it in with the idea of body location, and can show you that the light itself is not concerned about separate ideas of body formulation, but only the revealing of a new light that will be so intense that the idea of your black instant of devastation of pain and death will be converted. As it was just then, and will be from this moment on. And that's what a new continuum of time is.

Query: are we celebrating love together? Does it have anything to do with my own body formulation? Have you forgiven me, in the forgiving of yourself that we're actually not bodies at all? Can you recognize a healing of the process of the energy of our association of body that allows you to view me in the immediacy of a perspective of a new continuum of time, (listen) where everywhere (look with me) we begin to look in our ideas of our self, we begin to recognize memories of love that somewhere in time, we have shared? A little personal reference here: does that include the moment of love that I felt for my Japanese friend, who was previously a devastating enemy in my idea of my self, into which we found our selves in an association that was so devastating that it simply could not be stood? I was looking at your idea of the collapse of the Trade Center. It's going to be almost two years. Are you going to hear this with me: That's an impossible situation! Even now, as you live it within your own dream, you see over and over again this entering into that Trade Center. OK, listen to me. How does that compare with the devastation that I felt within my own mind, how does it compare with all of the devastation that you're feeling in the illusionary idea (you listening?) that this is life? It's not! This is not what life is. Here's just a moment about the hologram that you're contained in. Listen:

Black Hole Thermodynamics:

A central player in these developments is the Black Hole. Black Holes are a consequence of general relativity. Albert Einstein, 1915, geometric theory of gravitation: In this theory gravitation arises from the curvation of space/ time, which makes objects move as if they were pulled by a force. Conversely the curvation is caused by the presence of matter and energy. According to Einstein's equations, a sufficiently dense concentration of matter or energy will curve space/time so extremely that it rends forming a black hole. The laws of relativity forbid anything that went into a black hole from coming out again, at least within the classic non-quantum descriptions of the physics. The point of no return, called the event horizon of the black hole, is of course important, and extremely important, in the simplest case, the horizon is a sphere who's surface area is larger for more massive black holes. But listen. It is impossible to determine what is inside the black hole; no detail information can emerge across the horizon and escape into the outside world. In disappearing forever into a black hole however, a piece of matter does leave some trace. It cannot not, and that's what makes it interesting. If the matter is captured, while circling the hole, its associated angular momentum is added to the black hole's angular momentum. Then, both the mass and angular momentum of a black hole are measurable from their effects on space/ time around the hole. In this way the laws of conversion of energy and angular momentum are upheld by the black hole, since this is the fundamental law of the second law of thermodynamics.

Now, what I am presenting to you (listen) within the illusion of the formulation of entropy, human being, is the idea that you're going to retain the mass within your own galactic association – and use yourself up – in which you attempt to protect yourself within the idea of the containment within your black hole, that formulates a mass or energy of light that continually circumvents the idea of that containment. In a literal sense it's a formulation of galaxies, since each galaxy contains a black hole.

Say to me, "I am a galaxy." Sure! The relative association of the molecular association of the correspondence of the measurement of relationships between macrocosm and microcosm, would show you instantly that the relative distance between the "particlization" of your mind is totally meaningless, except in its own formulation of itself. Yes, it sounds like the Master Teacher. Why? I have had an experience of the illumination of my body form, in my new galactic association that I think I am going to call, through the light and love of my savior Jesus, "a quasar". Say to me, "Ah, I believe I just had a quasar experience!" When I look at your relative association out in the universe, I begin to spot, rather than circular galaxies, that are holding me in the density of separation, a moment of quasar. At that moment I lost my black hole! Now, as the quasar energy of re-association of light within extra galactic association begins to occur, it will effect, not at the speed of light, but in quantum, outside of it, the idea that, rather than trying to protect yourself from the black hole (now I am teaching directly from the source of the necessity for forgiveness within your own mind), there is an increase in the energy in the non defense of the non utilization of my self within the formulation. This is called forgiving yourself. Because in each moment I correspond to the extension of the light of my mind, which emanates from a single source, which we know of as God, since, (come on!) the source of our reality is eternal life, extending forever. Now, you have been included in with the idea of that light form, even though you were determined to reject it. Now, as you collapse into the black hole, you will always emerge further along than you were in time, until suddenly you come into the bright light, (are you listening to me?) of the realization of each other. That will express our moments of love for each other, in a quasar that's about to occur in you. Listen:

Truth has rushed to meet you since you called upon it. Here's your quasar. If you knew Who walks beside you on the way that you have chosen, fear would be impossible. You do not know because the journey into darkness has been long and cruel, and you have gone deep into it. A little flicker of your eyelids, closed so long, has not yet been sufficient to give you confidence in yourself, so long despised. Look with me. You go toward love still hating it, and terribly afraid of its judgment upon you. Look. And you do not realize that you are not afraid of love, but only of what you have made of it. Look with me. You are advancing to love's meaning, and away from all illusions in which you have surrounded it. When you retreat to the illusion your fear increases, for there is little doubt that what you think it means is fearful. Yet what is that to us who travel surely and very swiftly away from fear?

This from Jesus, in his Course, dear brothers:

You who hold your brother's hand also hold mine, for when you joined each other you were not alone. Do you believe that I would leave you in the darkness that you agreed to leave with me? In your relationship is this world's light. And fear must disappear before you now. Be tempted not to snatch away the gift of faith you offered to your brother. You will succeed only in frightening yourself. The gift is given forever, for God Himself received it. You cannot take it back. Look: You have accepted God. The holiness of your relationship is established in Heaven. You do not understand what you accepted, but (you listen) *remember that your understanding is not necessary. All that was necessary was merely the wish to understand. That wish was the desire to be holy. The Will of God is granted you. For you desire the only thing you ever had, or ever were.* (Chap 18:III)

And each instant that we spend together, will show you the new association that we have discovered with each other.

And in that discovery with each other, were the light and the love that we have now found in this moment of revelation. This organization of the procedure of the mind training of A Course In Miracles will now be available to you until the end of time. And if you share this with me as a Master Teacher of light and as you now begin to recognize our self, and we begin to share this moment of joy together, the gratitude that I am feeling by your willingness to accept the fundamental idea of the love I am feeling for you right now, and that we're sharing together, is going to be a merger so intensely bright in the passion of self realization, that this world is about to disappear, because it only lasted for that moment in your mind, and is now over and gone, and we're going to say together in this new continuum of time, "God bless us, each and everyone," in the recognition of the mission to come in to dark form of light that we accepted in the certainty that we could bring that light of conversion with us, just as we did right there, and all of the illusion of the pain and death that formerly constituted your dream of death, has become a dream of light and love that we share. Welcome Home, welcome to the light of love that at this moment dissolves the entirety of this universal idea of death.

The Paradox
of Eternal Life

The nature of the human consciousness is a definition of its existent self. Each one of us is evolved or involved in that definition of existence. What an exciting possibility! In the aspects of that, we suffer from the existent associations of ourselves. Is this true? Yes!

Good, now let's move to an admission of singular inclusion. I'm just curious to see whether at some point, as we progress in the nature of our individual transformations, this will be reasonably recognized as factual. The nature of the human consciousness is a definition of its existent self.

This is expressed in the fundamental teachings of Jesus of Nazareth from the very beginning of his ministry — you might say from the point of his illumination, allowing for his baptism at which time God said: *This is my beloved Son in whom I am well pleased.* (Matthew 3:17) Those of you to whom this has occurred are cognizant of what I am saying in this regard. All Jesus of Nazareth ever said from that moment on is that you are perfect as God created you and that all of your conceptual associations of existent form are not real. At no point, if you pick up any part of Jesus' teachings, does he say anything but this. Not only does he inform you from his own certainty that this is true, but he directs you that contained inherently in your existent human association, is the "self-certainty" by which you are using the power of your individual thought processes to both deny, and affirm, the Reality of God.

This is the message of his Sermon on the Mount. (Matthew 5-7). It is a statement of your entirety of Self and the manner of its recapitulation through defenselessness and extended service. All of the teachings of Jesus, obviously, as a whole human association transformed, are contained in Sermon on the Mount, and are directly and immediately and inevitably not accepted by your "objective conditional reality."

Listen to me. If we could start with the premise that the teaching is not acceptable to you, we could make progress immediately. As long as you believe some aspect of the problem, or the solution, can be determined within your own conceptual mind, you will suffer from the condition of conceptualism, which is inherently, if there is a source of total singular eternally-creative Reality, false! That is, separation is impossible if, in fact, God is whole and real and perfect. Now we have the dilemma. We also have the solution.

If the dilemma is separation, the admission of the separation and the inclusion of the entirety of you must afford you a solution to the problem, since you are obviously an expression of the problem. Why isn't it, then, if I pick up the Course In Miracles, or if I pick up the Sermon on the Mount, that there is not an immediate admission of the necessity for the totality of non-definition?

That is, why doesn't the consciousness immediately say, "Oh, I see what you mean. Do you mean that none of me is true?" Contained in the answer to that question is the illogical necessity to explain to any self-existent reality what it is!

"Oh, I see; none of me is real" is a sure indication that the self-association believes a portion of it is true. Otherwise it would not be able to, or indeed have need to, affirm that it was not! Into this impossible situation come the teachers of God. Did anybody hear this? I hope so.

Say to me, "I am a lawyer."

Say to me, "Lawyers always lie."

Is that the truth? "How can it be, if you always lie?"

"Well, not this time!" That's the whole problem. If this statement is the truth, then lawyers don't always lie. But if you're telling the truth, you're lying.

I'm not solving it for you; I'm just trying to let you see the dilemma of the paradox of attempting to teach in the separation of the cause and the effect. I'm not sure how clear that was to you.

A Course In Miracles teaches that any sequential association will bring a result that is not real because it is already past. That's one of the easier ways to avoid the dilemma of the paradox of an assertion of an unreality based on an attempt to make it real within the limited parameters of the consciousness. In any particular sense, obviously, all conceptual thought is paradoxical by the separation of cause and effect. There is actually no solution to the problem. Fortunately!

But, inevitably, the human perceptual mind will continue to spin around on the possibility that there is a definition that will gratify the totality of its own mind. It is literally not so. This is precisely and exactly why you need a miracle, or that the teaching must be only to the rejection of all of the definitions of yourself in order to have the experience of a new transformative reality. You are contained in the temporal invention of your own objective location. All of the apparent instructional modalities of intervention will appear to both verify and justify your meaningless conditional self-consciousness. What an impossible predicament!

Now, if I declare to you the falsity of the mechanisms of my teaching, it may not be understandable to you. I will give you an example: I am literally telling you that there is no reality in the method of teaching A Course In Miracles. That would have to be true if none of this is true. Obviously, the method by which you would come to know "this is not true" would also be not true. There is no solution to this problem, except the paradoxical statements that will be contained in the Course In Miracles. Very simply, "the impossible happened." Very simply, "the impossible did not happen."

Since you are trapped in space/time, in the association of the cause and the effect, you must be a part of the containment of the analyzation of the beginning and end, inherent in the possibility of the separation. Of course!

Say to me, "I've been a liar from the beginning."

That's true?

Well, you are a truthful liar!

Do you see what the conceptual mind is capable of doing? To that conceptual mind it will be true that he is a liar. Now he is caught in a continuing lying situation which will be true for him. What an incredible situation.

I love the solution of the Course In Miracles. It teaches you that time is over, and that your conceptual, temporal associations are always past. Let's see if I can take that to a quantum leap to "now" which is the only time there is. Ready?

All right, hold it! You're jumping my logic!

I see many of you are reaching my conclusions before I do. That's called revelatory thinking. It's a release of the necessity for your individual minds to determine what the hell I'm talking about! Because in truth, I'm not talking about anything! Reality is not about something. Reality is not about having thoughts; it is being who I am.

Obviously this is not acceptable to the human condition which must define the religion of its thoughts as separate from the holistic science of its fundamental awareness.

Teilhard de Chardin, the enlightened paleontologist/ priest, who is a positive assertion of "the evolutionary revelation necessary to remember your own Universal Mind," was rejected both by the Jesuits and by the scientific community, and wasn't allowed to publish anything until after his apparent demise. This is as recent as 1955. But the definitive correspondence in the action of his mind is a sure indication of his own certain self-realization that "the conceptual mind of man, by definition, physically, could be converted to the reality of Universal Mind." So we are in the paradox of judgment.

"All judgment is false" is a form of judgment. Wow! Let me try it in space/time for you. I'll show you the paradox of so-called growth: "At no single moment can you determine a change from one aspect to another." This is a simple fact of the matter. If you observe a child growing and you look at a picture of two years ago, and he has grown three inches, at no moment can you determine when that growth occurred.

Your attempts to determine when that growth occurred are what are locking you in space/time sequentiality. It doesn't seem as though it does, but your mind is incapable of instantaneousness, because your observation of the growth is contained in a past association of it, and must be compared to subsequent identities within the factoring of sequential time. Do you understand that? This is a statement of fact.

If I were to take a tadpole, if I had a sequence in frames of reference, and watched a tadpole evolve to a frog, at no moment could I determine when it was between being a tadpole and a frog. Why? Because at any moment its past is gone and its future not yet. It is, as Jesus calls it in the Course, a "Holy Instant of Singular Truth." It closes the gap between the causes and effects of any conceptual involvement. It is a moment of loss of necessity for any sequential continuity of thought patterns that justify the apparent progression from "tadpole to frog" or from "frog to frog on a lily pad." It is a quantum leap to "the certainty of perfect singular Self-Reality."

Here is the testament of Jesus, with that certainty, performing his healing ministry of instant communication through acts of love and forgiveness, using analogies and parables vitalized through the bright correspondence of his illuminate mind.

Listen to this simple reasoning that is so objectionable to your separated (sinful) worldly self-establishment: *Ye have heard that it was said by them of old time* (in memories), *Thou shalt not commit adultery; But I say unto you, That whosoever looketh on a woman to lust after her hath committed adultery with her already...* (Matthew 5:27-28) All of your apparent bodily actions, or those of "anybody" for that matter, can only demonstrate ideas about yourself. All of them are already always over and gone. I don't think that this simple admonition is acceptable to the structural objectivity of the human condition. But then how could or would it be? In fact, he demonstrates to you directly his certainty that anything that can possibly occur is already contained within the aggregate predetermination of your own conceptual identity of mind. He literally is saying, "Nothing is outside of you." "Outside of you there is nothing."

If you need to demand and demonstrate, through weakness and fear, "No, there is something outside of me that can be sinful, and I am not a part of that," all you are maintaining is that there is no totality of reality in the grace of God. This is the whole Sermon on the Mount. It will be repeated again and again and again that all of your judgments are what? Judgments about yourself! And further, a judgment about a self that has no reality. This is A Course In Miracles. All of your judgments are meaningless! If you sin here, you sin out there. Your brother is a reflection of your own mind. But this isn't any different than it was 2,000 years ago. Why is it not acceptable? The condition of rejection in perceptual mind is the verification for its reality. Do you understand?

Let's see if I can show you in another paradox. Here we go — you can spin this if you want to: *All ravens are black.* That obviously means that there are some white ravens. You can kick that around all you want, but there must be an alternative.

Otherwise you would just say: *All ravens are.* Can you hear that? All ravens are black has to mean that there is some raven that is not black. It cannot not be so. It is a paradox that cannot be resolved except by the admission of "What difference is it going to make?"

Saying *all ravens* will still necessitate a definition of your association with yourself — a self-conceptual identity that literally blocks the reality of wholeness from your sight.

In Sermon on the Mount, when Jesus says that you've got the beam in *your* eye, never mind the mote in your brother's eye (Matthew 7:4), he is saying literally that your mind is split in judgment, and because of that there is no way you can come to know the truth about yourself. No part of conceptual association is true. This is an astonishing idea and its admission can be truly enlightening.

Now you are going to try to teach this. The admission of the correspondence, that is, the necessity to teach at all, is where the paradox occurs. If I said to you that all of my teaching is totally meaningless, as Jesus would say in the Course — all of your concepts are totally senseless — *Your meaningless thoughts are showing you a meaningless world* (Lesson 11), perhaps to you, and certainly to most so-called Course In Miracles students, that becomes and remains a perceptual observation. What nonsense! A perceptual observation of what with what? Apparently a continuing analyzation of their meaningless perceptual discernment of a meaningless world!

Listen to this: *Everyone must come to know there is no world. You are perfect as God created you. You are not from here. There is no world.* (Lesson 132) Are these ideas acceptable to you? The requirement obviously is, and this is the teaching of Jesus, that it be acceptable to you, since you are the "adversary" contained within your own conceptual existence, and reasonably somewhere in time you will and did accept it. This world was over a very long time ago! That is, there is no separation or adversary to God in reality, except your own perceptual/conceptual association with the nothingness of yourself.

Let's try one more paradox:

Say to me, "I've only got a dime to my name."

Here's another dime. Now you have less than you had before.

I'll do it once more: "I only have a dime, I'm very poor."

Here's another dime. Now you are poorer.

Does everyone see this? Of course it's true. I'm twice as poor. The more dimes I have, the poorer I'll be, because I define myself as poor by the limitation of the dimes.

"Oh, that's nonsense. You keep giving me dimes until I have a truckload of them, and I'll come and dump a whole truckload of dimes and show you how prosperous I am."

All you really have is a truckload of meaningless memory of poorness or weakness or lack. It's a potential that you use to sustain your temporal mortality until self-annihilation is accomplished. I'll tell you that this is nonsense. You are just poorer and poorer because you are defining yourself by the limitation of the necessity of your own existence!

What is the solution? Give the dime away! God only gives. Many of you are experiencing the intensely happy necessity to do the same. In the act of giving the dime away, you will accumulate the wealth of Universal Mind, not based on the security of separation/possessing that the dime gave you in your own limitation of self-conception.

Wow! You're hearing me! You find this teaching very exciting!

To those who have less, less will be given. How does Jesus say it? *...from him that hath not shall be taken away even that which he hath.* (Matthew 25:29) This is the whole teaching. This is exhilarating to look at if you let it be! *Protect all things*

you value by the act of giving them away. (Lesson 187)
Your definition of yourself is the limitation of sickness, pain
and death that you believe are your inevitable endowment,
and indeed they are, within the containment of your own
separation.

Mind is idea because everything is an idea. Death is an
idea. Eternal Life is an idea. Your ideas about yourself are
simply unreal.

Remember that ideas leave not their source. You must
release them and set yourself free.

Obviously you are having experiences of the loss of your
conceptual identity. If you proceed with that, you will come
to see that the physical act of resurrection is going on in this
place at this time. It is a totality of conceptual realization, not
defined within the limitation of temporal location. It is the act
of the power of your mind expressed in the certainness of your
wholeness in Universal Mind.

So what is our premise here? That this teaching is not, in
this place and time, acceptable. But the question is not that.
The question is, is it acceptable to you? It's the whole teaching
of Jesus. He says, "Your kingdom is not of this world." He says,
you are not from here but from Heaven. All of the requests he
makes of you in His Gospel of Truth are always rejected totally
by this world very simply because the acceptance of them
is what salvation is. The moment they are accepted by you,
individually, in the consort of your own endeavor to remain
separate, you will spring into Heaven. Quite literally this world
is an illusion of the concepts of your own determination to
resist the inevitable transformation of you from separation to
wholeness. So the admonition "I need do nothing" is obviously
not acceptable.

The next one that will occur in Sermon on the Mount says
that if you judge your brother, they are going to lock you up and
throw you in the pit. That is inevitably going to be true, because
you are participating in the illusion of your previous associated

thoughts, and what you are doing unto your brother, you are doing unto yourself. If I need to read it to you, I'll read it.

It is going to rain on the good guys and the bad guys. (Matthew 5:45) God is totally indiscriminate as to the necessity for you to be perfect as you are created. Obviously that must be rejected, because you, as a conceptual consort, believe there are methods by which you can come to know the truth. That is literally impossible. If you could really be separate from God, there is no possibility that you could come to know of a singular Eternal Reality simply because there wouldn't and couldn't be any! Do you see? This is the entire teaching of Jesus Christ.

Now you can say, "Well, Martin Luther taught the same thing; salvation through grace, never by judgmental good works." Of course! So why don't you be graceful and come to God? Why are you not willing to admit that there are no devices by which you can come to know "who you really are," because "who you really are" is inevitable in the totality of your own mind? It is not open to the self-incriminating argument of limitation based on your own correspondence in space/time. Are you at last face-to-face with the impossible dilemma of not knowing your own Self? I hope so. Now you, individually, can begin to undergo the process of the release of the necessity for the defense of your own conceptual self. *Resist not evil.* (Matthew 5:39) *If I defend myself I am attacked.* (Lesson 135)

I am sure that the visitors here wonder what is going on. This, of course, is the Workbook of A Course In Miracles. The problem with this is that they will believe that somehow you are consorting together through interpretive judgment to reach conclusions about this teaching. Nonsense. This is to inform you, directly, that your human circumstance is only a denial and assault on the Source of your own Eternal Reality.

All of your establishments literally attack God! Do you see why the teachings of Jesus are not acceptable? For you to pretend they're acceptable to you must be nothing but a denial of what they say. Just as any interpretation of the Course In

Miracles is literally an attack on its author and his message. It says very simply that you are perfect and whole as God created you. That does not require a definition, and obviously any definition would be a denial of your own wholeness.

You are not a definition.

You are not a judgmental association of anything.

All judgment is false, including this statement.

Accept this process. Otherwise you are going to end up with: "All lawyers are liars." Is that true? Yes, except this one!

Now you are in the dilemma of determining which part of you is true, and which part of you is false. From that, there is no escape. Fortunately, if we can get you to see that all of your concepts are always only past each moment, and that if you don't continue to hold onto and organize them in the definition of yourself, you will not continue to sequence time to the certainty of your own temporal demise.

It is amazing that the human condition accumulates its own scarcity, because by its scarcity it defines its reality; that fundamentally the more security it apparently has, the more threat and doubt it must experience. I just came back to that one once more. Quite literally the more it has, the more poverty. It would have to be so, because its doubt is contained in its necessity to accumulate or possess factual information within its own mind to justify itself. None of it is true.

In reality, attack and defense are the same idea. No matter how much it accumulates, it cannot define when it will be complete, because accumulation is a denial of the completion. That's a very ancient paradox. You could never define what is the sufficiency of the association. The whole is not the sum of its parts.

I am teaching you that any single moment is a totality of time within itself, and that a pile of separate moments cannot arrive at a whole continuity of reality. It is impossible. But if that's true, my solution would be only to let myself be what I am as a wholeness in my own mind, without the necessity to justify the accumulation of my past grievous memories. This is the Gospel of the New Testament.

As you judge you will be judged. (Matthew 7:2) What goes around, comes around. Stop trying to get even. *You will believe that others do to you exactly what you think you did to them.* (Chapter 27) All pain is self-inflicted.

What a strange place you're in where this simple truth need be rejected! So, what if you decided not to judge because all judgment was only of yourself and false anyway?

Give to him that asketh...Love your enemies...be the children of your Father which is in heaven. (Matthew 6:42,44,45) These, the true teachings of Jesus of Nazareth. At last, the whole simple truth of you has found you out. You wouldn't dare to really begin practicing this, would you? Could you? You would begin to forgive immediately. Your self-imposed grievances would begin to disappear. You would begin to undergo the experience of your own resurrection immediately. Why would you not, except that you, individually, are in a denial of it, contained within your own mind?!

You are hell-bent on retaining a necessity for a definition of this teaching. Yet all the definitions of these teachings, according to the Author and His direction, are false and forms of denial. You are caught in "according to the teaching." Your accord in regard to the teaching has nothing to do with its truth or with reality in the slightest very simply because there is no such thing as your judgmental accord! You can go on insisting there is and say, "There is, too." All I would then admonish you is that whatever part of you you think is real is contained within the spatial/temporal identity you have given yourself in this association. It is impossible that it be creative because you remain perfect, *even as your Father which is in Heaven is perfect.* (Matthew 5:48)

Let's get to the possibility, just for a moment, that you, as a physical entity of consciousness thought, can undergo an experience whereby you can come to know your own perfect totality. Is that possible? Of course, how could it not be? It would be impossible that you do not know this. I'm looking right at this with you and telling you that the certainty of this is contained in the possibility of it. Very simply, any possibility must be a possibility of the totality of its association with itself, not with the definition of itself.

Consider the lilies of the field, how they grow, they toil not, neither do they spin. And yet I say unto you, That even Solomon in all his glory was not arrayed like one of these. (Matthew 6:28-29) They are absolutely perfect as created by God.

You say to me, "I am not a lily of the field." I say, what does that have to do with it?

May you not have a perfect thought of a perfect lily? All you are doing is denying the perfection of the lily and of yourself. The admission of the perfection of the lily would be the admission of the perfection of everything, because everything is perfect as created by God, not by your definition of the comparison of the lilies with the thorn. Do you understand me?

So the weakness is always only in the concepts, not in the lily or most certainly not in any action that you may perform. Obviously, any action in regard to the separation lays a double hiatus on the problem and literally becomes a cancel-out where no progress is possible at all, because you are basing your reality on the effects that are already gone. That's why Jesus says, if you lust in your heart, if you have any sense of committing the act, it has already occurred. Your denial of it, and the declaration that your brother caused it, is simply a denial of your own sinful, guilty, judgmental self. What a definitive way to teach it! "As a man thinketh..." is really all I'm saying.

So, these are the teachings of Jesus of Nazareth. The curiosity would be if it is possible that you could at some time pick this up and go out and actually teach the Sermon on the Mount. Obviously, the human consciousness mind is in the denial that it is an adulterer — adulterer in the sense of the totality of denial of God and copulation with idols of his self-possessed mind. Any adulation is obviously a denial of the whole eternally-creating Mind of God and of your own.

The necessity for the conceptual conglomerate to retain the separateness will begin to astound you.

Returning to Teilhard de Chardin — all he tries to teach is that "Nothing is more religious than the idea of evolution." How much more certainty could there be that "There is a God" than the idea that you were separate and are returning to God?! It solves your whole problem of "Who, what and why am I?"

Why does that have to be rejected, except in the limitations imposed by your human consciousness in its own conceptual identity, denying the creative necessity of its own mind to come to the truth of the inclusiveness of its individual Christhood with God and your neighbor? Or the necessity for you to admit to a single whole causation of Eternal Life?

What surprises me is that the religious establishment needs to deny evolution and proclaim that God created everything in an instant. Not that there is an objection at all to that idea, unless they maintain that God created evil things along with good things, which reasonably doesn't make any sense.

The entirety of God creating is not in question. All that is in question is the necessity for your own separate self-existence in an eternally creative singular relationship.

You are learning, then, a new manner of thinking. Is this true, human beings, of you and all of this world? Yes! Is that what is going on in your mind? Yes! It is not a definition of non-judgment — it is literally a moment, a Holy Instant, when you don't try to compare the previous associations with the present ones? Yes! It is that simple!

So any determination of progression or accumulation of precepts of self-conception is the falsity. This is the whole teaching of the Course In Miracles. You are already home in Heaven. Notice that it allows for the idea that "you might not have been" for just a moment. In that moment it will declare that "you never really left." Which is true? Both, of course. The question is not that. The question is who and where are you now? I am telling you that it's all contained within your own mind. This is what you are now finding very exciting.

But in the admission of "there is nothing outside of you" is the requirement for the forgiveness of your brother, quite literally, because it is the admission that his body form is a projection of your mind. That you are the cause of him! If you are indeed the cause of him, the necessity for you to forgive him would be obvious in perceptual association.

If you are the cause of him, you are the cause of his sin, sickness and death.

And as you do unto others, you do unto yourself. As you sow, so must you reap. These are the representative statements of Sermon on the Mount and the admission and practice of it is what Sermon on the Mount directs.

Forgiveness is only necessary because you believe that sin, that is, separation from God, is possible and that there is a choice in the matter. In the need to forgive, you justify the possibility of choice. We must then admit to you the possibility of choice, although it is not true. I'm teaching now directly from the certainty of my own singular whole reality that has evolved through a miraculous transformation.

It is not true that you can choose to be separate from God, Which is everything that is. That is not a true possibility. Therefore, any perceptual choice is not so. Do you understand? All choices will only be to "verify the separation" or to "sustain the single problem", which is what separation is.

One problem: Separation. One solution: Reunion.

If you never try to solve the problem of who you are, the problem will always be solved because there is no problem.

Any attempt to solve the problems of yourself or this world must be contained within the association of your definitions of your own self-consciousness.

I am not a body. I am free. For I am still as God created me. (Lessons 201-220) Now, with that declaration you are beginning to reap the harvest of the Holy Instants of Love that are an inherent part of the entire structure of the Noosphere, as our Jesuit mystic/priest teaches it. That is, an aggregate of the astral associations of definitions of our mutual divinity that surround us in our entirety of love and recognition of each other for the purpose of union with Universal Mind. He calls it Christogenesis.

What amazes me is that temporal prefaces will be written to what I am saying, and spatial prefaces and augmentations of conceptual identities will verify and interpret, in their own mind, the teaching of Sermon on the Mount without the simple admission of the whole truth of the Christ Jesus teaching. They are both the cause and the effect of their own identity in the process of a revolutionary rebirth and recovery from separation to an instantaneous reunion with the reality of Eternal Life. Yet this knowledge cannot not be known to each and everyone.

Behold, I shew you a mystery; We shall not all sleep, but we shall all be changed, in a moment, in the twinkling of an eye, at the last trump: for the trumpet shall sound, and the dead shall be raised incorruptible, and we shall be changed. For this corruptible must put on incorruption, and this mortal must put on immortality. (I Cor 15:51-53)

This will also begin to amaze your awakening minds. Listen to the inspirational instruction and direction offered by this God-realized mind. We're quoting from Meditations with Teilhard de Chardin published in 1988.

As a direct consequence of the unitive process by which God is revealed to us, God in some way 'transforms self" when incorporating us. So, it is no longer a matter of simply seeing God and allowing oneself to be enveloped and penetrated by God— we have to do more: we have to disclose God (or even in one sense of the word "complete" God) ever more fully. All around us, and within our own selves, God is in process of "changing" as a result of the coincidence of God's magnetic power and our own Thought. As the "Quality of cosmic Union" rises, so the brilliance increases, and the glow of God's coloring grows richer.

Disclose God through our cosmic union with Him? Be enveloped and penetrated by God? Are you listening?

God can in the future be experienced and apprehended (and can even, in a true sense, be completed) by the whole ambient totality of what we call Evolution. This is still, of course, Christianity and always will be, but a Christianity reincarnated for the second time (Christianity we might say, squared) in the spiritual energies of Matter.

Christ does not act as a dead or passive point of convergence, but as a center of radiation for the energies that lead the universe back to God through humanity, the layers of divine action finally come to us impregnated with divine organic energies. Organic energy? No wonder this Jesuit (Disciple of Jesus) had to be subdued, controlled and contained. Listen: *Not in a metaphysical but in a physical sense, the Energy of Incarnation was to flow into, and so illuminate and give warmth to even wider and more tightly encircling forms of embrace.* How incredible! He asserts there is an Omega point, a Holy Instant in space/time, where all of this comes together.

Starting from an evolutive Omega at which we assume Christ to stand, not only does it become possible to conceive Christ as radiating physically over the terrifying totality of things, but, what is more, that radiation must inevitably work up to a maximum of penetrative and activating power. The cosmic-Christ becomes cosmically possible. To sum up, Cosmogenesis reveals itself, along the line of its main axis, first as Biogenesis and then Noogenesis, and finally

141

culminates in Christogenesis. Look! This is the transformation and realization of your own individual objective reality!

What kind of Jesuit theology is this? Very simply, an admission of unqualified apostleship to the singular totality of Jesus Christ mind. Even more simply, "you are the only living Son of God."

Do you understand why this teaching requires a pretense of interpretation as a form of rejection? Holy mackerel. He's teaching physical resurrection! It's important that we go on with this.

There are two sides to this operation, the constructive and the destructive; and when Christ is installed at Omega Point it is both these two sides that are covered and permeated by a flood of unitive force. In one great surge, Cosmogenesis becomes personalized, both in the things it adds, which centrify us for Christ, and in the things it subtracts, which draw us out of our own centers onto him. A current of love is all at once released, to spread over the whole breadth and depth of the World; and this it does as a fundamental essence which will metamorphose all things, assimilate and take the place of all. And more. There is, in truth, a secret message, explanatory of the whole of Creation, which by allowing us to feel God in everything we do, and in everything that is done to us (God creating all things and being born in all things) can bring true happiness to our generation. Christ is incarnate; incarnate through the combined action of determinant and liberating factors, and of grace. He insists that our minds must perform this. You will do this with your own act of forgiveness.

Here is his definition of unconditional love: *Love is the free and imaginative outflowing of the Spirit over all unexplored paths. It links those who love in bonds that unite, but do not destroy, causing them to discover in their mutual contact an exaltation capable of stirring in the very core of their being all that they possess of "uniqueness" and "creative"power. Love alone can unite living beings so as to complete and fulfill them, for it alone joins them by what is deepest in themselves. All we need is to imagine our ability to love developing until it embraces the totality of the people of the Earth.* And of the Universe! This is a capacity that you must acknowledge in yourself! Wow!

Purity simply denotes the more-or-less distinct manner in which the ultimate center of their coincidence appears above the two beings in love. No question here of leaving one another, but only of joining in a greater than themselves. The world does not become divine by suppression but by sublimation. Its sanctity is not an elimination but a concentration of the sap of the Earth. Those of you who may still be suffering a little bit from your attempts to define special and holy relationships as presented by Jesus in A Course In Miracles, and you feel somehow uneasy because you have apparently specialized in what appears to be the uniqueness of your need to define yourself, be not concerned. If you have entered into this association, the admission of the possibility of the failure of your holy relationship is what affirms it — not the affirmation of the Holy Instant.

Can you hear this? I'll back this up a little. Here's what we've been saying:

It isn't necessary for you to affirm that you are holy. You already are as God created you.

The grace of forgiveness contained in what appears to be a holy relationship is only our certainty of the ultimate or total unreality of our earthly association. We then can allow ourselves the mistake of our continuing necessity to define it in some manner. Encompassed in that entirety will be the act of forgiveness, which is actually what Love is.

It is not the definition of the mistake, but only the admission that matters. We are redeemed in the totality of the admission of our fallibility, based on the certainty that you and I have come from outside of time to perform this act of saviorship through a miracle of forgiveness and loving service.

All holy relationships recognize the singularity and eternity of Mind. As you have answered this call, there is no question about the eternal nature of your mind, and therefore no real question about any manners, however apparently unruly, in which we attempt to insinuate into this unreal world of separation. This is true very simply because we are aware that our miraculous reparation of separation, while a necessary single happy solution, is in reality as unreal as the problem itself. With that, we are released from the necessity to define any method whatsoever by which we suddenly have become whole and loving with each other and the entire Universe.

You can make a mistake, but you can't sin, because this world of your own temporal identity is not real. So make some mistakes with me. I am a whole part of your own entire solution to the unsolvable problem of separation that is the nightmare of loneliness, pain and death, representing the nothingness of this world. I guarantee you that if your dedication is to remain mortal and suffer and die as your own body identity, that is exactly what you are going to do.

If you change your mind, there is nothing in the Universe that can contain, restrict or prevent your decision to use the potential of love, which is inherent in you, to come to know you are perfect as God created you. In other words, use up your potential of memories of pain and of loss. Don't project them into a future of nothingness! Don't analyze the Love of God! Utilize it as the whole of your creative reality! Your definitions are expressions of the limitations of the containment. If you want to be confined to your mind, you are going to be confined to your own mind.

God only gives. So what's your problem? Remember healing love is not in your definition of the giving, but only in the action. Definition is a form of retention of weakness and loss. Giving is creative energy that flows from you to the totality of Universal Mind.

All I am really saying is that all of your definitions are not true. Do you understand? I know you have a dilemma here. You've been a liar from the beginning. (John 8:44) And certainly you appear to be imprisoned in a cycle of self-termination because this has been your intention. Is this true? You are trapped in your own mind. If you will let a lie and truth be the same idea, you will have no problem. The totality of the lie is what truth is, not a definition of what a lie is.

You have been a liar from the beginning, but the beginning has nothing to do with reality. The idea that Life has a beginning is a lie. If Life is eternal, it could not possibly have a beginning. There is nowhere that the Father begins and the Son ends. You are at home in Heaven and have never left.

Your *organic Energy, then, becomes Presence. And so the possibility is disclosed for, opens out for, humanity, not only of believing and hoping but (what is much more unexpected and much more valuable) of loving. Co-existing and co-organically with all of the past, the present and the future of the Universe is in a process of concentration upon itself.* Within the reaches of your own mind. So this is an expression of your own totally personal transformation.

It is only toward hyper-reflection — that is to say, hyper-personalization — that thought can extrapolate itself. It is a mistake to look for the extension of our being or of the noosphere in the impersonal (that is, the objective). In any domain — whether it be the cells of the body, the members of the society or the elements of a spiritual synthesis — union differentiates.

Listen, this is one of the more difficult ideas you will encounter. If you believe you are separate and returning to wholeness remember: "The act of union will differentiate, but only in its entirety." "Union, as an abstraction, has no meaning."

145

The idea of objects coming together is impossible. It is in the personalization of the totality of the uniqueness of You as the only living Son of God that your salvation lies. In that sense, you are "totally unique in the entirety of You." Any definition of that uniqueness will be the falsity, or the impurity of perceptual mind.

In every organized whole, the parts perfect themselves and fulfill themselves. This is the whole quantum idea that each cell contains its own wholeness, that any single thought that you have will be perfect unto itself, and requires no other thought whatsoever.

Question: Can pure thoughts come together? Not without joining. If there is no separation in them, they will continue to combine within the separation of your defined uniqueness in recognition and celebration of the certainty of the divine uniqueness of the entirety of you in your own mind in relationship with Universal Mind.

In essence, what we are saying is: You are all the separation there is, and you are also all the wholeness that there is. Which would you rather be? Would you rather be perfect and whole and divine as God created you? Certainly this is an admission possible within the power of your own mind. Or would you prefer to remain in hell, manufactured by you in your determination to be separate? Ah, I see this is becoming comprehensible to you at last.

The solution is not outside of yourself, and obviously herein is what salvation is. All separation is only an attempted definition of Eternal Reality. This is what Teilhard intends to say, right here and now, at this time: All of your self-conceptions are unreal.

All I am trying to get you to do is not sequence your thoughts. Is it true that you can only have one thought at a time? Let me see you have more than a single thought right now. Attempts to do so are what delineate the past from the future, yet your future is as gone as your past since it is a continuing correlation of past thought form association. I'm just backed up to that paradox, so you can observe a distance between your thoughts that constitutes objective reality.

The distance between your thoughts is what space is. It is nothing but a separation of ideas of form you have established in the calibrations of your own mind. It is not true. Why? Your world has no causation. There is no cause for you within the confinement of space/time organization.

In every organized whole, the parts perfect themselves and fulfill themselves. It is a mistake to confuse individuality with personality. It's the only mistake you ever really make. I am the only living Son of God, is not a personality; it is a statement of fact. It is not who you think you are; it is who you are. *To be fully ourselves it is in the direction of convergence with all the rest that we must advance— 'toward the other."* Not toward ourselves; toward the forgiveness of the association. Not turned in, but finally turned out. First turn in, then turn out. First recognize yourself as the foundation, then extend that from you. *The peak of ourselves, the acme of our originality, is not our individuality, but our person;* "beingness" or "person itself." *...and according to the evolutionary structure of the world, we can only find our person by uniting together.* Since we are projections of our own mind. *Socialization means not the end, but rather the beginning of the Era of Person.* Of individual God-like associations! That's a true statement. Do you understand? This is not an ecumenical movement whereby you stay separate and define each other in your own perfection. Rather, it is the admission of a single perfection of which we all share and are each a total part.

Christianity does not ask us to live in the shadow of the Cross but in the fire of its creative action. This is, indeed, an inspirational mind! *But above all Jesus is he who overcomes structurally, in himself and in behalf of us all, that resistance to spiritual ascent which is inevitably part of all created reality. He is the One who bears the weight which is inevitably part of all creative reality. He is both symbol of progress and at the same time its heroic achievement.*

The full and ultimate meaning of redemption is no longer seen to be reparation alone, but rather further passage and conquest. To Reality. You cannot repair what is not real! Stop trying to repair it and you will progress to the certainty of what you are. That is what this says. In other words, the idea of reparation is the idea of the confirmation of separation! Of course. I am telling you there is nothing to repair. As long as you believe you can repair it, you can give value to the idea that sin can be atoned for, thereby making sin real and impossible to atone. If sin is real, Atonement is impossible. If there is such a thing as separation, there is no such thing as wholeness.

What I want, my God, is that by a reversal of focus which you alone can bring about, my terror in the face of nameless changes destined to renew my being may be turned into an overflowing joy at being transformed into you.

Transformed into God? Listen. Jesus is speaking: *Be ye therefore perfect, even as your Father which is in Heaven is perfect.* (Matthew 5:48) Listen again as this Complete Jesuit speaks: *What I want, my God, is that by a reversal of focus* (what is my attention going to be) *which you alone can bring about* (I give up), *my terror in the face of nameless changes* (this is what I am faced with) *destined to renew my being may be turned into an overflowing joy at being transformed into you.* My terror of nameless changes is actually destined to renew my being if I will let it! Acknowledgment of my fear is what my salvation is, not the avoidance of it. I am taught to live in that fearful moment all the time and be transformed.

I am going to deal with suffering for a moment because Teilhard deals with it as a Christian, as did Jesus of Nazareth. See if you can understand the necessity of suffering:

"Is suffering necessary?" You bet! But only because you asked.

"Then suffering is necessary?" Of course. What about it?

"What is the cause of suffering?" You are the one that

asks if suffering is necessary. The idea of "this necessity" is what suffering is!

Why do you ask, unless it is necessary for you to justify your own suffering? Query as to necessity is what suffering is. I suppose, without reducing to sacrifice, that's the whole question: "Why do I have to suffer to get this?" Obviously because it is the path you have chosen to justify your return to Heaven out of this hell of separation.

All I could ask you is why would you consider sacrifice a necessity in order to be perfect as God created you? "What can you in separation and denial possibly contribute to the perfection that you already must be?" Why would giving up hell to remember Heaven be viewed as a loss or sacrifice? What an insane upside-down perspective!

Let's take another turn and review our historic thesis of suffering if it's not sacrificial. *What a vast ocean of human suffering spreads over the entire Earth at every moment! Of what is this mass formed? Of blackness, gaps and rejections? No, let me repeat, it is formed of potential energy.* The idea of potential is actually what the suffering is, because the idea of potential is the idea of a form of limitation. Can you hear this? You can't really define it as gaps; it's not really form. He says all potential is suffering because it is the need to retain your self — objective existence, which is literally what suffering is.

"The need to define your self is what suffering is." This is the simple truth of the whole matter. It would have to be. You suffer from your own existent self-association. Let's see if this is admissible. It's called "The Great Reversal." Let me repeat: It is a formulation of potential energy. It is a matrix of thought form that suffers in retention of the association of itself, separate from God. A black hole. An ultimate impactness of creative energy from which your expanding universe originates each moment of time.

149

You are a self-definition of weakness and vulnerability by the reduction and retention of "possibility." Yet, there is no way that that potential coming from the total impactedness of ultimate suffering — which is what death is, and there is no death — is not fulfilled instantly in the realization of your mind.

In suffering, the ascending force of the world is concealed in a very intense form. That's the idea of sacrifice. In suffering, the ascending force of the world — the inevitability of your return — *is concealed in a very intense form.* And is what? Justified by your necessity to exist.

This whole world depends on suffering in order to sustain itself in the inevitable process of its return to God. It literally suffers by the necessity to be a potential of future possibility in the constraint of sequential space/time instead of simply admitting that none of my potential means anything if I am perfect as God created me.

The whole question is how to liberate it and give it a consciousness of its significance and potentialities. How can we both liberate it and give it a consciousness of its significance — in other words, why suffer if it's not for a purpose? And you would say to me, "I must suffer for a purpose," and begin to suffer. But the more you suffer, the more I'll ask, why is that necessary for you if God is perfect and whole? Obviously you respond, "No pain, no gain."

I'm not going to take the necessity for you to "bottom out" away from you. I'm just suggesting that you understand you are always at your own bottom or point of return to God if "You Will it be so" that "His Will be done." Admitting this world is hopeless is where your conversion to light occurs. You are always and only at the place and time where the total conversion of you is possible. *Time lasted but an instant in your mind, with no effect upon eternity. And so is all time past, and everything exactly as it was before the way to nothingness was made.* (Chapter 26)

You continue to suffer by the necessity to associate time with eternity. Indeed, that's what suffering is; you are separate from God, and you're lonely and you're alone in all the Universe. If being separate from God is not suffering, what is it? Not only is that so, but to you it is very real. You are what suffering is. You don't define love, you define manners in which you can retain your own suffering. Do you hear me?

This world is nothing but a manner of justifying the necessity for you to suffer. You call that love! *Swear not to die, you holy Son of God! You make a bargain that you cannot keep. The Son of Life cannot be killed. What he is cannot be changed.* (Chapter 29) You pretend that everyone must suffer so they can succeed in the denial of the inherent evolutionary process that's going on in them. In other words, you have invented time to keep from remembering the single terrifying moment when you imagined you were separate from God. You invented distance to protect your worship of death. This world is not what Life is!

Obviously I have offered you the totality of the solution, and obviously you have accepted it! Not only is that so, but I am telling you flat out that it is impossible that you did not accept it. All of your potential was never going to be real anyway. Not only that, but each moment you can use it up and live in the glory of your own mind as God. And that moment will have absolutely nothing to do with the manner by which you came to know this. My teaching, then, becomes totally meaningless. The truth is there is no perceptual manner by which you may return and remember Eternal Life!

All Jesus or any demonstration of Singular Reality could ever offer you is the totality of your own perfection in God. This is not acceptable to you. But it will be, and was! If it were, you wouldn't be here. And you're not! Each moment that it is acceptable to you, you are literally not here. I am here to tell you that you are not here. You need the practice of living "not here." There is no such place as this!

Most of you have evolved very simply to the recognition that there is no world. You don't know quite what to do with it, though you certainly are teaching that the world isn't true. Your joy and happiness and freedom of mind are in extending the healing Light and Love of God. Your gratitude for your freedom at last from the bondage of the meaningless self-possessions of your conceptual mind is the Light the world has longed to behold. Your potential for suffering is simply all used up!

The world would leap high towards God if all the sick together were to turn their pain into a common desire that the kingdom of God should come to rapid fruition through the conquest and organization of the Earth. Through the admission of the totality of themselves. If we're going to share pain together, let's share it for a purpose. "If you are going to stand with me to go to God," Jesus says, "let's stand for a purpose." Let's stand for the necessity of our convictions within our own mind so we can join in the inevitability of our return to God. In that, there is contained the structure of "a mansion in my Father's house." (John 14:2) And in that you are segregated by your uniqueness in yourself through the transformation of your own mind and body to the certainty that you are perfect as God created you. You are born again! *Put out your hand, and see how easily the door swings open with your one intent to go beyond it. Angels light the way, so that all darkness vanishes, and you are standing in a light so bright and clear that you can understand all things you see.* (Lesson 131)

May all the sufferers of the Earth join their sufferings, so that the world's pain might become a great and unique act of consciousness, elevation and union. All this says is, you have to admit that you are in a continuing cycle of struggle and resistance and rejection of the Eternal Reality of Happiness and Love that you really are. All it says is, there is no solution to your problem because your problem of separation from Eternal Reality does not exist.

And remember at the moment of no solution there is a spontaneous correction that occurs. It occurs simultaneously at that moment, not in the definition of what that moment is, because the definition of what that moment is what time and space are. Can you hear this? Simultaneously "it happens." Obviously there is no such thing as a "simultaneous event" in a sequential cause-and-effect relationship. Simultaneous becomes a paradox of the necessity for the definition, doesn't it? Just as Newtonian Physics trying to explain the action of Quantum Reality.

Do not brace yourself against suffering. Try to close your eyes and surrender yourself, as if to a great loving energy. This attitude is neither weak nor absurd, it is the only one that cannot lead us astray. Try to "sleep," with that active sleep of confidence which is that of the seed in the fields of winter. You are growing each moment. Healers!

Till the very end of time matter will always remain young, exuberant, sparkling, newborn for those who are willing. This is nothing but the conversion of your cellular body. *Till the very end of time matter will always remain young, exuberant, sparkling, newborn for those who are willing*...to let it be, rather than being trapped into the necessity to die. Your little willingness allows the cellular reassociation of your "place in time" without the necessity of the definition of the longevity that you press on your body in your determination to live in the limitations of your cellular cause and effect. Of course!

Because we are born and live in the very heart of this thing that is happening, we still find it quite natural not only to think with ourselves but also, inevitably, to think with all other persons at the same time: In other words, we can't move a finger without finding ourselves involved in the construction of a total human act that includes what we see and what we make. And what we do and what we are.

What a simple solution that in "every act of giving" is the totality of the creative energy of the Love of God. In that process, in each thing that we do in which we do not formulate and demand attention to our limitation, we are divine. It is impossible if there is a God, that all acts are not divine.

If I can teach you not to attempt to define the actions in your need to participate and distinguish between your acts, you will begin to teach the Sermon on the Mount, which allows you to admit that the causation is only contained within your own mind. Then forgiveness is very simple. You are doing this but to yourself.

"As a man thinketh" describes the Sermon on the Mount. Is that true? Yes! What goes around will come around. If you put it out there and cause pain, you are going to get it back. Why doesn't anybody believe that? They do, but only to the extent that they can justify the continuation of the necessity for it.

There is nothing in the Universe that can stop you from being what you pretend to be if you so choose, because nothing in the Universe knows anything about you. Come on, I'm reminding you of the lonely exclusion that you must be feeling in your own isolation from Eternal Life!

You attempt to share the separation with other associations of the projections of your own mind. That is impossible. You can't share separation. Separation is entrapment in space/time. You can make up things that share the separation, but you can't make them true because separation is not true.

I begin to distinguish the arrangement-curve... not the gentle drift towards equilibrium and rest, but the irresistible "Vortex" which spins into itself, always in the same direction, the whole Stuff of things, from the most simple to the most complex: spinning it into ever more comprehensive and more astronomically complicated nuclei. And the result of this structural torsion is an increase of consciousness, or a rise in psychic temperature. A rise in psychic temperature? These are attempts by Teilhard to express the increasing intense new passions of an all-new creative awareness into which his mind has entered. Much of which began with his "intolerable litter-bearer experiences" during the slaughter called World War I. What he is expressing is a death episode that he experienced. What a vivid realization!

So, in review, we have been directing our attention to the testimony of Jesus Christ wherein He declares that *"your kingdom is not of this world,"* and as a resurrected man, with the certainty of His own totality with God, He directs you from His whole mind to the certainty that you are whole with Him. Sin is only man's original idea of separation from God. This world is the result of your idea of sin. Your own mind is only the whole containment of the guilt of separation. *The wages of sin is death*. (Romans 6:23)

There is no admission in the entire Covenant of Atonement through Jesus Christ of any possibility that sin (separation from God) is real and can happen. You cannot die and Jesus proved it! If you are viewing it that way, you are intentionally misinterpreting it, just as you will misrepresent His message of resurrection as the necessity to suffer and die in order to become perfectly eternal. Obviously that is the antithesis of the proof of Eternal Life that Jesus demonstrates!

If I stood before you and said to you: *I am your resurrection and your life, and whosoever liveth and believeth in me shall never die* (John 11:26), what possible justification would there be for you to continue to suffer within the cyclical reasoning of your conceptual self? What reason for the necessity to terminate what you call life, in order to justify a temporal existence which is not necessary or even possible? This is the whole problem with attempting to teach His simple testimony of Love and Forgiveness. It's amazing.

The attraction of death holds you in that bondage. But the admission of the totality of resurrection, as a Christian, is literally what your salvation is.

Did Jesus Christ really rise up to Heaven? Of course! Then what are you doing here, Christians? *He that believeth on me, the works that I do shall he do also; and greater works than these shall he do; because I go unto my Father.* (John 14:12) If He rose, you've gone along with Him! Why do you attempt to continue to suffer your own self-inflicted crucifixion when the entire propitiation, by your own faith-filled admission, has been accomplished?

This world is over and gone and never was. You're back in Heaven! *Why seek ye the living among the dead?* (Luke 24:5) He is risen!

Many of you are experiencing the brilliantly thrilling microcosmic event of body transfiguration.

It's time for your resurrection! It's time to stand up and teach this to the Christian establishment. Let's try it. They may become very angry with you and attack you very simply because of the necessity for them to continue to *"take the useless journey to the cross,"* as Jesus teaches it in the Course — *The Last Useless Journey* — the idea that you would have to sacrifice something to be whole and perfect as God created you. It's simply not true.

Did we make some progress with this Bible lesson today? We went a little astray, but only so you can see the paradoxical impossibility of my teaching you perceptually of this. I have offered you the fact of this matter through my own recognition of singular Self-awareness and you have accepted it. This world is impossible and does not exist! Separation from Eternal Life is impossible! This will be revealed to you through your own revelation. I am reminding you of the simple truth of who you are as a part of the whole eternal Love that is God and you. Your denial of it will not make it less true.

Everyone must come to know there is no world. There is no such thing as objective reality. There aren't different kinds of life. That's the fact of the matter. This is the sole purpose of resurrection. Your own awakening will instantly confirm that you are not a part of the fearful insanity of this place in time. Obviously those who cling to any purpose whatsoever, in their necessity to justify this spot of suffering, pain, loneliness and death, will appear to remain separate from God. But not in reality. Remember: *A slave to death is a willing slave.*

Let those who can hear, hear. I am releasing you from the contingencies of your old non-existent self-constructed identity. You may still be very fearful of this simple message of total forgiveness and Love. But the fact is you did awaken, through your own Christ Mind, from the amnesia of your false, temporal reality.

It is impossible that I am not directing you to a perfect awareness of whole eternal Self that we share with Universal Mind through a transformative process of enlightenment of your own self-identified body/mind.

Sermon on the Mount is the greatest and only threat that the human condition could ever experience. It teaches you to love your enemies so you can discover you don't have any! Isn't that amazing?

Are you going to consider the truth of this Covenant of the Love of God for His creations? Until this moment you have had no intention of doing so. It's much too uncompromising as the complete opposite of your intentions to justify the existence of your own sick, suffering, dying self. Isn't it strange that you crucify Him simply because of His certainty and declaration that the establishments of this world are totally meaningless, and you are perfectly whole and loving as God created you!

Why would you insanely retain your resentment against God for not recognizing your dream of separation? Shame on you! Shame on those of you who continue to be resentful because life is perfect and whole and the universe is one act of Eternal Love that is all-inclusive of anything and everything that ever was, is or could be.

I can't do anything about your denial of perfect Love. This is true because it's true, not because anyone or anything says so. Your dream of death is over. You have lost the necessity of the defense of your own "self-nothingness."

"The beginning of time is the admission of its ending." All your pain and suffering is only a misappropriation and false application of eternally-creating Mind. The solution occurs when you can no longer tolerate your own miserable, possessive, self-justification in order to keep re-living the single moment of terror that seemed to validate your separation from the eternal Love of God. *Father, into thy hands I commend my spirit.* (Luke 23:46)

Thank you for this gathering. You are beginning to communicate at last. Remember, *communication must be whole to be real.*

Thanks for letting me compare the paradox of the idea of "entirety of possibility" with the instantly available evidence of a mindful fruition of "acts of singular inclusiveness" it can and will engender. ("What's that again?" Oh well...)

Where, in your own arrangement of existent mind, have you decided to retain and protect some temporal potential in order to augment your possibility of continuing cycles of life and death? Of sequential time and space?

Time is not sequential. I'm teaching you there is a single incarnation of mind and body, and it is going on right now. *There is no link of memory to the past.* You can and must remember the "right here and now." The idea of reincarnation can only be a repetition of a determination not to admit to the entirety of your own mind. Let your "re" be all the time. You will remain a moment "incarnate," and all time will be over. It is impossible to leave this continuum through so-called "physical death." There is no such thing as termination of life. *At no single moment does* your *body exist at all.*

The admission of the totality of your desperate surrender will rapidly accelerate your conversion to wholeness. Don't establish a false bottom of desperation (Biblically: your own Gethsemane at your own Calvary), and try to justify another cycle of futile worldly existence that is always "only over and gone." You will be trapped in the progression of your own mind as it awakens from this nightmare. Don't do it! Your time is up. Your enactment of another crucifixion will not avail. You've forgotten you are already resurrected!

Try to stay in your single moment of fear all the time. Salvation is dying each moment. Try to stay dead. You're dead anyway, and are resurrecting!

There is a whole world of direct instantaneous communication with the reality of your Creative Source going on all around you. Each moment that you admit to "no solution," the solution will be there. You follow the admonitions of the apostle Paul when he says: *I die daily.* (I Cor 15:31) Here is where your happiness abides. Here and now you escape this little box of time and space. *In this learning is salvation born: I do not know the thing I am, and therefore do not know what I am doing, where I am, or how to look upon the world or on myself. And What I am will tell me of Itself.* (Chapter 31)

If I have any problem with this, I will remember: *I do not know what anything, including this, means. And so I do not know how to respond to it. And I will not use my own past learning as the light to guide me now.* (Chapter 14)

The whole teaching is, you only have today. Today well-lived will be the only time that you ever have. So die into the eternal Mind of God each moment and you will live in Paradise forever. That is a literal truth. Don't sequence your time association. We've learned this, haven't we? Live one day at a time. We literally had to learn "Today is the only time there is." We thought our old past memories had meaning. Now we see that they had only locked us in an illusionary continuity of "temporal self-existence."

This world begins and ends only through forgiveness and non-judgment one day at a time. "Today I am going to get up, and I am going to take this Lesson Book called A Course In Miracles — it says "my thoughts aren't real," "that this world isn't real," and "that I'm still perfect as God created me" — and I'm going to turn to it and perform what I must have decided somewhere in time to undertake and complete." That "my happiness in a complete dependence on God" goes beyond expression. Since I am the cause of this world, this world will increasingly disappear into its own nothingness as my True Identity emerges in the Light of His Eternal Love. Not because of my doing, but by a miraculous undoing.

I need do nothing because there is nothing "need be done."

I am not a body, I am free. For I am still as God created me.

That's our Sunday School for today. What a joyful relief that your salvation is so magnificently uncompromising. You're just going to have to *let the dead bury their dead.* (Matthew 8:22) Not because I say so, but only because that's the way it is.

Quit trying to determine through some justification of your own association with yourself the outcome you want to be true in your own mind. I am offering you, and you accept in the certainty of whole mind, that all of your outcomes are totally meaningless, and all conclusionary outcomes are totally senseless and have no meaning. There is no such thing as an "outcome" to Creative Mind; it is an eternal extension of Itself.

Paradoxical thinking is strange to your mind. What we are saying is that our very teaching, itself, is, in actuality, not true. The mechanisms that I am offering you to employ are only because you believe it is possible to be separate from Singular Reality, and that is obviously why I am rejected as a teacher. And why Jesus of Nazareth is rejected as a savior. And most certainly why your separate existent identity (your ego) has rejected the awakening call from your holy eternal Self. Jesus testifies for you the utterly simple certainty that: *Truth is true and nothing else is true.*

Not only that, but all of your perceptual devices are a denial of the whole reality of a Single Truth. This is how Jesus represents you with his Covenant of eternal life. Stop being divisive in this!

The whole Sermon on the Mount is nothing but don't judge! Don't swear to anything. As you give, you will receive. As you condemn, you will be condemned. As you think, you will be. There is nothing outside of you. Simply include your self-concepts in with your own eternally-creating Reality.

That's all right as an Atonement principle, but at what point do you begin to realize the power of your own mind by the relinquishment, through non-defense, of your maintenance of self-termination? That's what we are teaching — it is more than just a surrender, it's more than just a supplication; it is rather an admission that you are whole and perfect.

Of course, the simple statement rejected by the world is that "your reality is a total dependence on God." Is that so? Yes! If your eternal creative reality is a dependence on God, why do you then continue to depend on your own devices? Ah, the question appears to validate your mechanisms of mind! Doesn't it? This you will embrace because I have authenticated the possibility of your devices as a means by which "you do not will with God!" An impossible proposition!

This is the paradox. The method by which you must be taught appears to offer you choice because you believe choice is possible. Your only choice is simply to "deny your own denial." Then this world will disappear and be gone forever because no part of it was ever real — not because a part of it was real by which you could determine an outcome that justifies your separation. Until you can come to know that, no progress can be made. If this is surrender to God, so be it. I suggest you begin to positively assert, using the power of Mind, that the realization of all of your love and happiness originates through your total dependence on your Creator! You suffer from an authority problem that is literally killing you. You did not make yourself!

You have learned through pain that whenever you depend on yourself it doesn't work. More and more you have experienced the miracle of turning your will and your life over to God and receiving the gratification that the problem was solved in a way heretofore unbelievable to you, to the point where you joyfully discover that salvation is nothing but a totally "unbelievable solution to an unreal problem!" This is a description of revelation. Here you are in the high metamorphosis of your cellular reassociation with the Light and Love that is all around you.

This is the New Christian Church of Full Endeavor. The New Christians are only expressions of the certainty of your uncompromising love of God and each other. This is the simple message of our savior Jesus. We are teaching Christianity — the return of Jesus of Nazareth as your Course In Miracles.

Jesus would love to have you realize and affirm that your Course In Miracles is the inevitable conclusive totality of mind of the "so-called historic Jesus of Nazareth," because that is the entire truth of the matter. Your fear of doing this is your fear of being assaulted by the world that is all about you. I can't do anything about that. If you can't see, or refuse to see or hear through denial or self-possession, or simply find "no problem" in your present existence of loneliness, pain and loss, so it will be with you. What is the sense in offering this simple ultimate solution to you when you have no need of if?

A Course In Miracles is only all about your own resurrection through the New Testament of our savior Jesus Christ.

Jesus only taught unconditional Love, or the certainty that you are whole and perfect as God created you. This is reasonably irrefutable except by apparent objective reality. Of course this world objects to total unconditional Love, but only because "any time and place" is the denial of it; not because it is denied by any particular means or fashion, but only because you, individually, have denied it in your own self-conceptual mind. "Temporal existence is the denial of eternal Life."

As you change your mind, you will see the world changing, not in joining in the uniqueness of you, but in the assertion by you of your individual uniqueness in the certainty of the discovery that you do not belong to and are not part of this time and place. You will discover that you are whole as God created you only through your personal illumination and transformation. You will be born again!

I know a lot of you are going to broadcast that we are teaching aggregate definitions of a new kind of reality. You are dead wrong. I am telling you that you are the total cause of the Universe. All of the associations of separation are contained only in your own mind.

See how easy the solution is. *And whatsoever thou shalt bind on earth shall be bound in heaven; and whatsoever thou shalt loose on earth shall be loosed in heaven.* (Matthew 16:19) If this is not true, no solution is going to be possible. The admission of that is very painful to you because you are the cause of your own pain. I can do nothing about that. But as you evolve to the certainty that you are the causation, you will no longer want the lonely isolation of a meaningless time and place that was the structure of separation from Life.

Your evolution to the certainty of your own Singular Self Reality will heal the sick and raise the dead. The salvation of this world depends on you. You brought this world with you when you came and it will disappear as you ascend to Heaven.

There is, as we say, a very serious authority problem contained within your own definition of yourself. Very early in the Course, Jesus says that, as ridiculous as it seems, you hold grievances in order to be in competition with eternally creating Mind. You fail very simply because God knows nothing of your hallucination of separation. Your conflict with your Creator, even unto death, is totally meaningless. It is only from your own self-entrapment of space/time that you are escaping.

For many of you, at last, this is far beyond conceptual instruction from Jesus, or from me, or yourself, or anyone.

You have emerged as a complete, new Self-Identity. It is a presence of holiness in which you are "participating in entirety each moment," rather than some old manuscript of conceptual mind about something that happened a thousand years ago or is happening a thousand years from now. All that is passed away.

Remember: There is no world without you! There is nothing outside of you. Outside of you there is nothing. Of course it is fearful! So let it be "joyfully fearful" that finally you are taking a step into the unknown in the growing certainty that the unknown must be Love rather than fear. If there is a Whole Anything, everywhere or anywhere, why couldn't and shouldn't It just as well be wholly lovable rather than totally fearful? Don't forget: There is no Heaven without you either!

So we take this journey together. We had lost our way for a moment but now we're back on track and Jesus is with us. We came from Heaven together and we are going home to Heaven together in the self-same certainty of the perfect eternal life that we are. -MT

Listen, Jesus is speaking:

I am with you always, even unto the end of the world. I will not leave you comfortless; I will come to you. Yet a little while, and the world seeth me no more; but ye see me; because I live, ye shall live also! At that day ye shall know that I am in my Father, and ye in me, and I in you!

And now come I to thee, Father; and these things I speak in the world, that they might have my joy fulfilled in themselves! I have given them thy word; and the world hath hated them, because they are not of the world, even as I am not of the world! I pray not that thou shouldest take them out of the world, but that thou shouldest keep them from the evil.

Of course they are not of the world, even as I am not of the world! Sanctify them through thy truth; thy word is truth.

As thou hast sent me into the world, even so have I also sent them into the world. And for their sakes I sanctify myself, that they also might be sanctified through the truth.

Neither pray I for these alone, but for them also which shall believe on me through their word; that they all may be one; as thou, Father, art in me, and I in thee, that they also may be one in us; that the world may believe that thou hast sent me. And the glory which thou gavest me I have given them; that they may be one, even as we are one! I in them, and thou in me, that they may be made perfect in one; and that the world may know that thou hast sent me, and hast loved them, as thou hast loved me.

Father, I will that they also, whom thou hast given me, be with me where I am; that they may behold my glory, which thou hast given me; for thou lovedst me before the foundation of the world! O righteous Father, the world hath not known thee: but I have known thee, and these have known that thou hast sent me. And I have declared unto them thy name, and will declare it: that the love wherewith thou hast loved me may be in them, and I in them.

Now look and listen as He speaks once again:

In me you have already overcome every temptation that would hold you back. We walk together on the way to quietness that is the gift of God. Hold me dear, for what except your brothers can you need? We will restore to you the peace of mind that we must find together. The Holy Spirit will teach you to awaken unto us and to yourself. This is the only real need to be fulfilled in time! Salvation from the world lies only here. My peace I give you. Take it of me in glad exchange for all the world has offered but to take away! And we will spread it like a veil of light across the world's sad face, in which we hide our brothers from the world, and it from them.

We cannot sing redemption's hymn alone. My task is not completed until I have lifted every voice with mine! And

yet it is not mine, for as it is my gift to you, so was it the Father's gift to me, given me through His Spirit. The sound of it will banish sorrow from the mind of God's most holy Son, where it cannot abide. Healing in time is needed, for joy cannot establish its eternal reign where sorrow dwells. You dwell not here, but in eternity! You travel but in dreams, while safe at home! Give thanks to every part of you that you have taught how to remember you. Thus does the Son of God give thanks unto his Father for his purity.
-Chapter 13

The Reality
Of Physical Resurrection

Herein are you, individually, verified as the entire cause of this apparent separation from reality, and presented with the manner of your personal escape from this world of pain and death through the unqualified affirmation of the resurrection of our Brother and Savior Jesus Christ.

Herein is the certainty of your very own Singular Self-Reality revealed through the illumination of your conceptual thought forms.

The Hero Of This Dream: Wherein Jesus reminds you that this nightmare of separation is yours alone, and vividly describes and explains His own physical resurrection.

Here we are once again together for an eternal moment at God's Country Place which is your own place and everywhere that you are in the temporal certainty that you are as God created you.

We are sharing the illuminate reality of the teachings of Jesus Christ of Nazareth, out of body, in eternity, out of time, speaking to you of the certainty that you are in a dream of separation from which He has awakened. This is an integrating of His awakened mind with your sleeping mind by which you will discover that you have been dreaming a dream of defensive self-containment in your effort to make real the apparent existence of this world, through your bodily identity, as somehow distinct from the single source of eternally-creating Life.

So the Course In Miracles is the awakening of you from your dream of death.

We've been reading from the Text of the Course a series of important correlations that indicate the direction of the miracle that your mind is now undergoing in its transformation, in its broadening inclusiveness of your self-identity. You are evolving from a limited fearful perceptual-mind consciousness to a wholly creative fully-endowed purposeful, powerful reality in the declaration that you are as God created you.

That's what the miracle is. Isn't it? Each moment you have sufficiently released your own conflict, your own identity, in your own dream as the dreamer of the dream to find yourself in a whole reconstitution of that association in your own mind.

We're going to get to this in Chapter 28. I'm going to read a little bit from the "Hero of the Dream" at the end of Chapter 27. Chapter 28 will deal with the certainty that all time is going on all the time and, in fact, all time was over and is over each moment.

This is a continuation of the readings for those of you who are listening to this sequence of tapes of the "Dreamer of the Dream" which we read on, I believe it was February the 6th. This then will be a back-date to the year 1998 A.D., or around 1,953 years after the completion of resurrection as we identify it in our historic reference. That is, the single man, Jesus, in our frame of temporal continuity reality, transformed as part of our total association, and this world was gone. We are gone from here. And this is what we were saying as we read yesterday.

Now the admission that this is so is what the Second Coming is as Jesus would identify it. Obviously, He has entered into a dream association of which you are apparently a part. He has come to show you that in reality He is you and that when one falsity in time, when one single self-identified man, one species Homo sapiens, transformed to the reality of Universal Consciousness, that was the end of time. Do you see?

There was only ever one real problem and that was only a moment of time versus eternity. Now you can dwell with that in your own time mind if you choose, and reach the conclusion that the solutions you have sought here in your own dream to bring about love, to bring about creative purpose, have been failing you, and that you've been dying, and that the dream that you have made for yourself, if you will accept that, is no longer tolerable, and that the necessity to change it is A Course In Miracles. And that through that necessity you have brought into your mind, quite literally, a Course in Conversion, then, from a later temporal sequence of your reality that will tell you that the only purpose you have here and now is to awaken and to remember that you are as God created you.

So we read in yesterday's episode about you being the dreamer of the dream. Now we are moving into an absolute truthful admission that you are the hero of this dream. That you are in totality both the cause and effect of this world. That you have identified yourself in objective reality and established space in your own mind. Now you listen.

The body, your construct of yourself, *is the central figure in the dreaming of the world. There is no dream without it, nor does it exist without the dream in which it acts as if it were a person to be seen and be believed.* Isn't this lovely? Who wrote this? Who but a resurrected mind? Increasingly as your own mind matures to brighter and brighter vision, you will actually look at this and you will readily see that its author could not possibly be a part of the meaningless temporal containment of this world. The authority of it is astonishing. It says that you're trapped in this little scenario contained within your own apparent objective reality.

It acts, your body that is, *as if it were a person to be seen and to be believed. It's the central figure,* isn't it? Why? It must take the central place in every dream. Yourself. In other words, the you that you think is you. Never mind someone else. You are going to give them an identity eventually, aren't you, as

169

projections of your own mind? But in the meantime, you must be the central figure of any dream that you're having. It doesn't make any difference whether you believe the dream is acting on you or you believe that you are acting on the dream, you will still be the central figure. Which tells the story about yourself.

It takes the central place in every dream, which tells the story of how it was made by other bodies... This is the whole history of mortality. ...born into the world outside the body, lives a little while and dies, to be united in the dust with other bodies dying like itself. Is it fair to say that's a description of the human condition? Absolutely! Human beings, out there, all over this dream of death: Is it fair to say that this Whole Mind has given you a description of yourself? I think so. Not only that, but you say, "Certainly that's true. What about it?" What can I say except to remind you that this is your dream? When you say, "Certainly that's true," it simply means that you're obviously not suffering enough in your own nightmare — that somehow you have figured out an answer within your own dream that gratifies your need of human self-consciousness.

It lives a little while and dies, to be united in the dust with other bodies dying like itself. In the brief time allotted it to live, and that doesn't matter how long it is, it could be a moment, it could be eighty years, it could be a thousand years, *it seeks for other bodies as its friends and enemies. Its safety is its main concern. Its comfort is its guiding rule. It tries to look for pleasure, and avoid the things that would be hurtful. Above all, it tries to teach itself its pains and joys are different and can be told apart.* And this is exactly what you do with the separate bodies that you have miscreated in your own mind. You teach them to defend themselves. You teach them when they're very young that the stove will be hot and burn them. You teach them not to take candy from a stranger. You teach them to associate in memories that you have about what this dream is as you have constructed it in your own mind. You teach your apparent offspring the imprisonment of objective separation.

Now. *The dreaming of the world takes many forms, because the body seeks in many ways to prove it is autonomous and real.* It's going to do whatever it can through its own thought forms. *It puts things on itself,* the body does, puts things on itself, *that it has bought with little metal discs or paper strips that its miscreated world proclaims as valuable and real. And it works to get them, doing totally senseless things, and tosses them away for senseless things it does not need and does not even want. It hires other bodies, that they may protect it and collect more senseless things that it can call its own. And it looks about for special bodies in its own dream that it has constructed in its mind that can share its dream. And sometimes it dreams it is a conqueror of bodies weaker than itself. But in some phases of the dream, it is the slave of bodies that would hurt it and would torture it.* And it lives in this continuing cyclical arrangement within its own mind.

The body's serial adventures, continually going on, from the time of birth to dying are the theme of every dream the world has ever had. It is a theme of every dream the world has ever had regardless of where it is in the dream. That is the central figure, as the world dreams itself. *The "hero" of this dream will never change, nor will its purpose.* The "hero" of this dream is you. No matter how you constitute yourself in the dream, you are the "hero" of it. You have constructed it in your own mind to correspond to your self-identity and it will never change nor will its purpose change because it is designed to keep you in the conflictual association of your own mind.

Though the dream itself takes many forms, and seems to show a great variety of places and events wherein its "hero" finds itself... and can present itself as a glorious over-comer of the evil things that are outside of it, and share the lovely passion that it feels in its determination to declare sickness and death a reality within its own mind ...*the dream has but one purpose* that is being taught in an infinite number of ways. Here it is. This single lesson does this split mind, the body identity, try to teach again, and still again, and still again, and still again. What is it? That it is cause and not effect. All of the things outside of you in your own dream are telling you that they are the cause of you. You let your body tell you that it is the cause of you. You want to look at the insanity of what you're saying? The body now can determine what you are for you. All of the other bodies that you've projected apparently outside of you will also confirm and determine their relationship with you.

Now, at last, you're going to declare that you are the dreamer of the dream, that you are the cause of them and can therefore change your mind and the world will change accordingly. But until now, you have been instructed in this dream that they are the cause of you. That you came into this world and found it here and that all the things that are going on will influence you and attack you or make you happy or cause you pain. And that's what you've been living over and over again, isn't it? *That this world is the cause of you and not the effect. And that you* in your own mind *are its effect, and cannot be its cause.*

You actually believe that the earth can have an effect on you. That it is where you are from. That it was here when you came. There's no sense in saying that you don't, because you do. Everything that you see in your own dream authenticates the fact of objective reality. That all of these objects are really real outside of you. That a boulder can actually fall on your head. That happenings outside of your control or direction can actually effect your very existence. That you must protect yourself from other associations in your own mind that are attacking you, and they from you, in an endless scenario of attack and defense.

Thus are you not the dreamer, but the dream. You're actually caught in the dream. *And so you wander idly in and out of places and events that it contrives for you* and from which you must defend yourself or share in for a moment or a lifetime. *That this is all the body does is true, for it is but a figure in a dream. But who reacts to figures in a dream unless he sees them as if they were real?* Obviously, that's what you have done. Now here's your transformation. *The instant that he sees them as they are they have no more effects on him, because he understands he gave them their effects by causing them and making them seem real.* Because he wanted them to be real to keep his own identity!

How willing are you to escape effects of all the dreams the world has ever had? All that the world has ever had?! You, individually, can escape all the dreams that all of the history of man has ever had. *Is it your wish to let no dream appear to be the cause of what it is you do? Then let us merely look upon the dream's beginning, for the part you see is but the second part, whose cause lies in the first.* You had to have an initial dream that something outside of yourself could actually effect you. That just for a moment there would be something separate from the wholeness of your own mind.

No one asleep and dreaming in the world remembers his initial attack upon himself. No one believes there really was a time when he knew nothing of a body, and could never have conceived this world as being real. He would have seen at once that these ideas are one illusion, and they're absolutely *too ridiculous for anything but to be laughed away.* Ah, *but how serious they now appear to be! And no one can remember when they would have been met with laughter and* with total *disbelief.* You can remember this if you want to. We must but look directly at their cause. There's no sense in hiding any longer from what has been causing our fear. And we will see the grounds for laughter. The ridiculousness that you could actually be separated or suffer sickness and die if you are Universal Mind and as God created you. And that there's absolutely no cause for you to be fearful at all nor was there ever any cause.

Let us return the dream he gave away unto the dreamer, who perceives the dream as separate from himself

*and done to him. Into eternity, where all is one, there crept
a tiny, crazy idea, at which the Son of God remembered not
to laugh. He remembered not to laugh.* He "remembered not"
to laugh. (Laughter) Good! We're remembering to laugh at the
idiotic absurdity of our apparent separation from eternal reality,
this entrapment in a box of time and space. *In his forgetting
did the thought become a serious idea, and possible of both
accomplishment and real effects. Together, we can laugh
them both away, and understand that time cannot intrude
upon eternity. And it's a joke to think that time can come
to circumvent eternity, which means there is no time* and
that's what eternity is.

Actually, we're sharing that single disastrous moment
together right now and laughing at it. It's interesting that it
really doesn't matter how you construct this scenario in your
own mind. It's very possible that you will want to view it as a
mistake; a break in communication ;something that happened
to you for just a moment. "A bump on the head." "Going east
of Eden." "Being lost in the horse latitudes." The story you
tell of your incursion into space/time is a parable description
of the Kingdom. Finally, the certainty must be that there is
one Universal Mind and you apparently lost communication
with it. Obviously, that would be impossible in reality. You
cannot be separate from what everything is and that includes
your self.

Since the beginning of all so-called human civilizations,
man has told his story of being lost or separated from his home.
Many of the ideas in folklore, fantasy or science fiction are of
this nature. That the earth and this section of the galaxy is a
penal colony, and because of your irresponsibility you have
been put in it. That you're guilty of an act against something
"other" for which you must be punished. Or perhaps the
idea that you have reached an advanced enough stage in the
evolution of your species, a maturity of reason, where you are
in enough harmony to be allowed to enter into the galactic

society. The truth of the matter is that you are evolving back each moment into the wholeness of life through the release of your own attack on yourself. *It is a joke to think that time through death can come to circumvent eternity, which means there is no* such thing as *time.*

A timelessness in which is time made real; a part of God that can attack itself; a separate brother as an enemy; a mind within a body all are forms of circularity— circulatory meanings — *whose ending starts at its beginning, ending at its cause.* It just keeps circling back on itself. *The world you see depicts exactly what you thought you did.* And have projected outside of yourself and it's now coming back to you somewhere in your own time associations. *Except that now you think that what you did is being done to you.* This is what objective reality is, isn't it? *The guilt for what you thought happened is being placed outside yourself, and on a guilty world that dreams your dreams and thinks your thoughts instead of you. It brings its vengeance, not your own. It keeps you narrowly confined within a body, which it punishes because of all the sinful things the body does within its own dream. You have no power to make the body stop its evil deeds because you did not make it, and cannot control its actions nor its purpose nor its fate.* Nor, in fact, anything that's happening. You're absolutely at the mercy of all the things that are around you. This is the fundamental teaching of a whole mind, Jesus Christ, in A Course In Miracles. The certainty of subjective reality. That there is no such thing as anything outside of your own mind that could possibly cause you travail or sickness and death. And further, the mind that thinks it possible does not exist.

The world but demonstrates a very very old truth; you will believe that others do to you exactly what you think you did to them. Past tense. But once deluded into blaming them you will not see the cause of what they do, because you want the guilt to rest on them. How childish is the petulant device to keep your innocence by pushing guilt outside yourself, but never letting go! Keeping it in your own mind so that you can play off of it. So you can give yourself an identity with it. *It is not easy to perceive the jest when all around you do your eyes behold its heavy consequences, but without their trifling cause.* You're letting the consequences of that horrible thought affect you. It's like you're in a nightmare, isn't it? And all of these things keep charging in on you.

Here then are the teachings of Jesus. As long as you defend yourself from them, or attack them in your own association, you cannot see that you are the dreamer of the dream. Do you see? This is much of the Sermon on the Mount, isn't it? This is: "Resist not evil." Don't defend yourself. Let go of it. Don't give this world reality by participating in reciprocity. "Your Kingdom is not of this world." "Be ye perfect even as your Father in Heaven."

Listen: There is no cause for this world and nothing follows after it. If you let its effects be your cause, those effects seem serious and sad indeed. *Yet it is their cause that follows nothing and is but a jest.* You are trapped as an effect of an effect with no cause because none of it is real. The separation did not occur.

In gentle laughter does the Holy Spirit, that is all of you, waiting for yourself, in total aggregate at the end of time, *perceive the cause, and looks not to effects.* You see? It has arrived at an inclusion of all of these perceptual thought forms in your mind. *How else could He correct your error, who have overlooked the cause entirely? He bids you bring each terrible effect to Him that you may look together on its foolish cause and laugh with Him for just a little while. You judge effects,* because they're in your mind, but a whole mind, your own whole mind, this mind, *has judged their cause. And by His judgment are effects removed.* This is how you change your mind. *Perhaps you come in tears. But hear Him say, 'My brother, holy Son of God, behold your idle dream, in which this could occur.*"*And you will leave the holy instant with your laughter and your brother's joined with His.* And did. And that was the holy instant of resurrection. And the earth was no more! And time was gone!

The secret of salvation is but this: Ready? *That you are doing this unto yourself. No matter what the form of the attack, this is going to be true. Whoever takes the role of enemy and of attacker, still is this the truth. Listen! Whatever seems to be the cause of any pain and suffering you feel, this is still going to be true. For you would not react at all to figures in a dream you knew that you were dreaming. Let them be as hateful and as vicious* (or as loving or as desirable) *as they may, they could have no effect on you unless you failed to recognize it is your dream.* That you are your own effects. This is the solution of salvation, isn't it? The problem is you. The solution is you.

This single lesson learned will set you free from suffering, no matter what form it takes. How could it not? Now, all we really do in your dream of death, all a whole mind does, all you will do with your brothers in your new Christ Mind, is to *repeat this one inclusive lesson of deliverance until it has been learned, regardless of the form of suffering that brings you pain. Whatever hurt he brings to you, you will make answer with this very simple single truth. You are doing this to yourself.* Cut it out! You are inflicting pain on yourself in your own dream and determined to make it real to keep your identity. *For this one answer takes away the cause of every form of sorrow and of pain.* Don't you see?

The form will affect your answer not at all. Look, I don't care what you bring me in this dream of yours, I'm telling you it's not real and you have constructed it in sickness, pain and death in your own mind. The form affects my answer not at all, nor will it affect yours for you have learned the single cause of all of them, no matter what their form. *And you will understand that miracles reflect the simple statement, 'I*

have done this thing, and it is this I would undo." And I
will undo it each moment by not demanding that a separate
human identity justify the projections of pain and grief of
human identity that I am inflicting upon myself. By not reacting
to my own projections, my mind will change in association
with my whole reality. Do you have this? Those of you who
are practicing your transformation through the Workbook
of A Course In Miracles? The miracle is nothing but your
reassociation in your own dream of how you want to look at
yourself. And it's happening each moment.

*Bring, then, all forms of suffering to Him Who knows
that every one is exactly like the rest. He sees no differences
where none exists, and He will teach you how each one is
caused. None has a different cause from all the rest, and
all of them are just as easily undone by but a single lesson
truly learned.* There are no degrees to miracles because
the sickness and pain in the world are literally not real, *and
salvation is a secret you have kept but from yourself.*
Everything else in the universe is saved except you if you're
in your dream of death. The universe proclaims it so. Yet to its
witnesses you don't pay any attention. All around you in each
moment in every conflictual idea you have about yourself is a
total witness to the truth of you somewhere in time, and in all
of time, reminding you that you are as God created you. It's
impossible that not be so. Yet to its witnesses you don't pay
any attention. *For they attest the thing you do not want to
know and are fearful to admit.*

When will you really want to confess that you are
absolutely whole as God has created you? This seems to be kept
a secret from you. *Yet you need but learn you chose but not
to listen, not to see.* The eyes, the ears — the objective mind
is designed not to hear the message of the truth of God. That's
why you need the transformation, don't you? Jesus would say
you are actually blind, deaf and dumb in a dream constructed
by yourself and are not communicating with anything except
your own thought forms somewhere in time.

How differently will you perceive the world when this is recognized! When you forgive the world your guilt, you will be free of it. Its innocence does not demand your guilt, nor does your guiltlessness rest on its sins. There's no sense in trying to combat sin. You are not guilty of anything no matter how you measure it. Why? This never happened. Do you see? If this really happened, obviously, you're going to be guilty. It never did.

This is the obvious; a secret kept from no one but yourself. And it is this that has maintained you separate from the world, and kept your brother separate from you. Now need you but to learn that both of you are either totally innocent or guilty. The one thing that is impossible is that you be unlike each other; because each of you has created the other one in his own mind, yet each of you is the only mind that there is. Each of you is singular in your entirety. And all and everything is perfectly whole and true. This is the only secret yet to learn. And it will be no secret you are healed. Why? You are the cause of this in your own dream. Mind is singular. You are a whole part of the eternal mind of God. (Chap 27:VIII)

How very reasonable that is beginning to appear to you now, isn't it? That you are actually in this dream. Many of you have known that there's a dream quality to this reality. And you've looked at the objective universe in your limited construction and you've looked out and seen a million suns or a thousand million stars and ten thousand million galaxies and a hundred million light years of distance and you've tried to measure yourself in your own limitation against the whole mind that is all around you. And finally, you have reached a conclusion somewhere in time of the futility of the human perceptual mind in the identification of the association of itself in a body. Your conceived and measured limitations of your human condition are simply too ridiculously unreasonable to be tenable to you any longer.

The reason that you're gathered with me here now is that this whole mind in you is demanding an answer to your existence in your own self-conceived split mind. You are no longer satisfied with the idea that your life must end in a pitiful death association; that you are a form of existence that is doomed to waste and die, that you must lose the things that you love and are defenseless against the ravages of time. Somewhere in your invention of time this has at last become intolerable to you. Now you gather with the other associations that you share in your own dream, who have also discovered that you are together in a mad house; that you're in a crazy unreal place; that you're dreaming a dream of death that lasted but for a moment.

And now you're going to experience the undoing of your own fear in your own mind. It will be undone. You will undo it because you're the one who was doing it. And it is undone. In that sense, obviously, the miracle doesn't do anything. Does it? The miracle, which is the remembering of your entirety, is obviously going on around you all the time. You are the miracle! You are returning into a present memory of your own divine association with God.

The miracle does nothing. All it does is to undo. What does it do in its undoing? *It cancels out the interference to what has been done.* You're interfering with your own whole return to reality that happened at the moment that you thought you were separated. You have created a lot of interference through your own perceptual mind about this atonement, about this immediate return and being with God. In fact, all of your self-construction is an interference that the miracle cancels out as you reassociate in your own mind. *It does not add, but it merely takes away. And what it takes away is long since gone, but being kept in memory appears to have immediate effects.* You keep bringing together all of your own self-contained concepts — all of your own memories that are in your mind that are already gone. And you're using them as the cause of you and giving them the effects in the present state in which you find yourself. Are you ready? Listen:

This world was over long ago. Some of you may be very happy to hear this. And to some of you, this will be very disturbing. If you want to start with the premise that you are only memory, it should help you to the certainty that this world was over long ago. Isn't it so? When you came into this room and sat down with me you were obviously just a memory of all the previous things that had happened to you in your own mind. The most that you could say about them is that they're gone. If they are gone, then all of the thoughts that you are having about them in relation to you in the future idea must also be gone. All right?

This world was over long ago. It really doesn't matter how long it was over, as long as it's over. Just as it really doesn't matter how soon you get this, as long as you understand that we have come to tell you right now that this is the time and space, at last, when you heard the timeless call. You are simply remembering your own eternal reality. What difference does it make how long your idea of a separate existence from eternal mind has been? *The thoughts that made it are no longer in the mind that thought of them and loved them for a little while. The miracle but shows that the past is gone, and what has truly gone* cannot possibly have any effects. *Remembering a cause,* trying to put it back together, remembering it after it's gone, *can but produce illusions of its presence, not effects.* So that everything that's happening to you is really having no effects at all because the cause of it is gone. Do you see? We're going to do what? Reverse cause and effect aren't we?

All the effects of guilt are here no more. For guilt is over. The idea that you made yourself. It's all gone. *In its passing went its consequences, left without a cause.* They couldn't be here because nothing caused them in the first place. Why would you cling to it in memory if you did not desire its effects? Obviously, you still want it to be true. *Remembering is as selective as perception, being its past tense.* You want to remember this and select the part of it that you want, to keep your own identity, and reject the rest of it. So you bring that grievance of thought, what it was to you, into your present condition. *It is perception of the past as if it were occurring now, and still were there for you to see. Memory, like perception, is a skill made up by you to take the place of what God gave in your creation. And like all the things you made, it can be used to serve another purpose* (since it's in your mind), *and to be the means for something else.* If you want it to be. *It can be used to heal and not to hurt, if you so wish it be.*

Nothing employed for healing represents an effort to do anything at all. Every time you try to do something in your own past association, you limit and restrict and deny the natural healing process that you are whole as God created you. Every time that you do it! Come on miracle workers. Every time that you give pain an identity in your own mind, you have denied the miracle. Now your mind needs an undoing of its own association with itself. Doesn't it? *Nothing employed for healing, to make whole, represents an effort to do anything at all. To do anything! It is a recognition that you have no needs which mean that something must be done.* The recognition that you are perfect as God created you must change the effects of your own mind which you have designed to be a part of the doing of your body in your own determination to stay sick and to die.

Okay, what is this healing process? I*t is an unselective memory, that is not used to interfere with truth.* It's a definition of the Holy Spirit. It's all the memory that the world has ever had, transformed in time to a moment of your union with God. And as you take all of your so-called selective memories that have held you in the bondage of the sequencing of time or cause and effect, they will be brought to a glorious union through the spirit of the Christ in you. Through the spirit of your own Whole Mind! And that's the miracle that's going on each moment. *All things the Holy Spirit can employ for healing have been given Him, without the content and the purposes for which* they have been made. Obviously, the whole perceptual mind was made in thought forms to stay autonomous; to be separate from God. So, all of those forms have to be brought to the whole mind to be recognized as products of the limited mind, so that the conflict can disappear in that mind that has chosen to be separate from God. *They are but skills without an application.* They're totally skillful each moment because they see no conflict in the thoughts within your own mind at the end of time. *They await their use. They have no dedication and no aim.* They are wholly going on all the time.

The Holy Spirit is literally the loss of objective reality or of the distance between cause and effect. The whole certainty of a whole mind is that cause and effect are the same and synonymous. That's God creating. The Holy Spirit is nothing but the taking of apparent sequential perceptual time and bringing it, for just a moment, together in a congruous reality that doesn't suffer the conflict of judgmental identity. This, then, is the moment in time, and the only moment in time, when you remembered that you were whole. Because that's the terrible moment you wanted to forget, and that's what you've brought together now in this holy instant in your own mind.

The Holy Spirit can indeed make use of memory, for God Himself is there. Because God is everywhere. And using that memory of that terrible thought that you had about yourself. Do you see? *Yet this is not a memory of past events, but only of a present state.* Why? There is only a present state. What is this present state? The moment when you forgot God. That's what this present state is that you're now remembering. Yet this is not a memory of past events, but only of a present state.

You are so long accustomed to believe that memory holds only what is past, that it is hard for you to realize it is a skill that can literally remember now. And if it doesn't defend itself and cause a conflict of its own association with its past thoughts, it will remember now. Why? This is the only thing there is to remember. This. Right now. In your dream.

As you are. Here. This is really all that you need remember. Why? It's all there is! Oh my, what a miracle!

The limitations on remembering... Remember we're giving remembering a moment's reality. Your mind is so split up in its various thought form members that it must be "re-membered." It has to be put totally back together in association with itself by remembering that each thought is whole in your own mind and not separate thoughts of your past association. *The limitations on remembering the world imposes on it are as vast as those you let the world impose on you.* Because they are a simple declaration of the conflict of objective reality. Listen to this sentence: There is no link of memory to the past. Got it? Some of you can hear that. It's a revelatory idea.

There is no link of memory to the past. All memory is going on right now, in your own dream, and you've brought it together. You've brought all of these old past associations, all the future ones that were going to happen in your sequential time, and you're remembering them all at one time. Do you see this? You can really only have one thought at a time, right? Can we get you to look at this? So the more inclusive that thought is, the happier and more creative you will be because you haven't rejected anything from your own mind. Since you are the product of what you think is your own mind outside of yourself, when you stop identifying it, you'll spring into Heaven. You will become whole, won't you? Why? *There is no link of memory to the past. If you would have it there, then there it is.* You can remember it if you want to, but you can't make it real because it's gone. But remember that only your desire made the link, and only you have held it to a part of time, where self-identity, where guilt, where the need to make yourself appears to linger still but is actually gone.

Now the Spirit's use of memory is actually apart from time, which is the sequencing of thoughts. *He does not seek to use it as a means to keep the past, but rather as a way* to let go of it. This is the whole teaching of "forgive your brother." Let go of your past associations in your memory that are causing the grievance of sickness and death in your own mind. Why? *Memory holds the message it receives, and does what it is given it to do.* They cannot not do that. *The memory does not write the message, nor appoint what it is for.* The memory is nothing but an accumulation of body thoughts. But the thoughts are given them by the mind who wants to dictate the terms of its own identity. In fact, this is a good definition of the body.

The body is held together by previous memories of the disassociation, and the necessity to keep that disassociation in some sort of memory form. *Like to the body, memory is purposeless within itself.* It is purposeless within itself because every memory is false. All of the memories that it has are but reflections of its own false memory. *And if it seems to serve to cherish ancient hate, and gives you pictures of injustices and hurts that you were saving, this is what you asked its messages be and this is what you will experience.* This is the whole idea of human establishment, isn't it? Of culture? Of races of men? Of civilizations? The need for you to hold this grievance in your mind.

Committed to its vaults, the history of all the body's past is hidden there. All of the strange associations made to keep the past alive, the present dead, are stored within it. Do you understand "the present dead?" That you're dead each moment that you're here in an existent identity? I promise you, you can hear this now if you simply choose to do so. If you keep the past alive, the present must be dead because it's based on the past and the past is dead and gone and never was. This world is not what life is! Everybody got this? This is the same idea as Jesus declares in the New Testament, "Do not look for the living among the dead." What He says is, don't look for a present frame of reference in the past dead associations. It's not there. Do you see that? That it's gone away? *All of the strange associations made to keep the past alive, and the present dead...* Let's take a quick look at it.

I know objective mind has the idea that the body dies and at the time of resurrection all of those dead bodies are going to rise up. From where to what? I'm going to give you what death is: "Death is this temporal existent body that you find yourself in." Why? Because it's nothing but memories that are already gone. *At no single moment does the body* really *exist at all.* In that sense, it is literally nothing. This is what death is: "Nothing." Do you understand?

Now, I am going to work the miracle of raising the dead. See how simple it is? By not giving that body an identification of my previous dead experiences, it rises up in my mind in the glory of the certainty of my saviorship. Is everybody with me on this? All of our minds are actually a single self-reality. *It is God's Will that He has but one Son. It is God's Will that His one Son is you.* Now, as I go around in my mind as the savior of the world, I raise the dead by not giving it my previous dead associations that have nothing to do with God at all. See how easy and joyous? We are raising the dead here, now, together, you and I. So really all that happens is that the dead, being a limited association of the mind, in a single flash, in a single moment, are transformed into the bright reality of God.

This is what Paul means in Corinthians in that lovely sentence, "Behold I show you a mystery." (I Cor 15:51) In a moment the body will be totally changed to the bright light of reality. That's what he's trying to describe, as an illuminate teacher of God, which Paul was. Paul had his Damascus experience, didn't he? Many like to ignore the personal transformation through the Love-of-Jesus part of Paul, and instead remind everybody that Paul said that ladies should sit in the back of the church and keep their hats on. They like to identify with the Saul part of Paul. Just as they like to identify with the Saul part of you. When you declare your own Paul reality, your own total Damascus experience, or even more completely, as Jesus declares, your own Saviorship, they may not be ready to hear you. They may crucify your saviorship, and the Christ in themselves, through holding you in the bondage of their previous dead associations with themselves and this meaningless world of isolation from reality.

Notice how you like to associate with the new bright self you find now in your own time. This is your God's Country Place; your borderland between worlds. That's a need for you now in your own re-identity to have the healing experience of the now — of remembering the now, together, as the time when you stepped out of time to eternity.

Let's continue: *All of the strange associations made to keep the past alive, the present dead, are stored within* your genetic memory (see?), waiting your command that they be brought to you, and lived again. And they can be projected from your own mind and give you back a reflection within your own dream. *And thus do their effects appear to be increased by time, which took away their cause.* And now you're nothing but a big bundle of effects of illusion. The effects increase more and more. Why? You stored them in spatial/temporal computers identified as particle/wave energetic light formulations that constitute your objective conceptual reality. You actually harbor interlocking grids of sourceless memory; thought forms that you can call on to keep your objective limited identity with yourself. Oh my goodness sake! You are trapped in the substance of your own illusionary conditional thoughts!

Your continuing association of separate pieces of mind binds you to sequential time. But remember that *time* itself *is but another phase of what does nothing* at all. Neither side of time is really real. There is no beginning and end. *It works hand in hand with all the other attributes with which you seek to keep concealed the truth about yourself.* You invent time to keep your thoughts apart. It then becomes space — one thought out there that is separate from you. A distance between your own thoughts! Isn't that something?

It works hand in hand with all the other attributes of your own mind with which you seek to keep concealed the truth that's actually you. *Time neither takes away nor can restore*. How could it? It doesn't pass. "Oh time is passing and taking things away from me, and I can find them later on." Untrue! There is no such thing as a past. *Time neither takes away nor can restore. And yet you make* real *strange use of it, as if the past had caused the present*, and that's crazy when you really look at it. What would the past have to do with the present? So you sequence time in your own mind and really are dead at that moment. The truth is you're not really here or anywhere at all. *And yet you make strange use of it, as if the past had caused the present, which is but a consequence in which no change can be made possible because its cause has gone.*

There's nothing really more frustrating to the perceptual human mind than to believe that it is being caused by its past association and can't go back and change it – that it's condemned to get old and sick and die, that it can't or won't forgive a single mistake that it made thirty years ago or last week (It's a terrible way to be trapped in time.), and that the time is actually sequencing. It is but a consequence in which no change can be made possible because its cause has gone and it's caught with what it did. And it might just as well resign itself. It can't change itself now. Brother, what a state to be in! So you try to change your mind, but nothing is happening. You simply re-illusion into this fearfully hopeless maze of separation that always ends where it begins.

Yet change must have a cause that will endure, or else it will not last. No change can be made in the present if its cause is past. And darn you minds that keep securing yourself and trying to change yourself based on your past references, that are really illusions of nothing because all of the thoughts that you are having are already past, and are associated with your own past self. *Only the past is held in memory as you make use of it, and so it is a way to hold the past against the now:* to hold onto the grievance, not to see the glory of you that's all around you now, to defend yourself by your past associations against the Love of God that's going on all around you.

Remember absolutely *nothing that you have taught yourself, for you were badly taught. And who would keep a senseless lesson in his mind, when he can learn and can preserve a better one? When ancient memories of hate appear, remember that their cause is gone. They are causeless. Once again. When ancient memories of hate appear, remember that their cause is gone. And so you cannot understand what they are for.* You keep trying to hold yourself together in judgment of yourself and the separate world around you. But you've been "a liar from the beginning."(John 8:44) You keep trying to put together in your mind all the causes that are already gone and judge them in the association of your now. *And so you cannot understand what they are for. Let not the cause that you would give them now be what it was that made them what they were, or (better) seemed to be. Be glad that it is gone, for this is what you would be pardoned from.* And it's already gone. *And see, instead, the new effects of cause accepted now, with consequences here.* You can do it right now. *And they will surprise you with their loveliness.* This is the holy instant. This is the transformation of your mind, isn't it? These are the new vistas that are opening up in your perceptual mind as you release your hold on your own death form association. Listen: The ancient new ideas they bring will be the happy consequences of a Cause so ancient that it far exceeds the span of memory which your perception sees. It's the original great thought of joy and happiness that you were never separated.

Listen to this once more, this sentence right here: *The ancient "new" ideas...* They seem to be new, but actually they're all an accumulation of all of the whole ideas of joy and loveliness when you realized instantly that you really weren't sick and dying. Can you hear this? The reason that many of you associate death with happiness is because at the time of your physical death many of you experienced that joyous moment. Can you see that? Since you are holding your conceptual self together, you might as well hear this: You are dependent on physical death. You are holding together the memory of your body and getting older and older with it, but it's going to fall apart, isn't it? What happens when it finally falls apart? It uses up all of its own memory potential of longevity that was always over and gone a long time ago — and never really was at all. Then it has a moment of revelation, when all of the forms that held it together spring up in a bright light.

Those of you who have been with a body/mind human consciousness experiencing the departure from body form may have seen the bright light that comes about them as they have a death sequence experience. You can understand well what I am saying. And many of those who are revived from apparent life/death associations will recall the glory of that moment when they see the guardian hosts around them, or perhaps even Jesus, or perhaps old and new friends of happy memories come to greet them.

Through this Course in Transformation there is a plan to transport this entire "spatial aggregation of thought form" to and through that glorious moment of escape from time. We help provide the miracle experience now, so that you can recapitulate the entirety of your sojourn of separation as you undergo a conversion of your "conceptual self" directly in the death experience, followed instantaneously by the whole new bright identity that turns and converts the memory forms of your mind. This is the resurrection. Do you see?

Not only is this immediately possible, but as Jesus declares in His resurrection message, the newly awakened can then make another appearance in a whole new constitution of body somewhere or anywhere in time. What a lovely mystical step to reality. This is very much the message that Jesus gives to the scribe, Helen Schucman, who scribed the Course, when she asked about the physical resurrection. What I'm reading here is what Jesus actually describes about His own physical resurrection. In fact, I think we'll read it as part of this tape and it will help you see that actually, in time, you are undergoing a whole re-resurrection of your body each moment. This is why we teach physical resurrection. Do you see? That the dead will rise up and be healed and are being healed each moment. *Remember nothing that you taught yourself, for you were badly taught. And the ancient new ideas they bring will be the happy consequences of a Cause so ancient that it far exceeds the span of memory which your perception sees.*

This is the Cause the Holy Spirit has remembered for you, when you would forget. It is not past because He let It not be unremembered. It has never changed, because there never was a time in which He did not keep It safely in your mind. Its consequences will indeed seem new, because you thought that you remembered not their Cause. But you really did. Yet was It never absent from your mind, for it was not your Father's Will that He be unremembered by His Son.

What you remember never was. It came from causelessness which you confused with cause. It can deserve but laughter, when you learn you have remembered consequences that were causeless and could have no effects and were never real. The miracle reminds you of a Cause forever present, that's going on right now, the holy instant, *perfectly untouched by time and interference.* Never changed from what It is. And you are Its effect, as changeless and as perfect as Itself. Its memory does not lie in the past, nor waits the future. It is not revealed in miracles. *They but remind you that... It will no longer be denied.* It's always present with you all the time.

You who have sought to lay a judgment on your own Creator cannot understand it is not He Who laid a judgment on His Son. You would deny Him His Effects, yet have They never been denied. There was no time in which His Son could be condemned for what was causeless and against His Will. What your remembering would witness to is but the fear of God. He has not done the thing you fear. No more have you done it to Him. And so your innocence has not been lost. You need no healing to be healed. You are

191

healed. *In quietness, see in the miracle a lesson in allowing Cause to have Its Own effects,* and not what you think yours are, *and doing nothing that would interfere with it,* and you'll spring up and remember that you are in Heaven.

The miracle comes quietly into the mind that stops an instant and is still. It reaches gently from that quiet time, and from the mind it healed in quiet then, to other minds to share its quietness. And they will join in doing nothing to prevent its radiant extension back into the Mind Which caused all minds to be. See how it reflects? You're getting a reflection now of your own Whole Mind. *Born out of sharing,* born out of forgiving, born out of giving, *there can be no pause in time to cause the miracle delay in hastening to all unquiet minds,* all self-justifying, resentful perceptual minds, *and bringing them an instant's stillness, when the memory of God returns to them. Their own remembering is quiet now, and what has come to take its place will not be wholly unremembered afterwards* and each time you remember it, you convert more and more of your own dark thought forms, more and more of your own ancient hate thoughts into the glorious remembering of that instant when, for just a moment, you thought that you were separate, and now you laugh it away as you spring joyously into Heaven.

He to Whom time is given offers thanks for every quiet instant given Him. For He knows that in that instant is God's memory allowed to offer all its treasures to the Son of God, for whom they have been saved. How gladly does He offer them unto the one for whom He has been given them! And His Creator shares His thanks, because He would not be deprived of His own effects, of His own creation. *The instant's silence that His Son accepts gives welcome to eternity and Him, and lets Them enter where They would abide.* And They come together. *For in that instant does the Son of God do nothing that would make himself afraid.* And in that instant is he whole and perfect as he has always been.

How instantly the memory of God arises in the mind that has no fear to keep the memory away! Don't be afraid. *Its own remembering has gone.* It simply disappeared. *There is no past to keep its fearful image in the way of glad awakening to present peace.* It doesn't try to deal with its own conflicts. It doesn't give reality to the earth, to the sickness and pain and death and chaos and hatred and loss that it formerly possessed as its own self-identity. What it thought was a necessary inevitable temporal association. What happens? *The trumpets of eternity resound throughout the stillness,* yet don't disturb it at all. Because you hear that lovely trumpet in your own mind. *And what is now remembered is not fear, but rather is the Cause that fear was made to render unremembered and undone. The stillness speaks in gentle sounds of love the Son of God remembers from before his own remembering came to get in the way in between the present and the past, to shut them out.* And not let them come together in a glorious moment of awakening from this nightmare of death.

Now is the Son of God at last aware of present Cause going on now and Its absolutely benign effects. He doesn't attack himself. *Now does he understand what he has made is absolutely causeless, and is having no effects at all.* Why? *He has done nothing.* He's done absolutely nothing. The world was never real. What is happening? He's waking up from his dream, isn't he? *And in seeing this, he understands he never had a need for doing anything, and never did.* You never had a need for doing anything and therefore never did anything. Not that you had a need to do something that was not yet complete. Not that you needed to be separate in order to come home. Not that you needed an identity that you thought was separate. No! *He understands he never had a need for doing anything, and never did.* Why? *His Cause is Its Effects. There never was a cause beside It that could generate a different past or a different future. Its effects are changelessly eternal, beyond fear, and past the world of sin entirely.*

What has been lost, to see the causeless not? What can you lose by not seeing something that never was real in the first place? *And where is sacrifice,* that you're actually giving up something, *when memory of God has come to take the place of loss?* (And death!) *What better way to close the little gap between illusions and reality than to allow the memory of God to flow across it, making it a bridge an instant will suffice to reach beyond?* And each time you forgive your brother, and each time you let go of the necessity to defend yourself, you actually flow through your own perceptions to eternity. And this is the bridge out of time, for God has opened it with Himself. *His memory has not gone by, and left a stranded Son forever on a shore where he can catch glimpses of another shore that he could never reach.* And this is what I could never stand or understand in my own human mind. And this is what many of you can no longer tolerate in your minds. In this time and place, you found yourself with a memory of perfect Love and of God, yet you were being taught by your own memory thoughts that you could never reach Him or really know Him. You were being told that a price of fearful loneliness, loss and pain, and finally death, had to be paid; that there were happenings beyond your control you must battle in order to get there. You were being told that you had to overcome terrible obstacles that were designed to keep you from eternal happiness or even that you were condemned for a crime you knew nothing about. No wonder you were in pain and sickness and finally demanded an answer not of this world. Now at last you are discovering that all of those things were only in your own mind. And it was your dream of death that was keeping you from seeing that this bridge to Heaven was always right with you — that this bridge out of time to eternity is right here and now.

His memory has not gone by, and left a stranded Son forever on a shore where he can glimpse another shore that he can never reach. His Father wills that he be lifted up and gently carried over. He has built the bridge, and it is He Who will transport His Son across it. All of the thought forms that you have designed originally in your own evil memory, separate memory, to keep you separate, are now marshaled to show you, in the bright reality of you, that you can cross safely across this bridge. And God obviously is there, because He's everywhere. And He's in this bright reunion with your own mind. *Have no fear that He will fail in what He wills for His Son. Nor that you will be excluded from the Will that is for you,* and was designed explicitly for you in your own dream of death.(Chap 28:I)

Listen, you so-called "searchers for meaning and purpose" in a place where there is no possibility of finding any. Listen to this. Here is a description of the present condition of your conceptual reality and of this objective continuum you appear to inhabit. Listen:

Without a cause there can be no effects, and yet without effects there is no cause. The cause of cause is made by its effects; the Father is a Father by His Son. Effects do not create their cause, but they establish its causation. Thus, the Son gives Fatherhood to his Creator, and receives the gift that he has given Him. It is because he is God's Son that he must also be a father, who creates as God created him. The circle of creation has no end. Its starting and its ending are the same. But in itself it holds the universe of all creation, without beginning and without an end.

Since you need it, that is the simplest most lucid description of the Singular Universal Reality of Eternal Life that you will ever hear.

Now comes the solution that requires only your willingness that it be so. Listen:

Nothing at all has happened but that you have put yourself to sleep, and dreamed a dream in which you were an alien to yourself, and but a part of someone else's dream. The miracle does not awaken you, but merely shows you who the dreamer is. It teaches you there is a choice of dreams while you are still asleep, depending on the purpose of your dreaming. *Do you wish for dreams of healing, or for dreams of death? A dream is like a memory in that it pictures what you wanted shown to you.*

Now stand by.

Here is a description of the present condition of your conceptual reality and of this objective continuum you appear to inhabit. Listen:

This world is causeless, as is every dream that anyone has dreamed within the world. No plans are possible, and no design exists that could be found and understood. What else could be expected from a thing that has no cause? Yet if it has no cause, it has no purpose. You may cause a dream, but never will you give it real effects. For that would change its cause, and it is this you cannot do. The dreamer of a dream is not awake, but does not know he sleeps. He sees illusions of himself as sick or well, depressed or happy, but without a stable cause with guaranteed effects. (Chap 28:II)

Your mind is the exclusive and inclusive cause of this entire fiasco of attack and defense that you pretend is life.

So this is the time of your resurrection, isn't it? And you can actually see this happening, now, in your own dream. Let's look at how intense we really are with this. This is a declaration that objective reality, where you are, is actually being resurrected each moment in a quantum leap, in a total reassociation of your mind, in a transfiguration of your body through the dedication of your mind to remember and return to Heaven and the eternal love of God. And this is what the message of Jesus Christ is and has always been — that if I don't resist the evil associations outside of myself, if I don't lay up the stores that have imprisoned me through the possession of my own conflictual mind, that I will remember that my Kingdom is not of this world, and I will no longer participate in serving my own hateful, vengeful thoughts even unto death. I have discovered that I cannot do both. If I am as God created me, I cannot have created myself. And the creations of myself are only memories of my own mind which I can transform, through my own whole mind, into remembrance that I am as God created me.

Making the connection between this quantum leap, this stepping from objective time to eternal reality, the movement from the dark particle form to the certainty of the wave of creative light energy, is only an acknowledgment of a unified force field or a Holy Spirit — a totality of the continuing unity reassociation of time and eternity. There're lots of different ways to express this in personal or historic philosophical, temporal associations, or, of course, quantum physics. Or a great variety of so-called spiritual paths or methods or purposes that all vouchsafe the inevitable necessity of the transformation of your own individual self-awareness.

But this course is for you. Isn't it? This is very directly a required course. This is the way you will remember you are still at home in Heaven. This is A Course In Miracles by the resurrected, objective man, Jesus Christ, in your historical frame of reference, returning in a full sense to you, because you are ready to hear this, in your own mind and declaring to you that He is resurrected and that so are you. And that He has always been with you in this single memory that you had together, both of the atonement principle, which is at the beginning of time, and the actual resurrection of the man, Jesus, in your own mind. And this is the incredibly freeing, joyously happy reality of Your Course.

So that perhaps we can read this now to you, that this resurrected man, this historic Jesus is the same Jesus in the Course In Miracles speaking to you from "out of time" from His resurrected eternal reality. And perhaps this is a little step in faith, isn't it? Perhaps it is a step of faith for you to declare, "Wow, I'd certainly like to believe that A Course In Miracles is coming from the mind of Jesus Christ of Nazareth." Perhaps this requires some faith and a little willingness that it be true. But those of you, in all of time, who have professed yourselves as Christians certainly have demonstrated a tremendous amount of faith in an apparent historic spiritual occasion that is now 2000 years old. It has been misconstrued and reduced and corrupted in the human conditional mind in a great variety of cultures and languages still containing all of the elements of rejection, opposition and crucifixion that constitute this world. But it simply will not be denied. See how it continues to communicate all of His gospel message of your salvation by Love through forgiveness that is finally our whole memory of His Saviorship and our resurrection if you will simply allow Him to be who He is and mean what He says.

Remember that you, as you are conceived in your own perceptual mind, must be a denial of the resurrection. So here we are in that physical sense of denial. But when this conceptual mind of Helen Schucman, ego mind, human mind, split mind, who is scribing, is taking the dictation of this total message of truth being brought into this chaotic continuum of darkness; this wondrous event that allowed the exposure of creative totality to be brought to this changing continuum of objective separation, when she asks directly in this time containment, of the eternal mind of Jesus Christ of Nazareth, specifically if the "resurrection was physical." "Did it actually happen to your body?" And I'm going to read for all of the world the response of the Jesus Mind. Not only as it is happening now and did happen two thousand years ago, but as it actually was brought to the supra attention of yourself in your own dream of awakening. This is from the Ken Wapnick story (Absence From Felicity) about the inception of the Course:

Helen speaks: "Jesus was there really a physical resurrection?"

Jesus speaks in response:

My body disappeared because I had no illusion about it. This is exactly what we just read about. This is exactly it. He did not have any illusions from His past reference as a man. Do you see? *The last one had gone. It was laid in the tomb, but there was nothing left to bury.* Now, and I'm going to try and give you this step. The association in the limited thought forms could very well have seen the body that they were laying in the tomb. But in the whole mind of their association with the resurrection of Jesus, it actually disappeared, as did they. *It was laid in the tomb, but there was nothing left to bury. It,* the body, did not, and does not, disintegrate because the unreal cannot die. The body was never there in the first place or in any real place. The resurrection, then, is the remembering of the total illusion of objective reality. *It merely became what it always was.* Which was what? Nothing! Got it? *And that is what 'rolling the stone away" means.* That the body is a vault where all of the perceptual memories are kept and buried in your own conceptual self — this is the whole idea of the crucifixion and resurrection. *This is what 'rolling the stone away" means. The body disappears, and no longer hides what lies beyond.* It is not held in the constriction of its own thought forms. *It merely ceases to interfere with vision. To roll the stone away is to see beyond the tomb, beyond death, and to understand the body's nothingness. What is understood as nothing must disappear.* And will and does and did.

And now listen to these explanations. *I did assume a human form with human attributes afterwards* — this is the actual return of the whole physical body of Jesus — *to speak to those who were to prove* to the rest of those still sleeping in split mind, *the body's worthlessness to the world.* To demonstrate His re-vision of the temporal continuum. To show that all He ever taught was that this world is not real. To establish, if necessary, a church, a momentary spatial context, which while still an entrapment of eternal life energy, as an establishment of mans' objective mortality, could be used as an instrument or light impetus vehicle of the Second Coming (full awakening). That, in fact, the body identification they possessed was not real, as demonstrated by the resurrection of this man, Jesus. *To prove the body's worthlessness to the world. This has been much misunderstood. I came to tell them that death is an illusion, and the mind that made the body can make another since form itself is an illusion.*

When Jesus appeared to the disciples behind closed doors, He appears as a very solid, apparently real, body. Does everyone understand this? Jesus declares to Helen what He demonstrated to His disciples. What was accomplished? He says, "The body is an illusion and I will prove it by undergoing a resurrection and then appearing as a continuing whole body. You have witnessed my apparent death in your own mind, now witness my resurrection." And this is exactly what each of us is demonstrating. That this body is actually a resurrected body each moment. Isn't it? That the bodies that we apparently are formulating around us are actually whole and resurrecting everywhere, all the time, in all of space/time in every holy instant of reality. This world was over long ago. You have been but reliving that single moment when fear came to take the place of Love.

This is much misunderstood. But I came to tell them that death is an illusion, and the mind that made the body can make another since form itself is an illusion. They did not understand. But now I talk to you and give you the same message. The death of an illusion, the loss of the world, the disappearance of these shadowy human figures that surround you, *means nothing.* They all *disappear when you awaken and decide to dream no more. And you still do have the power to make this decision as I did.* And this is the experience of our illumination and transfiguration through His Course In Miracles. That you are dreaming this dream of death, and it's not real, and that each moment that it appears to be real, you can transform it totally from a dream of loss and death to the happy realization of your own resurrection and return to Heaven.

God holds out His hand to His Son... I'm continuing to read Jesus speaking here about the resurrection. Listen to how incredibly lucid this is. *God holds out His hand to His Son to help him rise and return to Him. I can help because the world is an illusion, and I have overcome the world. Look past the tomb,* past *the body,* past *the illusion. Have faith in nothing but the spirit and the guidance God gives you. He could not have created the body because it is a limit. He must have created the spirit because it is immortal. Can those who are created like Him be limited? The body is the symbol of the world. Leave it behind. It cannot enter Heaven. But I can take you there any time that you choose* because I am always with you. *And together we can watch the world disappear and its symbol vanish as it does so.* Its symbol being only your body. *And then, and then* — and then it's very difficult for me to speak of this because it's joyously beyond conception. And Jesus says to Helen, *'I cannot speak of that.'* Nor do I have a need to speak of that. Soon I need not speak of this at all because you have lost your body associations and now are with me where you have always been in a place that you had never lost. And you are then completely whole and remember you are still perfect as you were created and this little world spins away to nothing.

What a beautiful message from our dear brother and teacher, resurrected man, Jesus Christ, and I'm glad this will be a part of a very bright coherent possibility contained in this very analog of conversion because I really want you to hear what you are being told in your ancient dream of death. So that you, individually, in the construction of your own body/mind, as it has been projected from you and has made other bodies still self-contained within your own thought forms, can undergo the resurrection through the transformation of your mind. And this is the message that you can hear now, because this is the message that is being offered to you now at this time in this place to awaken you personally from your own nightmare of hell that is your present futile dream of loneliness, loss and death.

When will you hear it? Now! When did you hear it? Now! How did you hear it? Through this message from Jesus, through the declaration of your own mind that this is true. This is A Course In Miracles. A course in the transformation of your mind from time to eternity. A beautiful, incredibly conceived thought form time association brought together in a continuum block of unreality that is to be transformed. The saving of time. The holding together through forgiveness of variant thought forms of your mind that you have projected somewhere in your own disillusionment and resentment of self-construction, but now are willing, because of the message you are hearing and have directed to your own mind, from out of time, to stand for a moment and let the grace of God descend on you in this time and in this place.

Thank you dear ones and Jesus. Thank you for joining in this awakening to the memory of God, and dreaming together for a very little while this new true dream of love which we shared, and share now for a moment. We are remembering, through the forgiveness of each other and our Father, and in the laying down of our ancient memories of hate and death, the reality of eternal life. We have become One Self together and remember our home in Heaven before time was. As we awaken, this world disappears and we step into eternity.

We hope that you will join this great awakening as Teachers of God and Saviors of the world. We are and will be everywhere that you are each moment. In your mind is the full resurrection going on of your entire body, if you will allow it to be, by not continuing to construct in time the old historic you and projecting those memories and this little objective nothingness forward into some sort of unreal time association to protect your insane need to defend your conceptual self-identity from resurrection by crucifying your own Christ Self once again.

We're together at the end of time and this dream is over and all of the pain and suffering that you have been undergoing has now become needless and valueless to you. And you see that there's no need for you to lose the things that you love. There's no need for you to suffer from cancer and there's no need for you to get old and slowly deteriorate. And, in fact, since time does not pass, it's impossible to age at all. The idea of getting old and dying was just a dream of death that you were holding in your own mind, and it's passed away, and we're together in Heaven. What a celebration! The revival of the dead ones! The rising up of your spirit of wholeness to the dream of the truth that you are still and always have been perfect as God created you and that nothing ever really happened, and all of all Universal Mind is only your mind as God created it, perfect in this new vision. Thank you everyone.

We know we'll be seeing you much sooner than you previously planned, if you'll only let it be so. The close of this continuum is very near. Those of you in all of the universe that would share in this new enlightenment, this contagion of the light and mind of creative reality that's spreading throughout the galaxies in quasars of eternal energy, can jump into this late dream with us and discover your own beautiful Light of God. What a reunion! What a celebration! God bless us everyone. MT

Here are but two directions you can take,
while time remains and choice is meaningful.
For never will another road be made
except the way to Heaven.
You but choose whether to go toward Heaven,
or away to nowhere.
There is nothing else to choose.
God gave His Teacher to replace the one you made,
not to conflict with it.
And what He would replace has been replaced.
Time lasted but an instant in your mind,
with no effect upon eternity.
And so is all time past,
and everything exactly as it was
before the way to nothingness was made.
The tiny tick of time
in which the first mistake was made,
and all of them within that one mistake,
held also the Correction for that one,
and all of them that came within the first.
And in that tiny instant time was gone,
for that was all it ever was.
What God gave answer to is answered and is gone.

Jesus Christ of Nazareth, The Third Patriarch of Zen, and You

"Whatever Happened To This Dream Of Death?"

We hope that at last you are beginning to look at the out-of-this-world assertion of Jesus in His *Course In Miracles*. You understand that it says initially, and in the totality of the expression of it, that this objective world is not a reality. Does everybody understand that? Is there anyone here — I'm curious — that has a question that that's what it says? This has nothing to do with the acceptance or the denial of it. It has to do with the fundamental admission that objectivity is illusionary, that any association of cause and effect that gives form or location or temporal-ness in a relationship with apparent passage of time is an illusion. Once more I'm going to do this because for some reason or other this has always been accepted conceptually as the picture or representation of any human being who has come to some form of sanity. Any human being that comes to any form of sanity may ultimately describe it in conditions relative to his vocabulary possibility. But what he will express through revelation is the self-certainty that he is a whole part of Eternal Reality and that this world is simply not real in any regard whatsoever.

It is very important that you get this so that you will stop doing conceptual comparisons of religious or philosophical associations dedicated to expressions of the truth in relationship to the illusion rather than the experience thereof.

If you are going to teach *A Course In Miracles*, the great discovery that you will make is that the *Course In Miracles* is the *Rig Veda*, for example. For goodness sake, philosophers, all we really are teaching you is that your subjective mind, in the totality of your own individual cause-and-effect relationship, has miscreated an objective association. That's exactly what we are saying.

Now, whether you're interested in this or not, I don't know. But somebody is going to come to you finally and say, "Oh, I know now what you're doing. You're teaching the same thing as the Third Patriarch of Zen." Well, I am the Third Patriarch! I'm teaching from the same mind. If you can hear the Third Patriarch of Zen and you read Chapter 7 of *A Course In Miracles*, they will express exactly the same thing. The Third Patriarch of Zen, or any mind in the discovery of wholeness, indeed including Jesus in His Sermon on the Mount, is not going to say anything different from what you will and must and did come to know in your own illusion to be the truth of your own reality.

The problem, obviously, is the necessity at this time in space for your personal admission of the necessity for you, individually, in your own constructed delusion, to pay attention to what the Third Patriarch of Zen tells you. Zen is an active Buddhism. That is, it is active to the extent that it teaches the possibility of vacant mind. It teaches to the immediate experience of awakening through a constancy of divine negation. The whole *Course In Miracles* teaches, "Vacate your mind." The whole *Course* is to vacate your mind. In the *Workbook*, it says, "Just for a moment don't correspond with the illusion." And if you vacate your mind, it will immediately be filled with Reality. Well, that's what the *Course In Miracles* says, that your objective self concepts are dark barriers that blind you to the eternal Light that is all around you.

The act of the vacation of the objective association is what the miracle is. Zen may say that it is transcendence. And then along comes Jesus and says, "You bet! Not only is it transcendence, but it involves the totality of your individual personal identity." So does the Third Patriarch. The Fourth Patriarch said, "No, that's not so." So all the Patriarchs got various ideas about what the teachings are.

The truth of the matter is there is no real association, except in a totality, between objective spatial time reality and the essence of a creating God, except in the inclusion of your own objectivity through the miracle of the non-association of your objective form. If you are going to teach this with me, you can throw out all the other stuff. You are teaching the action of the conversion of the individual human objective man.

It has nothing at all to do with *Course In Miracles* groups. It doesn't have anything to do with groups at all. It has to do with the transformation of your own individual objective mind. Don't search in there. "All your searching," says the Third Patriarch of Zen, "will just cause you to re-illusion because you are basing your objective reality on the continuation of the illusion rather than the release of it."

I ran into him over in Portage. The Third Patriarch is making noodles in the Chinese restaurant in Portage. Yes! Of course. He's a nice young fellow. He looked at me and just went right into a totality of his association. He wears some sort of tress. His name is One Hung Lo! It's a step. Then you take the step to: None Hung Lo! Don't try to separate your ancestral memories. You are learning to release the necessity for the objective correspondence in the previous associations of your bodily identity and you are experiencing the joy and happiness of the eternity that is all around you. How very simple.

It will astonish you, that if you got a specialist in Zen who shaves his head and puts his two fingers together — he has absolutely no intention, none, of reading the Third Patriarch of Zen. He couldn't possibly have any intention of reading the Third Patriarch of Zen because I found the Third Patriarch of Zen's little booklet. I didn't know I had it. It has coffee stains all over it. He handed this to me when I went over for Chinese food.

This says, Sing Sing Ming, verses. *Faith Mind by Seng t'san, the Third Zen Patriarch.* I'm going to take a look at this. I wonder what this is about. Look here what it attempts: *Make the smallest distinction, however, and heaven and earth are set infinitely apart. If you wish to see the truth, then hold no opinions for or against anyone.* That sounds very much like the very fundamental teachings of Jesus. This is what you are practicing, isn't it! You say, "How can I not hold any opinions? Not holding opinions will be the same as holding opinions." I am sure he will probably say that. And that will become very obscure, then, to the Zen specialist. So he will try to define what not holding opinions means. And, of course, being a specialist in the definition of Zen, he does.

The Way is perfect, like vast space, where nothing is lacking and nothing is in excess. Indeed, it is due to our choosing to accept or reject that we do not see the true nature of things. Live neither in the entanglements of outer things nor in the inner feelings of emptiness. That's not totally acceptable to the Buddhist establishment. Since that's what the Third Patriarch says, I'm sure he didn't last very long. *Be serene in the oneness of things* and what will happen? *And such erroneous views will disappear by themselves.* That sounds very familiar. That's the whole *Course.* Jesus says they will disappear by themselves. If you don't hold them in your own mind, they will simply disappear because you are the cause of them in a relationship of your own mind. You are the correspondent. You respond to them according to the dictates of your previously projected mind. No wonder you are an illusion.

This will say you are nothing but effects of effects. You are in an illusion. That's what this says. Well, it's said that for 3000 years, 3800 as a matter of fact. It has said for 3800 years that you are in a nightmare of your own dream. The problem, obviously, is there is no one here who has awakened through the auspices of Zen. If they have, they are not here. That was the provision of Jesus of Nazareth 2000 years ago, which is nothing but the activity of Zen, which he will attempt to express in here. The Third Patriarch says passivity is totally active. He says that. Then he was really rejected because they thought to sit and be passive in your mind was the way.

Virtually everyone in this new mind association has far surpassed any so-called Zen master there ever could be. Zen is not going transcendent. I am talking about Zen Buddhism now. That's just crap. It is not going transcendent and then coming back into the world. Zen is the transformation of the illusion to the certainty of wholeness. Don't be misled. So in that sense, when somebody asks you what you are, you say, "I'm a Zen master." Don't make such a big deal about it. Not only that, you have become active in your physical Buddhism, or what you call Shaktipat — that you can, in physical activity in Buddhism, change the correspondence of your own illusion. Is that so?

This is a nice little pamphlet. *Those who do not live in the single way fail in both activity and passivity, assertion and denial. The changes that appear to occur in the nothing world we call real are only because of our ignorance. Do not search for the truth. Only cease to cherish opinion. In the chase of this and that the mind essence will be lost in confusion. Although all dualism comes from the One, do not be attached even to this One.* That is an out-of-time statement. And that's being translated from something 3800 years old. That's how simple this is. Listen:

When the mind exists undisturbed in the miracle, which is *the Way* — he calls it "the Way," the holy instant — *when the mind exists in the* miracle, *nothing in the world can offend. And when a thing can no longer offend, it ceases to exist in the old way.* The thing ceases to exist. He is teaching Zen. He is teaching, "Change your mind and the world will change." Isn't that amazing?!

209

When no discriminating thoughts arise — this is the whole *Course.* When no discrimination — when you walk in here as a human being and have practiced your own conversion to the reality of universal mind sufficiently so it is no longer necessary for you to discriminate your own cause and effect relationships, all of which are caused only by your illusionary mind, *the old mind ceases to exist.* Once more: The human mind ceases to exist. Of course. Its existence depended on a discrimination of the associations of the objective form. Has anybody tried to teach Zen Buddhism this way? Wow! This is an astonishing sentence. *When no discriminating thoughts arise...* "I will not let my old thoughts be a guide to me now." Everybody got that? Do you understand? This is from the Zen master. *...the old mind ceases to exist. When thought objects vanish, the thinking subject vanishes.* That is going into Light and disappearing! Obviously the thinking subject would vanish because he is the cause of his own objectivity. That's literally true. Isn't that amazing? You didn't know that was in this. Thousands of these have been printed from Virginia Beach and distributed, thousands of them. Of course, a million *Course In Miracles* have been printed.

Do you understand me? You are going out into a world that has refused to hear the very fundamental essence that is the requirement for the transformation from objectivity to creative reality, to a universal mind. There is no other manner in which it can be done. That is why we say there is no other manner in which it can be done by the associations of your own mind. How simple the solution! Is that Zen Buddhism? A moment of Zen and you're gone from here. That is what a miracle mind is!

When thought objects vanish, the thinking subject vanishes, as when the mind vanishes, objects vanish. That's saying cause and effect; it's saying it both ways. In case you didn't get it one way, he gave it the other way. You are both the cause and the effect in your own association. *Things are objects because of the subject mind. The mind subject is such because of things object.* This is the whole *Course In Miracles!*

It's a cause and effect relationship. The form is never real. It's an illusion of your own mind. *Understand the relativity of these two and the basic reality, the unity of emptiness.* Understanding the relativity of these two is true perception. You understand the association in its entirety.

Someone called me on the phone last night and was expressing the Third Patriarch of Zen, saying, "What do you do when you have the certainty of the wholeness of your own mind?" There obviously is no manner in which you as the Zen master, as the savior of the world, as Christ, are going to be able to express this to a perceptual association. But you can show them through the unity of your mind the unity of theirs, first of all because they are objects of your mind. I'm into healing for a minute. And you have caused them to be objectively sick and to die by the definition of yourself — that's what this says — and when you change your mind, the entire objective association will undergo a radical re-association because the body at no single moment is real at all, but only an illusion contained within the objective form.

What's the big deal about what we just said? The salvation of the world depends on you, not as some sort of abstractedness of transcendentalism but as an existent reality contained within your own self-identity. The savior of the Christ, the savior of the Son of God, is yourself, *yourself,* your objectivity. Of course!

In this emptiness the two are indistinguishable, and each contains in itself the whole world. That's about as good as you will get. He's trying to express something that he has experienced, just as you are going to try to attempt something that you are experiencing. That is what you call a holy relationship. It is a direct admission of the totality of the association without any possibility of anything more than a momentary necessity for a correspondence of the limitation, which is the provision for the miracle. Without that provision, you're gone. So all you really do is convert the objectivity constantly into a new condition of reality. That's what I'm doing with you right now. That is what I do. I am a Zen master. But instead of sitting on my buns and humming, I have brought Christianity — which is the conversion or the resurrection of my body — into the association.

Obviously transcendentalism is a step, because if you go back to *Rig Veda* what happened is in the correlation of an attempt to correspond objective reality. We evolved from the *Rig Veda*, which says exactly this. If you go to *Veda*, it will say this. The other *Vedas* begin to slide off and suddenly you've got a caste system. Suddenly you have associations all working to bring about associations with each other — Hinduism — the admission of the possibility of an ascendance based on definitional associations of limitation expressed within the entire congruity of space/time. When you do that, you will need Buddhism to get out. Hinduism couldn't possibly work. How could it? It is a definition of the objective association. It is the admission of the possibility of evolution from the untouchable to the Brahmin, but there is no element of transcendence in it. And that is how Buddhism came about. Christianity obviously followed that. How could it not, once you have the admission of the possibility of the transcendence regardless of the condition, which is what Buddhism is. Buddhism was not obviously concerned about any caste system whatsoever. All it formed then was a priesthood of an entirely different caste in order not to admit to the simple truth of what it says. I see we have a new Dalai Lama. He's seven years old and they have a big fight going on because the Communist Chinese have their own Dalai Lama, and the Dalai Lama here has got his own Lama. Why don't you call him on the phone and tell him you are the reincarnation? Are you? You bet! In its entirety. Boy, talk about definitions limiting associations. Do you see how incredible that is?

If you do not discriminate between coarse and fine, you will not be tempted to prejudice an opinion. That means "look through it." When you see something coarse, don't attempt to distinguish between something that is rarer and something that is thicker. This is the whole *Course In Miracles*. Don't distinguish. It is the admission of the objectivity, with the certainty that any discrimination will be a form of opinion that will hold you in the bondage of your own conceptual mind. Isn't it? And that's obviously what you have done. In this translation from the Chinese, "coarse" and "fine," are not a very good translation. Another translation of "coarse" and "fine" probably would be better. Probably "particle" and "wave" would be closer. Can you hear that? Don't distinguish between the particle and the wave because they are both finally going to be the same thing. When he tries to express it in translation, it came out from the Cantonese, it came out more like Chop Suey. So we are smoothing that out for you. Put a little sauce, a little soy in it. We are trying to smooth out your mind so that you won't get caught in your own Chow Mein, or in your own prognostications.

You find it in fortune cookies. I would love to see *Course In Miracles* fortune cookies. *The world you see has nothing to do with reality.* You crack them open, and you have an experience. You can improvise: *Stand by. We are beaming you up.* Isn't that amazing? How many oysters will you crack looking for a pearl worth any price? It's the same idea: we're always searching for that one truth. And finally we discover that it's in us. That's what this says. Isn't that lovely?

To live in the Great Way, to live in the holy instant, to live with the will of God, *is neither easy nor difficult. It is only different.* Isn't that amazing? Who would have thought that they would say that? *It is only different. But those with limited views are fearful and irresolute. The faster they hurry, the slower they go.* That's the exact truth. It's just going to take them that much more time because they are frantically looking for the solution here.

Are you ready? *And clinging*— what you call attachment, what he calls objective reality, limitations, ego, clinging, attachment — *cannot be limited at all.* If there is any clinging at all, it will be a totality of clinging, is what this says. Ah so! This is very extreme. This sounds just like the *Course In Miracles. Even to be attached to the idea of enlightenment.*

213

Don't depend on the means. The means are also an illusion. Don't depend on them. *Even to be attached to the idea of enlightenment is to go astray. Just let things be in their own way, and they will be neither coming nor going.* This is the whole *Course In Miracles*. You appear here, you let things be what they are, and you couldn't possibly have a problem because you are not going to associate with your own effects. If you do that, there will not be a coming or a going. You simply cease to be here at all. This is the statement that this is a coming and going, in case you would like to know.

Anyone attempting to describe what is occurring in your own mind might very well write this in Chinese. Why wouldn't he? He needs to express it some way. *Obey the nature of things...* your own nature *...and you will walk freely and undisturbed. When thought is in bondage, the truth is hidden, for everything is murky and unclear.* So much of the *Course* teaches this. You can't get a decent reflection because your thoughts cloud up the simple truth through the projections of your own mind. Wow! What an amazing idea. *...for everything is murky and unclear. And the burdensome practice of judging brings annoyance and weariness.* Jesus asks this all the time: *What benefit can be derived from distinctions and separations?* He is just trying to express the futility of dealing with human beings that are looking for a solution to the problem when the only benefit you could possibly get from your own objective association is your own termination. What possible benefit could you get from your own identity?

If you wish to move in the one Way, listen. The wise man strives to no goals, but the foolish man fetters himself. There is one dharma, not many. This idea of the reduction of Buddhism to multiple dharmas really annoys me. The whole teaching is there is one illusion, not many! How could a Buddhist possibly put on a red robe and bang gongs when it says that? Then again, how could somebody pick up the *Course In Miracles* and not immediately spring into Heaven? All he would have to do is make the admission that it came from out of time. Is it that simple? "Well, nobody seems to have gotten it in 3800 years." What did this just say, dummy? This says the only one that hasn't gotten it is you! It says there is only one dharma. "Well, is dharma the effect of karma?" I just read you, they are interchangeable. The whole *Course In Miracles* says dharma and karma are the same thing. That's what it says!

First you don't depend on the dharma and then you transform your own karma. That's what we are really saying. Initially you intermix what you call environment and heredity, which is dharma and karma. They've got a show. They're going to put on a show on Saturday night, *Dharma and Karma.* Can you get it? Karma does the lyrics and Dharma does the music. It's a melody all mixed up and the words are simply the karma of your own mind. That was pretty good, wasn't it?

There is one dharma, not many. Distinctions, separations, (objective reality) *arise from the possession or clinging needs of the ignorant.* Quite literally, nothingness. *To seek mind* (reality) *with the discriminating conceptual mind is the greatest of all mistakes.* And finally the only mistake. There's no sin connected with Buddhism because there is no necessity for conversion. Sin comes about with an attempt to associate the objective with the subjective — the idea that a sin could be corrected outside of you. No wonder the *Course* isn't accepted. The *Course* teaches you flat out if sickness is real, it could never be corrected, and that by the acknowledgment (this is Chapter 27) of the sickness you kill it rather than heal it. The acknowledgment of the disease is an acknowledgment of the correspondence. What an amazing idea.

To seek reality with the discriminating conceptual mind is the greatest of all mistakes. Rest and unrest derive from illusion. In enlightenment there is no liking or disliking, just the realization of your eternal singularity. All dualism comes from ignorant inferences. They are like dreams or flowers in the air, foolish to try to grasp them. Let them go.

Gain and loss, right and wrong — such thoughts must finally be abolished at once. There was another sentence in there. The translation, very simply, is: "It has to happen now or it's not going to happen." It is not a future thing that can be abolished. It is right now. *If the I never sleeps, all dreams will naturally cease. The mind makes no discrimination, as the ten thousand things are as one. To understand the mysteries of this one essence is to be released from all entanglement. No compromising, no comparisons or analogies are possible in this causeless, total reality. Consider movement stationary and the stationary in motion.*

Consider movement stationary and the stationary in motion. That's the most difficult thing to teach, isn't it? Obviously, we are in a form of stationary instantaneous recovery in the totality of the momentary reformation of our totality of form. *Consider movement stationary and the stationary in motion.* Particle and wave. *Both movement and rest disappear. As such dualism ceases to exist; Oneness itself cannot exist either. In this ultimate finale, no law or description applies. With a unified mind in accord with the Way, all self-centered striving ceases. Doubts and irresolution vanish and life in true faith is possible. With the single scope, we are free from bondage. Nothing clings to us, and we hold to nothing. All is empty. Self clear, Self illuminating, with no exertion of the mind's power at all.* Then the power of the universe emerges. *To come directly into harmony with this reality* — this is the whole *Workbook* — *just simply say, when doubt arises, Not-Two.* Not true, not so, not two. It cannot be so.

In this 'Not-two" nothing is separate. It doesn't teach you to attempt to bring them together. The whole *Course* teaches you Not-two, not objective reality. Do you understand? It is never this! The whole salvation is simply Not-two. The idea that you can be separate from God is what two is. Since you think you are separate, you think there are two. There would have to be a distance between them. All you must teach is

Not-two. What an amazing idea! *In this "Not-two" nothing is separate, nothing is excluded. No matter when or where, enlightenment means entering into this truth. And this truth is beyond extension or diminution in time or space. In it a single thought is 10,000 years.* This is the whole *Course In Miracles!* Wow!

Infinitely large and infinitely small...no differences for definitions have vanished, and no boundaries are seen. So, too, with being and non-being. Don't waste time in doubts and arguments that have nothing at all to do with it. It actually says that! I am not telling you this. That's what this says! Don't waste time in doubts and arguments. Practice "Not-twoism". That's from *Universal Publications*, Virginia Beach, "grateful acknowledgment required for permission..." This is the whole lesson of salvation. Do not underestimate the insanity of the conceptual mind. It is formed with the full intention to retain the objective identity. Absolutely. That is what this says!

At no single moment does the body exist at all. A cancel-out has already occurred because of your split mind. I don't think that you are teaching *A Course In Miracles* here still. If you don't begin with the assumption of the unreality of this, it becomes very difficult to teach. *Course* groups now are writing letters still maintaining the idea that the *Course* groups have something to do with the *Course In Miracles*. You can't get out by teaching that. Groups have nothing to do with the *Course In Miracles* at all. The *Course In Miracles* is the de-grouping, your coming to the certainty of your own whole mind. Power cannot oppose.

This is Chapter 27. I'm going to give you just a sentence to see if you can get an idea. *Your function is to show your brother sin can have no cause. How futile must it be to see yourself a picture of the proof that what your function is can never be! The Holy Spirit's picture changes not the body into something it is not. It only takes away from it all signs of accusation and of blamefulness. Pictured without a purpose, it is seen as neither sick nor well, nor bad nor good.* That is what I just read you. *No grounds are offered that it may be judged in any way at all. It has no life, but neither is it dead. It stands apart from all experience of love or fear.* That is the whole teaching.

The simple way to let this be achieved is merely this — Brother, by your hand I live — *to let the body have no purpose from the past, when you were sure you knew its purpose was to foster* (your own identity) *guilt. For this insists your crippled picture is a lasting sign of what it represents. This leaves no space in which a different view, another purpose, can be given it. You do not know its purpose. You but gave illusions of a purpose to a thing you made to hide your function from yourself.* Brother, there is no death! If you don't begin with the fundamental assertion, you couldn't possibly teach *A Course In Miracles.*

To witness sin and yet forgive it is a paradox that reason cannot see. For it maintains what has been done to you deserves no pardon. And by giving it, you grant your brother mercy but retain the proof he is not really innocent.

Forgiveness is not real unless it brings a healing to your brother and yourself. (Chap 27:II)

Power cannot oppose. There is no opposition to power. Power is God Mind. There is absolutely no opposition to it, and it cannot oppose anything. There is no such thing as reciprocity or exchange. There is one Universal Power of which you are a whole part. You may utilize it in your own limitation, but if you do, your opposition will be to your own limitation, not to the power of the mind. *For opposition would weaken it, and weakened power is* totally ridiculous! Yet the whole basis of your present condition is the idea that there are various degrees of power and that one power will be weakened by the assertion of another power. What an absurd idea. It is simply an attack on God. *Weak strength is meaningless...* All of your competition is based on weak strength. You have a million different categories where you decide where the participation of the association should be in a definition of the goals that you set up in the limitations to what? Limit the power of your own creative mind, and derive the benefit of the accomplishment of a limited goal, based on a previous association. Listen to me: It is not real! I don't care what you do within your own associations of cause-and-effect, any goal that you set would be absolutely and totally meaningless. Your goal here has only been to retain the existent association of the correspondence of the hitherto determined cause of you — which was over and gone a long time ago.

And therefore it must be limited and weak, because that is its purpose. It is designed to what? Protect its own location! To defend itself in its own limitation. If I defend myself, I will be attacked by my defensive posture. It's the whole *Course.* Do you hear me? Is there a question about what this says, human being? I am telling you that you are a human being in a condition of being attacked by your own projections. It is going to say that in this book. I need your fundamental admission of the necessity for you, as an apparent objective mind, to undergo the experience of a whole mind perfectly creating as God created you. That is where we begin our teaching. That is where they end their teaching. That is where you begin! *And therefore it must be limited and weak, because that is its purpose. Power is unopposed, to be itself.* And I assure you, power is itself. It has no contradiction. The power of your mind, teacher of God, is totally unlimited and contained by nothing. You are ruler of the Universe! Until you accept that, you will believe that some sort of alien power outside of you can set the terms on what the definition of you, in the entirety of you, is. And you will never be happy doing that. How could you be? It is impossible!

No weakness can intrude on it without changing it into something it is not. This is going to say that opposing power cancels. It is going to say that you are setting up conditions of nothingness in a relationship with yourself. *To weaken is to limit,* to define, *and impose an opposite that contradicts the concept that it attacks.* You are going to be attacked by *Course In Miracles* teachers who don't agree with your concepts. And they will contradict the concept of their own concept, because that's what their mind does. Their mind is not capable of releasing to a non-conceptual association. Do you hear me? That's what this says! *And by this does it join to the idea a something it is not, and make it* totally *unintelligible.* Any association of form becomes unintelligible. The association between that chair and that rug is literally unintelligible. There is no way possible that you, as a human being, are going to be able to explain to me your existent association based on a comparison between that chair and that rug. You will set up another form that is exactly as illusionary as the forms that you pertain to in order to keep your identity. That is the Third Patriarch of Zen. Don't do that! That is not what reality is. Can you teach it or not? You would have to believe it, and you have to have the experience of the non-necessity for your own objective association because this is a course that says very simply all of your objectivity is not real. It says it page after page after page. The very least you have to do is say that this is what it says. You will be ridiculed, attacked, you can be killed, you can be crucified each second, anything. But unless you teach it, there is no way you can come to know it. How could you? Each moment you are allowing for your own reality, based on your own illusionary objective associations. Yes or no? Who is doing that? Point to your nose. You!

And by this does it join to the idea a something it is not, and make it unintelligible. Who can understand a double concept, such as "weakened-power" or "hateful-love"? You can pretend to understand it. All you will find is degrees in your own non-existent association. Degrees, aspects and intervals have nothing at all to do with what I am telling you. I am teaching you to awaken from your own objective unreality. That is all. Please do not present me, either, with the objects that you believe are real, or the manner in which you believe you can come to the truth. None of them are real. I am talking directly to you. That is called faith in God!

You have decided that the guy out there — your mother, your uncle, your cousins, your brother — the phantom figures that you have brought with you to define within the correspondence of both your objection and acceptance are going on equally to create an image that literally does not exist. Your mind is split trying to determine a distinction between your rejection of it and your acceptance of it. Yet any objection or rejection simply cancels out the whole thing! You think it doesn't do that, but it does. It is a cancel-out. Ideas leave not their source. If I forget something from my mind that I rejected, it hasn't gone anywhere. But, obviously, having rejected it, it is no longer a part of my mind — nor is the thought by which I rejected it. I may have loved it for a little while, and then rejected it. Yet, I live in my mind with both the memory of loving it and hating it simultaneously. That is impossible! Nothing is happening when you do that. What a psychology! It is called forgiveness. How simple is salvation. All you have to do is release your imagery of it, and it will immediately spring into light because you are not defining it. Any definition will limit.

You have decided that your brother — all humans do this — *is a symbol for "hateful-love," a "weakened-power," and above all, a "living-death."* Can you believe that? You are going to lock that guy in the electric chair, and you feel both sorry for him and justified in not being sorry. And you are caught. You are bound. Now you have to decide whether he should be punished or not. You will never get out of it. What am I telling you? It is not real! Stop trying to get out of it. You can't get out of it through any judgment at all. All of your judgment will literally be nothing because it is a distance between nothing and nothing. This is *A Course In Miracles*. Stop trying to locate yourself. All of your locations are dissolving — am I teaching the Workbook of the *Course?*

You have decided that your brother is a symbol for "hateful-love," a "weakened-power," and above all, a "living-

death. 'He is both alive and dead. He is dead because he is going to be dead. But he is not dead yet. Yet when a thing dies, you distinguish between what is dead and gone and what is still here. What could you possibly be comparing but dead with dead? You couldn't possibly be comparing with life because life is eternal. If life is eternal, why do you compare the dead with the dead? Let the dead bury the dead. All of the associations here are nothing but correspondences of an attempt to identify eternity with time. He formulates time and cancels out everything. It literally does not exist. Your objective association does not exist. This world does not exist. How do we come to know that? Don't resist your own association with yourself. The only problem you will ever have teaching this is you refuse to press on them that they are the cause of this. All of the letters we get will entirely ignore this. Listen to me. They will ignore that you are the cause of this. They will ignore the teachings of the Third Patriarch of Zen, that the objective association is totally illusionary and is caused by your subjectivity. When the phone rings and somebody says, "Come and teach," why don't you say, "The salvation of the world depends on you." They will say, "No, it depends on these phantom figures that I love and hate. The *Course In Miracles* teaches me to love my brother to death." It is exactly the opposite! It teaches you not to judge your brother so you can see he is perfect as God created him.

I am getting nods from you, but I am giving you the facts. I am telling you that you can make that decision in your mind and the world will disappear. I am not teaching you from a 3800 year old tablet. I am standing here in your own mind telling you that you are in an illusion, a nightmare, of your own making.

And so he has no meaning to you, for he stands for what is meaningless. You can fight it and fight it, and you can do everything you can, but you cannot give meaning where no meaning is. Everything that you value here does nothing but bind you to your own condition of pain and death. Everything! There are no exceptions to that. None! You are either free as

God created you, or you are nothing. *He represents a double thought...* This is real lucid stuff. In a double thought, both have to be cancelled out. Can you see that? Listen to what this says: *And so he has no meaning to you, for he stands for what is meaningless. He represents a double thought, where half is cancelled out by the remaining half.* If you take God as a whole thing and break off a piece of God, the half that is left is cancelled out by the other half because you have got two pieces. So when you are separated from God, all you can see is a piece of God broken out. You can't see the whole God. Who sees that? You may see Him as almost whole, but the piece that will be missing will be you! All you can see is where the piece was broken off. Otherwise you couldn't be separate. Here's the borderland. You keep getting closer and closer to the piece that has been broken out. But as long as you keep it separate, you will be dualistic in your own association. Holy mackerel. You literally can't get there because you are trying to get to something that you cancelled out by attempting to determine in your own mind what it is. Who sees this?

God keeps pushing on you. "I am not God." "You are, too." That's all that really says. The "you are, too" part of it authenticates the separation of your own mind. It verifies what? Your own separation. It is nothing. You have cancelled yourself out entirely. Certainly wholeness doesn't know anything about it. But for the instant that you thought you were separate, you got what? A reflection of the separation. That is what we are repairing here. The reflection was off just a notch.

And so he has no meaning to you, for he stands for what is meaningless. He represents a double thought, where half is cancelled out by the remaining half. Yet even this is quickly contradicted by the half it cancelled out, and so they both are gone. Obviously you can't tolerate the impossible position of the judgment of yourself. Quite literally you are struggling trying to find equanimity between love and hate, between the reality that you are and the conflict of yourself. You cancel it out initially by separating yourself entirely from it. This is exactly what you do. But you can't even stand that; you must continue to separate it in an effort to maintain a balance within your own mind in the separation. Once you begin to do that, you will do comparisons with comparisons with comparisons. That is what you as humans call "mind" or "thinking". You are dead wrong. You are dead. That is not what thinking is. Conceptual associations in the human condition are not what mind is. What are they? Nothing! Each moment is being cancelled out by something else. What a terrible place! So you live in the illusion and attempt to balance the forms of your own association. You maintain that they are real within you, you suffer the consequences of the illusion, and you die. What is that?

Aren't you finally going to ask what is going on here? Aren't you finally going to begin to question your own aspects? Don't you really want to know why you are so limited in this box of time? You asked for what else there was. This is what else there is! I am telling you that what you thought is not real. Totality is all around you. The joy that you are discovering is very simply that this is not life! This is not what life is. It existed for a moment in whose mind? Yours! Now what do you do? You are transforming through the release of the association. What are you experiencing? The joy and love and happiness of Universal Mind.

Yet even this is quickly contradicted by the half it cancelled out, and so they both are gone. Here's a description of objective reality. *And now he stands for nothing.* Why? *Symbols which but represent ideas that cannot be must stand for empty space and nothingness.* He is literally an illusion. You were not even attempting to correspond with his body. You are too fearful to do that. What you are corresponding with is an illusion of your own mind. He does the same. You create illusions of your own mind and pretend that is what life is. What nonsense. *Yet nothingness and empty space can not be interference. What can interfere with the awareness of reality is the belief that there is something there.* There is not anything there! Are you going to try to teach this to the world?

All of these phantom figures — the picture of your brother that you see is totally and absolutely meaningless. There is no such thing as a person. There is no such thing as separate minds living within a containment of the body. That is the First Law of Chaos, that there actually are separate persons contained within themselves. Why does the separate person maintain that? Because he has separated himself from himself. Having separated himself, all he could possibly be meeting is what? Himself! He is meeting himself. Yet if he is not real within his own mind, who he will meet will also be an illusion. So he shares the illusion of his own identity, and because he doesn't want, through judgment, the other association, he gives it a reality separate from himself. He pretends that he didn't make it in his own mind, and lives in the conflict of his illusions with his illusions.

I can't read it any plainer than this. I don't know if I can express it any plainer than this. It is not real. Let it go. That is what forgiveness is. Stop making it real and trying to atone it. What makes illusion is illusion. The entire association is illusionary because: *The world I see has nothing to do with reality. It is of my own making, and it does not exist.* (Lesson 14) What are you going to do now? Apply a little Third Patriarch of Zen. When that works, it will be working; when it doesn't, it is simply because you reillusioned. But the solution is to continually release because all of it is illusionary! It is impossible that you fail; the whole thing is not real. It is another way of saying the separation did not occur. If the separation did occur, there is no way you could ever get back. You could get back temporarily until some more conflict came up. What a weird idea that you were cast out of Heaven by God — that there was a fight. Nobody kicked anybody out of Heaven. Nonsense. Anything not in Heaven is not real. Anything that kicks anything out of Heaven is also not real. Did you get that? You are kicking yourself. It is a weird idea that somebody forced you out of Heaven. Who is that somebody? The guy that you have rejected outside of yourself — your brother, who you now must hate and love at the same time, has rejected you. Do not underestimate the insanity of the human mind. You are in a dream of death, brother, and you are waking up from it. It was actually over a long time ago and you are discovering it, and you are no longer going to participate in the nightmare of your own mind.

The picture of your brother that you see means nothing. Are you ready? You are not going to like this. Don't tell me you can stand up in front of a seminar of physicists and read this. What are you teaching? Personal atonement. I would be surprised if the world didn't begin to catch on, at least fundamentally, that you are teaching that the subject is the cause of the objective association. Individually you are the cause of this in your own mind. Any aggregation is not true.

The picture of your brother that you see means nothing. There is nothing to attack or to deny... This sounds like the Third Patriarch. There is nothing to love, there is nothing to hate. There is nothing *...to endow with power or to see as weak.* That's what I read you in that little pamphlet. And the moment that you saw that, you awakened from the dream and were in Heaven. This is over and gone. And now you are discovering that was so — when it becomes so for you, it will always have been so. You are not doing anything that you have not done. You are entirely one mind. It is impossible that you are doing anything that you have not done since there is only your mind. It would have to be true. What a strange idea that power could oppose and there could actually be something in the Universe — I am looking right at your mind now, holy Son of God, Creator in the Universe — that would actually stop you from being as God created you. It is crazy. But remember, you are the one that is telling me that you are as God created you. I am just agreeing with you. You are as God created you. There is only one. There is nothing to attack, there is nothing to deny, there is nothing to love, there is nothing to hate, there is nothing to endow with judgment or power or to see as weak. Why? *The picture has been wholly cancelled out, because it symbolized a contradiction that cancelled out the thought it represents.* It would have to be true. So you are possessed by some thoughts that you don't look at. You bring them up in your own mind when you decide to use them, then you distinguish which thoughts you want to use and which you want to reject. This is the body. Holy mackerel! And you think that if you don't look at them at all that they're not involved in what you are. Therefore you cannot use them as a potential literally because you are fearful of the entirety of your own potential — you are actually afraid to let all of your possessive thoughts be a part of you. Why? All of your possessions would become whole with you in your own mind. You are afraid of your own enlightenment. What an astonishing idea. Wow!

The picture has been wholly cancelled out, because it symbolized a contradiction that cancelled out the thought it represents. You might want to do, "Don't look at the frame, look at the picture" out of Chapter 17. That is what this is describing. It is nothing but a series of reflections within your own mind. It becomes a frame to keep you from seeing through into the Light. That is what this says. *And thus the picture* — the picture that you make using the frame as a reference — *has* absolutely *no cause at all.* It is gone. Wow! *Who can perceive effect without a cause?* No one! Nothing can conceive of effects without a cause except something that is equally causeless. Since the cause of the earth was gone the moment that it came into being, you are only the effects of the effects of the cause that is already back in Heaven. You have every right to be upset about that. But there is nothing I can do about it because the guy that planned this whole expedition is already back in Heaven. That's true. You are going to have to forgive him or you can't get out of here. You don't like that. I'm giving you the concrete evidence that the schism is real to you through the assertion of the power of an agreement that was made somewhere to retain the illusion. That is where you are trapped.

And thus the picture has no cause at all. Who can perceive effect without a cause? What can the causeless be but nothingness? The picture — that guy. You're going to read it, but you are not going to believe it. That picture of you, the identity, the form in your own mind, what you call a human being that's actually changing each second that you are holding concrete in your own objective illusion of yourself... I lost my place. I don't want you to read it conceptually. I want you to understand that we are sharing an objective unreality. Actually if we let it go, we simply would disappear. All we are doing now is retaining momentarily, like the Third Patriarch says, a totality of causation that has no objection to it, because the objection was only in our individual mind. We are literally saying we are going home to God. Nothing in the Universe can stop us from doing that except our determination to deny the association to come with us. All you have really done is include everything in rather than attempting to judge it in relationship with yourself. It is nothing but an inclusiveness of your own mind. We call it forgiveness. Look at what forgiveness offers you! If you don't judge it, it will become a whole part of your mind. Wow!

I'm getting warmed up here — I am reading the *Course In Miracles* to you! Is that all there is to it? Absolutely! What is happening? You are having the miraculous experience! I don't have to explain the *Course* to you. The *Course* means exactly what it says. This gets better!

The picture of your brother — the solid body, your body, his, you are only seeing yourself, right? You agree? You've got all different guises. Whatever he is, he is just an image of your own mind. You are meeting yourself in another moment in time. Use time. Time is valuable here. Remember you are trying to associate the contemporary with what you rejected. Although a contemporary is always gone, all of your thought forms are actually in different associations of time. In that sense, every guy that you meet has a totality of both your rejection and your acceptance. This is on the third to the last page of our *Out of Time* Journal where I said to you that you can't meet a stranger. You are meeting associations from all over in your own mind. Any difference that you see is only an attempt to be different from God. Quite literally, it is an attempt to be different. By being different, everything outside of you will also be different.

It will be different, different, different, different, different. But none of it is real. Can you see this? I know this reduces in the *Course* to "you are not different." We wrote all of this together. There is no difference. We are all as God created us.

The picture of your brother that you see is wholly absent and has never been. Not only is it not there, but it was never there since the correction was made at the time. You are in a dream. Do you want to look at it that way? You know you are in a nightmare and you are waking up. That is why you are having all the joyous experiences because you are not paying any attention to your old dream. Is that so? Is it that simple? Yes! Positively. It is positively that simple. *The picture of your brother that you see is wholly absent and has never been.* Listen: *Let, then, the empty space it occupies be recognized...* through the release of your necessity of the correspondence as being what? *...as vacant...* Since you cannot know what totality is — I am doing Third Patriarch here — since totality is everything, you must just for a moment, the holy instant, vacate the closure of your own mind in the reflection of yourself. Do you hear me? Stop mind-snapping on me. The new guys here always mind-snap. All human beings mind-snap. They literally come into the association having already judged it. That's hopeless. The practice is that they begin to release that necessity — they do the *Workbook* — and finally they discover that by not holding or snapping their mind into a definition, that they experience the miracle of the wholeness of their own whole mind. Isn't that what I am teaching? I am telling you that all of your concepts are what your restrictions are because you are restricting yourself in your own conceptual objective association. Isn't that what this says? Is that what I am telling you? Do you want that to be true? If you want it to be true, it will be true because it is true. Why else am I telling you that you are the cause of your own pain? Because later on, on a page back there, you are going to have to admit that there is no need for you to suffer sickness and pain. Dummies?! There is no need for you to suffer sickness and pain and loneliness and death because they are only effects of your own non-reality. You've got that in your Church creed. It says right there: ...*misery and death do not exist.* Sickness and death are not real. They have no idea that you mean that. Why? There's a God. God is a fact.

Let, then, the empty space — that instant that you keep filling in order to protect yourself — *it occupies be recognized as vacant, and the time devoted to its seeing be perceived as idly spent, a time unoccupied.* I will tell you what that says. That says that everything you do as a human being is totally meaningless. Everything! Don't try to con yourself into the idea that there is value in your conceptual association. The value is not a con job, it is a reality. If you don't value this and don't try to justify yourself, you will be whole and real. Why? Isn't the miracle going on all the time? In all time? Yes! Wow! Release yourself from the bondage of self. ...*and the time devoted to its seeing be perceived as idly spent, a time unoccupied. An empty space that is not seen as filled, an unused* (you are doing nothing) *interval of time not seen as spent and fully occupied...* Because you are always only spending time — spending, literally, spending means exchanging — you are spending a part of your mind on your retention of something else, spent in idolization of your own association. Did you learn to do that? Yes, you learned to do that. Now you are beginning to feel the happiness of the non-necessity to define yourself. Yet your reality, heretofore, was based on the necessity of the conflict of your own definition. You don't have to study that. I am giving you the fact of it. There is no such thing as a human being. You do not exist. You are just in a transient moment. That is the whole teaching!

An empty space that is not seen as filled, an unused interval of time not seen as spent and fully occupied... Look what the human being does. And watch them come up here and attempt not to occupy their space for a moment. They are looking for some sort of relief and they are going to define it as a temporary freedom, so they then can go back and continue the conflict. Do you see that? So the vacation is a better illusion. But if that is so, and God is and this ain't, why not stay entirely in the vacating, or the vacation, of your own mind? I am teaching you to vacate your occupation. It is a vacation! I have told you to stay on vacation. You are all worried about things that are out there. You can't know you are the cause of them until you go on vacation. This is active Zen! Instead of vacating, you are opening and allowing all of the previous illusions — it is called atonement or resurrection of your own form. What an astonishing idea. Transcendental Existentialism! I exist in a continually transcendental reassociation. What a lovely idea.

An empty space that is not seen as filled, an unused interval of time not seen as spent and fully occupied, become a silent invitation to the truth to enter, and to make itself at home. Very silently. And how immediately it will come. You are being instructed by yourself to let yourself in. It is impossible that not be so. I wouldn't go to abstraction at this point. If you have to, let it be totally abstract. You are still going to discover yourself in a correspondence with yourself anyway. How much that reduces I don't know. The fact of the matter is we vacate our mind and we enjoy the experience of the Light association that is all around us. How do we vacate? We don't give an identity to the association. That is the teaching of this. Why don't you start teaching it! Go out in the world. Go anywhere. Take your Journals. Start out with the fundamentals. Get out of all that other perceptual junk of, "I have got to forgive my brother" and "We are all coming together to retain the family." Teach this. Don't you see? You don't have to teach that Jesus only taught you've got to hate your family and get out of here — that is what He says and everybody ignores that. Why should you remind them of that? They didn't hear Him 2000 years ago and they sure aren't going to hear it now — any more than they heard the Third Patriarch of Zen. You let *yourself* be whole in your own mind. This is *A Course In Miracles*. There is no doctrine in this *Course* at all. None. It doesn't exist. It says all doctrine is illusionary. All associations are not true. Time is not real.

For what you leave as vacant God will fill, and where He is there must the truth abide. Unweakened power, with no opposite, is what creation is. For this there are no symbols. Nothing points beyond the truth, for what can stand for more than everything? For goodness sake! Isn't that lovely?! Wow! *Yet true undoing must be kind. And so the first replacement for your picture is another picture of another kind.*

As nothingness cannot be pictured, so there is no symbol for totality. (Chap 27:III)

All questions asked within this world are but a way of looking, not a question asked at all. It is all propaganda. A question asked in hate cannot be answered, because it is an answer in itself. A double question asks and answers, both attesting the same thing in different form. The world asks but one question. It is this: 'Of these illusions, which of them is true?'(Chap 27:IV) The truth of the matter is that none of them are true. This is called *A Course In Miracles!* Are you now able to pick it up and read it from your new viewpoint? You have opened that door now so you can see it. I hope so. The form is never real. The question is not that, the question is: are you now, individually in your mind, willing to direct attention to the release of your own perceptual self? Until then, no salvation is possible. You can write all the letters you want about objecting to the manner in which I am teaching this. I am not teaching in any manner at all. I am telling you that you are not real and do not exist.

What you are literally teaching is, "Give with no result." That's what I just taught you. Don't accept a reflection of your own mind in your own limitation because if you do you can't be healed or heal.

Why am I telling you to give up the world? Because you're perfect as God created you and the world is not real. That's the fact of the matter. It is not open to a discussion with you. Why? You are possessed with yourself. Yet the only manner in which you can experience a miracle is to be de-possessed. There is no other way you can possibly do it. How could you do it any other way? I can't understand the value of a perceptual mind. Virtually no one in this room can understand why you remain possessed. It makes absolutely no sense. Don't shake your head at me. Get into it! If you are here, for goodness sake, this is a chance for you to have faith in God. You spend all of your time in this conflict and call it existence. Why not simply release it and at least find out what it is? It can't be any worse than where you are now. This is a negation. *Not this.* What is the real alternative? *Not this.* That's making most of you very happy. By not being this, it is everything that is. If it is this, it is nothing. No compromise is possible in this. Why? Reality is no compromise. You can't compare time with eternity. Why? Comparison is what time is. Isn't it? Well, it would have to be. Comparison is judgment. I am teaching you the freedom of Universal Mind. That is what is making you happy. If it makes you sad, then be sad. All I am telling you is you can't escape the reality of Universal Mind. That's all I'm telling you.

You think you are going to die again. That is ridiculous. What dies is nothing. Can you teach that to a human being? You say, "We are all going to gather around to die." No, you are not. Why? You can't die. Why? Because you are nothing. Amazingly enough, if you were something, you might be able to die. But that would be the loss of your own self. Nothing compares with nothing and is gratified by nothing. I know that went multiplistic as soon as I confronted that association. There is nothing I can do about it. You remember this when you are teaching this. That totality, right there, is responsible for everything there is in the Universe. It will either be attacking and denying and be nothing, or it will be whole as God created it. And I mean that mind, right here. I don't mean some other one. I just got through reading you, there aren't other ones. There aren't separate minds. So your freedom is in giving it away.

Thanks, dear ones. We got a little excited here. You all hear what I'm saying? Releasing animosity is fun. It is accomplished by the admission that the historic reference is only in your own genetic makeup. That is not a big deal. Release your own cellular memories of body and they will be perfect because every single cell is an entirety both of the memory of the chaos and of the reality of God, sitting side by side, being caused by your mind. This is that healing page in the Journal, page 13. Don't specialize. All of your specialization is a limitation. Does that say that in this book? Does it mean that? Does the Third Patriarch of Zen mean that when he said that you are in an objective illusion and it's not real? All the scientists teach is that they are in an objective illusion and it's not real. Now they have discovered another trillion-galaxy universe, and all they do is sit in this little gaseous condition, contained within a body, and observe how many angels are on the head of a pin. It makes no sense. It is senseless.

If you didn't learn any other lesson today, learn this: All human beings are totally senseless and do not exist. It is a transient moment of coming from chaos to the truth. That is what it says in the Journal that I read from Endeavor Academy. It says it; that it is a moment in time where you thought you were from both time and eternity. That is impossible. Why? Because you will either become eternal or you will cancel out both time and eternity. This is what I just read to you. Do you understand me? I'm going to do it once more. One or the other is not true. Any definition cancels out both because definition is what cancellation is. Holy mackerel! I just keep going around it again for you.

So you say to me, "What's the solution? Don't judge?" I don't know what you are talking about. Judge until you can't stand it. I don't know how you could turn on the television and want to be a human being. How do you keep from being a human being? Don't associate in your own mind with humanness. Never mind the action. Listen to me. I am not at all concerned about what you do. The change of your mind comes by not associating with it, saying, "I don't want that. It is an insane place. People are dying. There is murderousness in it. I don't want to be a human being. I don't want to have to do that." At that moment it worked. Come on! The moment that you said you didn't want to be that, it worked perfectly. Why would you now want to continue to associate, which is only going to be the nothing of your own mind, anyway? I am telling you literally this is true. The power of your own mind is all around you. The simple assertion, "I don't want to be human," springs you into Heaven.

As the Zen master says, "Not-two." Just God. Otherwise you reduce it to a 5000 year old phantom. If you perceptual guys want to struggle with it, struggle. I am telling you the struggle is non-existent. I am telling you, you are each holy in your own mind. You don't have to struggle. You want to piss and moan? Go ahead. Read Chapter 27. You want to blame somebody else for your suffering and pain? You want to get old and sick and die? Go ahead. I am telling you, you have only yourself to blame, and the self you blame has nothing to do with God's laws. There is no blame in them. You are not guilty of anything. Salvation is that none of this is true. If any of it is true, there is no salvation. If you can be separate from God, there is no God. Certainly not a god that I would have anything to do with. He is a god that you have to do with because you believe that separation is real. You then have to do with that god. To hell with you! I don't like your god. He is weak. He knows about separation. He knows about sin and sickness and death. He judges it. Come on. I will match mine against yours any day. This is Mary Baker Eddy. She says God is in the son, because God is everything. I don't care what you think about it.

Boy, some of you guys are really bright. Are you all fine? That's our lesson for the day. What are you guys doing right now? You are communicating. See how simple it is? You're beginning to live in the joy and the light of the conversion of your individual body association. It will work perfectly. Sometimes it seems as though you are participating in the world. Seems to who? Don't try to define your own participation. Be inclusive with it. All of your actions must be directed to the inclusiveness of your own mind. That is a fact of the matter. It is not open to a discussion. What an amazing idea that you're becoming willing to use your own power, which is what love is, because there is no objection to the power of love, which is nothing but the unity and joy of the wholeness of your own mind. Isn't that fun? Is there an objection to that? Why would you object to the circle of love and of God? For goodness sake! Love is letting go of fear. When you are fearful, you are what? It says that in the Preamble. When you are fearful, you are non-existent! There isn't any such thing as fear. You are what fear is in its totality. What are you really afraid of? God. Your own wholeness. In your own nightmare, you really believe that somehow you got separate. It didn't happen. And I'm in the dream to tell you that it didn't happen.

If you get out of the way of your own cause and effect, you would just spring into Heaven. Did you all just spring to Heaven? You are in Heaven! Notice how you can't tell the difference between this place and Heaven. There really isn't any difference. For just a moment there appears to be a difference because this is the coming out of the illusion to reality. But what a perfect illusion! There's no conflict in it. If it's illusionary, why should there be conflict in the illusion? All illusions will have to be totally inclusive, anyway. You can't be separate from the wholeness of God. You have learned to include yourself in rather than objecting to yourself. What an amazing idea! Do you mean to say you've really only been doing this to yourself? No communication whatsoever is going on here? Is that what you are telling me? That all of this is only a reflection of your own mind, that you have been locked in here and haven't been talking to anybody, and those who answered you weren't anything, either? That the whole thing is gone? Anyone that answers your question in the illusion verifies your illusion. It is time to let the unhealed teachers go. Anyone that gives you any allowance for this is simply unhealed in his own mind. For goodness sake! Did you want that to be so? Go find someone that will verify you. There are plenty of them out there. How many? Everyone!

All you really had to decide was this was your last chance and you had no problem at all. You couldn't possibly have a problem if this is your last chance. This is your last chance. "Well, no, there's another way." No, there's not. "Oh, yes, there is." I am watching you, scrinching. "Oh, absolutely. I can figure it out." The hell you can. "Well, I am going to go out again. I have a lot of things I still have to do." You have nothing to do with me at all because you are nothing. I am offering you a real world. You actually think you can still go out in the world and I just got through telling you, you are non-existent. You absolutely do not accept it. The moment that you did, you would come into the real world, which is all around you. You keep defining these associations by your own cause-and-effect, and make them real so they can die with you. Enough of that.

The momensity of the human condition can be very gratifying because it is a dependence on God. God is a fact. Is that so? Is there really a Universal Mind? We are all of that? Isn't that amazing? Yes. That's a true thing. Yet the dead one has nothing to do with it. But the dead one has nothing to do with anything. I am telling you, the human has nothing to do with anything. I just got through reading you this. What does that reduce to? Give everything away. Give yourself away. God is. You ain't. *Father, into Thy hands I commend my spirit.* (Luke 23:46) You are not going to do it. Why won't you do it? You would rather die. Because everything you do verifies yourself. You don't want to die. You say you don't want to die, but of course you do because that's why you are here. Don't tell me you don't want to die. You've got cancer. I told you that you had cancer. I got you into a remission but you are going to go out and die again. I can't do anything about it. I just have to tell you that you are not real. Yet everything here will verify your capacity to remain in time, in this little, teeny, nothing place.

Are you ready? Are you ready to hear this, you? There aren't other guys. There aren't other people. Once more: There aren't other people! God does not make all sorts of separate things. You are perfect. Then you say, "Well, there's a lot of other people, and they are all perfect." There aren't any other people. You are whole in your own mind. There is no other. Salvation is, there is no other — there's not another mind.

I'm doing a healing with you. Chapter 7 and Chapter 28 are a lot about healing, and how you keep your brother sick in his body by refusing him the light of the extension of your own mind. The fact of the matter is, it is impossible that that association, defined by me, be sick except by my definition. That's a fact. If I mean that, I say, "How are you doing?" It's the same as saying, "How well are you holding yourself together?" If I want to heal, obviously, I would release my definition. I am going to show you how to heal. Wouldn't I do that? And just as obviously, you are fearful — this is Chapter 28 — of what? Of being well. Not only are you fearful of being well, but if you got completely well, you would probably kill yourself rather than be completely well. You will find another way to be sick because the reality of that body association depends on fear. It is totally meaningless. It is contained within itself. Yet it uses all the projections of its own mind to condemn them to another form of the disease, which they don't suffer from. So you have bodies together suffering from disease. Into this insane place we have come to tell you: That's absurd! Don't formulate yourself in that association. It is not real. They are products of your mind.

So you notice I make no attempt to heal. I just release you from your own crap. That is exactly what I do. But you don't want to be released. You want me to give you a sick association in order that you can stand next to me, an illusion of your own mind, and condemn me to a reflection of your own crap. It's what I just read you. Didn't I just read that? The two forms will stand together and authenticate their individual associations and just set up forms, neither of which is real. It is like they put a facade out in front of them and they hide behind it, and they present that picture of themselves and they walk around, pretending that is who they are. That is crazy! Now I'm at: You are just playing a part. I am not going to go into that today, but that's the fact of the matter. You recognize that as a part, that is not a part of you, and you will live in the joy of being in Heaven. You will not actually interact with your own projections. You will convert them to the Christ who is always with you. The Christ is always all around you, anyway, and by merging that together in your own illusion, you become, for a moment, a whole reality of your mind, in which your old projections must share because they are projections of your own mind. Now you've got a circle of Atonement that simply admits to the oneness of your own mind, the Universal Mind. That's not hard to do, is it?

What a delight this is! At least you can feel it. You guys actually have a borderland of Light that you are entering into. It is hard for you to see that you are actually sharing in it, but you are, because in the intensity of this, you are experiencing love and release. Actually there's a step beyond that, which many of you are in now, where the world will simply look unreal to you. This is not a real world. And the idea that you would actually have to battle it and measure it makes no sense. You have lost your capacity, which is the same as necessity, isn't it? You have lost your necessity to defend the meaninglessness of you. Where is God? All around you. The Light is all around you. Wow, you guys are pretty exciting. You are really telling a lovely story here. You came to a place in Wisconsin and you opened a restaurant and a lovely Healing Center. It's a good story. Quit trying to be somebody else's story. Be your own story. You *are* your own story. This is your mind. Jesus says what worked for somebody else has nothing to do with you. Why? There isn't anyone but you. There is not someone else. If it worked for someone else, he's gone. If he is gone, he is not someone else, he is you, gone. Did you get that? There isn't any such thing as someone else. The someone else that got it some other way is gone. He is now you, having already learned it. So this is the way. Forgive!

There's a lot of light here. We will go to some real lovely light. I just want to be sure the new guys are all happy. Be happy, newgies. Don't decide to go back out into the world. If you have to, go ahead, but remember that you are taking yourself with you. The conversion will be very easy if you don't insist on trying to repair it. Don't try to repair it. You are beyond that now. You are not going to acknowledge the sickness in order to repair it. That's called a miraculous healer. Walk into it and let it change in correspondence with the totality of the capacity of the moment that you are in, remembering that that moment is always going to be gone, anyway, unless you are determined to set up a result you want within the old association of yourself. If you do that, all you will do is slow yourself down. You can't stop yourself because the only thing you are really going to do is come to Light. Don't get distracted or tempted to formulate cause-and-effect relationships. You are not doing anything for any reason at all, except for the release of the necessity for the purpose for which you are doing it. Is that all right with everybody? So the whole thing is nothing but the release of your necessity. It is working all the time if you will let it. It would have to be. Yet it can't work if you insist on binding it. How could it? You are the obstruction. It is an amazing idea that if you don't do that, you will just be Light.

Are you looking over there? Quit looking at your projections. Some of you guys at high levels have a tendency to verify yourself at the wrong time. When I'm looking at you, you don't have to look at me. You don't have to do that with me. I know who I am. In this case, many of you are introducing me to your new Light associations. I appreciate that. I am much aware that you have real Light associations. It is not of this world at all. You can travel in the universe. You can go anywhere you want. You've freed your mind now to be free. There's nothing in the universe you cannot do. There's no obstruction to this. There's nothing out there preventing you from springing into Heaven, nothing, from awakening from this dream. You are dreaming.

This is individual. If you want some acknowledgment from me, I'll give it to you, but I want you in the totality of yourself. I am not measuring you. I am releasing you from measurement. That is fun if you are willing to do that. All I know is that you never left Heaven. You know perfectly well there is a God. All the things you do, all the music, all the art, verifies the perfection of mind. Isn't that amazing? I am not taking any of your humanness away from you at all. I am telling you that humanness in its entirety is what God is, because God is an entirety. The thing is He is not at all concerned about how you have defined your humanness. In that sense, you just have to be you. Everything is perfect.

There is a light in you which cannot die;
whose presence is so holy
that the world is sanctified because of you.
All things that live bring gifts to you,
and offer them in gratitude and gladness at your feet.
The scent of flowers is their gift to you.
The waves bow down before you,
and the trees extend their arms to shield you from the heat,
and lay their leaves before you on the ground
that you may walk in softness,
while the wind sinks to a whisper round your holy head.
The light in you is what the universe longs to behold.
All living things are still before you,
for they recognize Who walks with you.
The light you carry is their own.
And thus they see in you their holiness,
saluting you as savior and as God.
Accept their reverence, for it is due to Holiness Itself,
Which walks with you, transforming in Its gentle Light
all things unto Its likeness and Its purity.

Emerson
The Over-Soul and Circles

Over-Soul teaches to the inevitable nobility of the human spirit. That can be expressed in overcoming obstacles – a father going out and working, a mother's love for her children. It's expressed in the War. It's expressed in everything we do. So there's no regard in Over-Soul for what a man does. There is no judgment in it of the mean spirit of man but only that contained in the meanness is that inherent nobility.

Here's your criterion: *I am God's Son, complete and healed and whole, shining in the reflection of His Love. In me is His creation sanctified and guaranteed eternal life. In me is love perfected, fear impossible, and joy established without opposite. I am the holy home of God Himself. I am the Heaven where His Love resides. I am His holy Sinlessness Itself, for in my purity abides His Own.*

This is a perfect description of a human being, not of the Son of God, but of a human being, because it says, "healed." It says, "I am healed." It says, "I am that." Otherwise I wouldn't have to recite it. The reason I have to recite it is so that I can remember that I am. I suppose there are people sitting back there who say, "We already know that." I don't know that. I constantly must remind myself of my own perfection. I must remind myself of the mission that I have here. I must remind myself that the nobility of God Mind is expressed through me. And when I say, "me," I'm not speaking of me. I'm speaking of you, if you can hear this. I'm speaking of us in aggregate, in the discovery of our human condition, because the human condition is a discovery. The idea that time is associated with an eternity is the inevitable discovery that you made in your own mind.

I titled that Confession of Perfection because it's a confession whether you believe it or not. If you don't believe it, at least confess it. What's wrong with this? Is that okay? You let that be okay with you. There's no measurement in it. There's no one to measure you. There's no one who can judge you in saying that. Why? What did I just read? That is you. Who would judge that? Who could possibly judge what I just read? That criterion is the one that human associations compare themselves with. Every time we meet, we are comparing ourselves with that perfection. If I can get into this, this will describe it much better than I can. Stay with me.

Emerson's Essays: English Traits and Representative Man. This book is a very treasured book of mine. It came from my grandfather. I was allowed to deface it. I wrote in it a little bit. These are the kind of books that, when you were a little kid, you would look at in the bookcase, or you would hold, even though you couldn't read them. I did. I just liked the idea that it was a book. I was always fascinated by the idea that it said things. I knew that it said something in there, even though I couldn't read it.

Remember when you discovered that you could read? Can you? And suddenly the word meant something. Boy, that's an amazing thing. Was yours connected to a symbol? Like ● = ball. Was it? Oftentimes it would be. So you had learned what a ball looked like. And then you learned to say, "ball." But putting it together was a fascinating thing.

So what happened? You discovered your consciousness of Self. And every-where you go now, you're taking that consciousness. But somewhere there's a criterion. It doesn't appear to be here. But it is. That, in this little epistle, is called the Over-Soul.

There's a little quote from Henry Moore, who is a Sixteenth Century English poet, who says in the Prologue:

'But souls that of his own good life partake,
He loves as his own self; dear as his eye
They are to Him; He'll never them forsake;
When they shall die, then God himself shall die;
They live, they live in blest eternity."

There is a difference between one and another hour of life in their authority and subsequent effect. Our faith comes in moments; our vice is habitual. Yet there is a depth in those brief moments which constrains us to ascribe more reality to them than to all other experiences. For this reason the argument which is always forthcoming to silence those who conceive extraordinary hopes of man, namely the appeal to that experience, is for ever invalid and vain. We give up the past to the objector, and yet we hope. He must explain this hope. We grant that human life is mean, but how did we find out that it was mean? What is the ground of this uneasiness of ours; of this old discontent? What is the universal sense of want and ignorance, but the fine innuendo by which the soul makes its enormous claim? Why do men feel that the natural history of man has never been written, but he is always leaving behind what you have said of him, and it becomes old, and books of metaphysics worthless? The philosophy of six thousand years has not searched the chambers and magazines of the soul. In its experiments there has always remained, in the last analysis, a residuum it could not resolve. Man is a stream whose source is hidden. Always our being is descending into us from we know not whence. The most exact calculator has no prescience that somewhat incalculable may not balk in the very next moment. I am constrained every moment to acknowledge a higher origin for events than the will I call mine.

As with events, so it is with thoughts. When I watch that flowing river, which, out of regions I see not, pours for a season its streams into me, I see that I am a pensioner;

*not a cause, but a surprised spectator of this ethereal water;
that I desire and look up and put myself in the attitude of
reception, but from some alien energy the visions come.*
Isn't that lovely?

*The Supreme Critic on all the errors of the past and
the present; and the only prophet of that what must be, is
that great nature in which we rest as the earth lies in the
soft arms of the atmosphere; that Unity, that Over-Soul,
within which every man's particular being is contained
and made one with all other; that common heart of which
all sincere conversation is the worship, to which all right
action is submission; that overpowering reality which
confutes our tricks and talents, and constrains every one
to pass for what he is, and to speak from his character and
not from his tongue, and which evermore tends to pass into
our thought and hand and become wisdom and virtue
and power and beauty. We live in succession, in division,
in parts, in particles. Meantime within man is the soul of
the whole; the wise silence; the universal beauty, to which
every part and particle is equally related; the eternal One.
And this deep power in which we exist and whose beatitude
is all accessible to us, is not only self-sufficing and perfect
in every hour, but the act of seeing and the thing seen,
the seer and the spectacle, the subject and the object, are
one. We see the world piece by piece, as the sun, the moon,
the animal, the tree; but the whole, of which these are the
shining parts, is the soul. Only by the vision of that Wisdom
can the horoscope of the ages be read, and by falling back
on our better thoughts, by yielding to the spirit of prophecy
which is innate in every man, we can know what it saith.
Every man's words who speaks from that life must sound
vain to those who do not dwell in the same thought on their
own part. I dare not speak for it. My words do not carry its
august sense; they fall short and cold. Only itself can inspire
whom it will, and behold – their speech shall be lyrical,
and sweet, and universal as the rising of the wind. Yet I*

desire, even by profane words, if sacred I may not use, to indicate the heaven of this deity and to report what hints I have collected of the transcendent simplicity and energy of the Highest Law. Wow!

If we consider what happens in conversation, in reveries, in remorse, in times of passion, in surprises, in the instructions of dreams, wherein often we see ourselves in masquerade – the droll disguises only magnifying and enhancing a real element and forcing it on our distinct notice – we shall catch many hints that will broaden and lighten into knowledge of the secret of nature. All goes to show that the soul in man is not an organ but animates and exercises all the organs; is not a function, like the power of memory, of calculation, of comparison, but uses these as hands and feet; is not a faculty, but a light; is not the intellect or the will, but the master of the intellect and the will; is the vast background of our being, in which they lie – an immensity not possessed and that cannot be possessed. From within or from behind a light shines through us upon things and makes us aware that we are nothing, but the light is all. A man is the façade of a temple wherein all wisdom and all good abide. What we commonly call man, the eating, drinking, planting, counting man, does not, as we know him, represent himself, but misrepresents himself. Him we do not respect, but the soul, whose organ he is, would he let it appear through his action, would make our knees bend. When it breathes through his intellect, it is genius; when it breathes through his will, it is virtue; when it flows through his affection, it is love. And the blindness of the intellect begins when it would be something of itself. The weakness of the will begins when the individual would be something of himself. All reform aims in some one particular to let the great soul have its way through us; in other words, to engage us to obey.

What a twist! Did you see him twist that? Boy, I wish I had written that! That's nice. That's nice!

Of this pure nature every man is at some time sensible. Language cannot paint it with his colors. It is too subtle. It is undefinable, unmeasurable; but we know that it pervades and contains us. We know that all spiritual being is in man. A wise old proverb says, 'God comes to see us without bell;" that is, as there is no screen or ceiling between our heads and the infinite heavens, so is there no bar or wall in the soul, where man, the effect, ceases, and God, the cause, begins. The walls are taken away, we lie open on one side to the deeps of spiritual nature, to all the attributes of God. Justice we see and know, Love, Freedom, Power. These natures no man ever got above, but they tower over us and most in the moment when our interests tempt us to wound them.

What a great sentence that is! Most in our moments when our interests tempt us to wound them. Isn't that amazing? That's when we feel that. Isn't that lovely!

The sovereignty of this nature whereof we speak is made known by its independency of those limitations which circumscribe us on every hand. Can you hear this? The soul circumscribes all things. *As I have said, it contradicts all experience. In like manner it abolishes time and space. The influence of the senses has in most men overpowered the mind to that degree that the walls of time and space have come to look solid, real and insurmountable; and to speak with levity of these limits is, in the world, the sign of insanity. Yet time and space are but inverse measures of the force of the soul.* That's Course In Miracles, guys.

The spirit sports with time – "Can crowd eternity into an hour, or stretch an hour to eternity."

Wow. Wow! I really like this, guys. I really like it. I think I'll just go on and read it by myself.

We are often made to feel that there is another youth and age than that which is measured from the year of our natural birth. Boy, is that loaded! *We are often made to feel that there is another youth and age than that which is measured from the year of our natural birth. Some thoughts always find us young, and keep us so. Such a thought is the love of the universal and eternal beauty. Every man parts from that contemplation with the feeling that it rather belongs to ages than to mortal life. The least activity of the intellectual powers redeems us in a degree from the influences of time.* That's the holy instant. Wow, is that ever nice!

Is the teaching of Christ less effective now than it was when first his mouth was opened? And so always the soul's scale is one, the scale of the senses and the understanding is another. Before the great revelations of the soul, Time, Space and Nature shrink away. In common speech we refer all things to time, as we habitually refer the immensely, sundered stars to our concave sphere. And so we say that the Judgment is distant or near, that the Millennium approaches, that a day of certain political, moral, social reforms is at hand, and the like, when we mean that in the nature of things one of the facts we contemplate is external and fugitive, and the other is permanent and connate with the soul. Otherwise you wouldn't know it. The things we now esteem fixed shall, one by one, detach themselves like ripe fruit from our experience, and fall. The wind shall blow them none knows whither.

The soul looketh steadily forwards, creating a world always before her, leaving worlds always behind her. She has no dates, nor rites, nor persons, nor specialties, nor men. The soul knows only the soul; the web of events is the flowing robe in which she is clothed.

One mode of the divine teaching is the incarnation of the spirit in a form – in forms like my own. I live in society; with persons who answer to thoughts in my own mind, or outwardly express a certain obedience to the great instincts to which I live. I see its presence to them. I am certified of a common nature; and so these other souls, these separated selves, draw me as nothing else can. They stir in me the new emotions we call passion; of love, hatred, fear, admiration, pity; thence come conversation, competition, persuasion, cities and war. Persons are supplementary to the primary teaching of the soul. Wow! What an amazing idea!

In youth we are made for persons. Childhood and youth see all the world in them. But the larger experience of man discovers the identical nature appearing through them all. Persons themselves acquaint us with the impersonal. In all conversation between two persons tacit reference is made, as to a third party, to a common nature. That third party, or common nature, is not social; it is impersonal; it is God. And so in groups where debate is earnest, and especially on great questions of thought, the company become aware that the thought rises to an equal level in all bosoms, that all have a spiritual property in what was said, as well as the sayer. They all wax wiser than they were. It arches over them like a temple, this unity of thought in which every heart beats with nobler sense of power and duty, and thinks and acts with unusual solemnity. All are conscious of attaining to a higher self-possession. It shines for all. There is a certain wisdom of humanity which is common to the greatest men with the lowest, and which our ordinary education often labors to silence and obstruct. The mind is one, and the best minds, who love truth for its own sake, think much less of property in truth. Thankfully they accept it everywhere, and do not label it or stamp it with any man's name, for it is theirs long beforehand. It is theirs from eternity.

The soul is the perceiver and revealer of truth. We know truth when we see it; let skeptic and scoffer say what they choose. Foolish people ask you, when you have spoken what they do not wish to hear, 'How do you know it is truth and not an error of your own?" We know truth when we see it, from opinion, as we know when we are awake that we are awake. This is A Course In Miracles. *'How do you*

250

know it is truth and not an error of your own?" We know truth when we see it, from opinion, as we know when we are awake that we are awake. It was a grand sentence of Emmanuel Swedenborg, which would alone indicate the greatness of that man's perception – 'It is no proof of a man's understanding to be able to affirm whatever he pleases; (everybody does that) *but to be able to discern that what is true is true, and that what is false is false – this is the mark and character of intelligence." In the book I read, the good thought returns to me, as every truth will, the image of the whole soul. To the bad thought which I find in it, the same soul becomes a discerning, separating sword, and lops it away. We are wiser than we know. If we will not interfere with our thought, but will act entirely or see how the thing stands in God, we know the particular thing; and every thing, and every man. For the Maker of all things and all persons stands behind us and casts his dread omniscience through us over things.* It's a dread omnipotence. That's our conscience. We're very fearful, finally, to acknowledge that He's right here with us, reminding us constantly of that. Wow!

But beyond this recognition of its own in particular passages of the individual's experience, it also reveals truth. And here we should seek to reinforce ourselves by its very presence, and to speak with a worthier, loftier strain of that advent. For the soul's communication of truth is the highest event in nature, for it then does not give someone from itself, but it gives itself, or passes into and becomes that man whom it enlightens; or, in proportion to that truth he receives, it takes him to itself. Wow. Is that nice, guys. Wow!

When he speaks on this page, he speaks for a moment about how all of us have these experiences and how all religion and thought is formulated on it. It's kind of nice to look at that.

*We distinguish the announcements of the soul, its manifestations of its own nature, by the term 'Revelation."
These are always attended by the emotion of the sublime.
For this communication is an influx of the Divine Mind into our mind. It is an ebb of the individual rivulet before the flowing surges of the sea of life.* When he writes that sentence, he's suddenly got himself into something! I'll try to get into that for a minute. *It is an ebb of the individual rivulet before the flowing surges of the sea of life. Every distinct apprehension of this central commandment agitates men with awe and delight. A thrill passes through all men at the reception of new truth, or at the performance of a great action, which comes out of the heart of nature. In these communications the power to see is not separated from the will to do, but the insight proceeds from obedience, and the obedience proceeds from a joyful perception. Every moment when the individual feels himself invaded by it is memorable.* What do we call these in the Course? Holy instants: *Every moment when the individual feels himself invaded by it is memorable. By the necessity of our constitution a certain enthusiasm attends the individual's consciousness of that divine presence.* At least it does in my case. *By the necessity of our constitution a certain enthusiasm attends the individual's consciousness of that divine presence. The character and the duration of this enthusiasm varies with the state of the individual, from an ecstasy and trance and prophetic inspiration – which is its rarer appearance – to the faintest glow of virtuous emotion, in which form it warms, like our household fires, all the families and associations of men, and makes society possible.* Once more: It makes society possible. I don't care whether it leads you to ecstatic states of revelation that cause you not to be able to feed yourself, or run naked through the streets, or reduces itself to a glow of welcoming somebody home or into your house. It's all one and the same. Okay. Why am I explaining him? I'll just read it.

A certain tendency to insanity has always attended the opening of the religious sense in men... Oh, yes, we pretty much agree with that. *...as if they had been 'blasted with excess of light." The trances of Socrates, the 'union" of Plotinus, the vision of Porphyry, the conversion of Paul, the aurora of Behmen, the convulsions of George Fox and his Quakers, the illuminations of Swedenborg, are of this kind. What was in the case of these remarkable persons a ravishment, has, in innumerable instances in common life, been exhibited in less striking manner.* We don't care how it strikes you. What we want you to see is that it's going on all the time. "Well, I don't want to run naked through the streets." Don't worry. You won't until you do. Can you hear that? You let the soul set the standard and don't worry about it. This is beautiful stuff!

What was in the case of these remarkable persons a ravishment, has, in innumerable instances in common life, been exhibited in less striking manner. Everywhere in the history of religion betrays a tendency to enthusiasm. That must be restrained. "I'm feeling good!" "Be quiet!" "You're going to a concert!" "Shut up!" We are always constrained, aren't we? Somewhere we are always afraid to express God. Isn't that amazing? Wow. What a place to be! It's true.

Everywhere the history of religion betrays a tendency to enthusiasm. The rapture of the Moravian and Quietist; the opening of the internal sense of the Word, in the language of the New Jerusalem Church; the revival of the Calvinistic churches; the experiences of the Methodists, are varying forms of that shudder of awe and delight with which the individual soul always mingles with the universal soul. The individual soul mingles with the universal soul! Isn't that fun? It mingles with it. Did you hear that? It doesn't do anything but mingle. You can tell when a guy's in spirit; mingling souls is kind of good. When you guys mingle together in soul, in recognition, you're mingling with Universal Soul. Isn't that nice?

The nature of these revelations is always the same. They are perceptions of the absolute law. I love it! Notice how he went to law. *They are solutions of the soul's own questions. They do not answer the questions which the understanding asks. The soul answers never by words but by the thing itself that is inquired after.* Tricky. Tricky. You're only really asking one question, and that's the question it always answers. The question is whether you're willing to accept it. The question is always, "Who am I?" The answer is, "I am the Holy Son of God." Everything in between is what you decide you hear. But what are you using to do it? Your whole soul. You bet!

Revelation is the disclosure of the soul. The popular notion of a revelation is that it is a telling of fortunes. In past oracles of the soul the understanding seeks to find answers to sensual questions, and undertakes to tell from God how long men shall exist, what their hands shall do and who shall be their company, adding names and dates and places. But we must pick no locks. That's nice: *But we must pick no locks. We must check this low curiosity. An answer in words is delusive; it is really no answer to the questions you ask. Do not require a description of the countries towards which you sail. The description does not describe them to you, and tomorrow you arrive there and know them by inhabiting them. Men ask concerning the immortality of the soul, the employments of heaven, the state of the sinner, and so forth. They even dream that Jesus has left replies to precisely these interrogatories. He has not. Never a moment did that sublime spirit speak in their patois. To truth, justice, love, the attributes of the soul, the idea of immutableness is essentially associated. Jesus, living in these moral sentiments, heedless of sensual fortunes, heeding only the manifestations of these, never made the separation of the idea of duration from the essence of these attributes, never uttered a syllable concerning the duration of the soul.* Not one time did He tell you you had to be here and get sick and die. He always only told you: "I am the soul

254

of you. I am the Life of you." This is from a guy who obviously knows that to be true. Isn't that nice?

It was left to his disciples to sever duration from the moral elements, and to teach the immortality of the soul as a doctrine, and maintain it by evidences. The moment the doctrine of the immortality is separately taught, man is already fallen. Once more: The moment the doctrine of the immortality is separately taught, man is already fallen. In the flowing of love, in the adoration of humility, there is no question of continuance. No inspired man ever asks this question or condescends to these evidences. For the soul is true to itself, and the man in whom it is shed abroad cannot wander from the present, which is infinite, to a future, which would be finite. He lives in the now. Imagine this being written! It's incredible stuff.

These questions which we lust to ask about the future are a confession of sin. Is that so? Of course! Planning for the future is what sin is. *These questions which we lust to ask about the future are a confession of sin. God has no answer for them. No answer in words can reply to a question of things.* The question doesn't make any sense. *It is not in an inarbitrary "decree of God," but in the nature of man, that a veil shuts down on the facts of tomorrow; for the soul will not have us read any other cipher than that of cause and effect.* What you do will come around. Wow! *By this veil which curtains events it instructs the children of men to live in today.* That's the answer to all that you could ever ask.

The inevitable nature of man: *By virtue of this inevitable nature, private will is overpowered, and maugre our efforts or our imperfections, your genius will speak from you, and mine from me. That which we are, we shall teach, not voluntarily but involuntarily. Thoughts come into our minds through avenues which we never left open, and thoughts go out of our minds through avenues which we never voluntarily opened. Character teaches over our head.* Isn't that lovely? Isn't that lovely!

This is called Speaking From Within: *It is of no use to preach to me from without. I can do that too easily myself. Jesus speaks always from within, and in a degree that transcends all others. In that is the miracle. I believe beforehand that it ought so to be. All men stand continually in the expectation of the appearance of such a teacher. But if a man does not speak from within the veil, where the word is one with that it tells of, let him lowly confess it.* "I don't know what I'm going to do." Let him say so. Wow!

But genius is religious. It is a larger imbibing of the common heart. Wow! Is that nice! *But the soul that ascends to worship the great God is plain and true; has no rose-color, no fine friends, no chivalry, no adventures; does not want admiration; dwells in the hour that now is, in the earnest experience of the common day – by reason of the present moment and the mere trifle having become porous to thought in the sea of light.* Wow!

Converse with a mind that is grandly simple, and literature looks like word-catching. The simplest utterances are worthiest to be written, yet are they so cheap and so things of course, that in the infinite riches of the soul it is like gathering a few pebbles off the ground, or bottling a little air, when the whole earth and the whole atmosphere are ours. Nothing can pass there, or make you one of the circle, but the casting aside your trappings and the dealings of man.

Now we'll read what we wanted to read to you: *It is the highest compliment you can pay. Their 'highest praising,"* said Milton, *'is not flattery, and their plainest advice is a kind of praising."* He's speaking of Teachers of God – a Teacher of God as you will become. Your highest praising is not flattery when I tell you you're the living Son of God. ...*and their plainest advice is a kind of praising.*

Ineffable is the union of man and God in every act of the soul. The simplest person who in his integrity worships

God, becomes God; yet for ever and ever the influx of this better and universal self is new and unsearchable. Even it inspires awe and astonishment. How dear, how soothing to man, arises the idea of God, peopling the lonely place, effacing the scars of our mistakes and disappointments.

The simplest person who in his integrity worships God, becomes God; yet for ever and ever the influx of this better and universal self is new and unsearchable. It inspires awe and astonishment. How dear, how soothing to man, arises the idea of God, peopling the lonely place, effacing the scars of our mistakes and disappointments.

When we have broken our god of tradition and ceased from our god of rhetoric, then may God fire the heart with his presence. It is the doubling of the heart itself, nay, the infinite enlargement of the heart with a power of growth to a new infinity on every side. It inspires in man an infallible trust. He has not the conviction, but the sight, that the best is the true and may in that thought easily dismiss all particular uncertainties and fears and adjourn to the sure revelation of time the solution of his private riddles. He is sure that his welfare is dear to the heart of being. In the presence of law to his mind he is overflowed with a reliance so universal that it sweeps away all cherished hopes and the most stable projects of mortal condition in its flood. He no longer hopes for anything. What an amazing idea! Wow.

That's an incredible thing: *In the presence of law to his mind he is overflowed with a reliance so universal that it sweeps away all cherished hopes and the most stable projects of his mortal condition in its flood. He believes that he cannot escape from his good.* I don't know where you hear that. He's got caught. He's caught in God. He can't escape. He didn't mean to get there. It's sort of like God caught him. That's what happened to me. There's no way I would have intentionally done it, but I got caught. I got trapped by God. When you read the Course tomorrow, there's a lovely description that God is chasing you. The Christ is always chasing you. There's a beautiful passage where Jesus, in the most irony that is expressed in the Course, says, "Maybe He's finally caught up with you, brother." He actually says, "Maybe if you stand still just for a moment the thing you fear most to see is going to entrap you." What is it? The eternal good! You are going to get caught being good. And heretofore you've been fearful of your total goodness, if you would like to hear that. Boy, it's nice to hear that said here.

He believes that he cannot escape from his good. The things that are really for thee gravitate to thee. You are running to seek your friend. Let your feet run, but your mind need not. If you do not find him, will you not acquiesce that it is best that you should not find him? For there is a power, which, as it is in you, is in him also... This is an example. This is the whole teaching of A Course In Miracles! It's exactly what this says. Wow. *The things that are really for thee gravitate to thee. You are running to seek your friend. Let your feet run, but your mind need not. If you do not find him, will you not acquiesce that it is best that you should not find him?*

For there is a power, which as it is in you, is in him also, and could therefore very well bring you together, if it were for the best. You are preparing with eagerness to go and render a service to which your talent and your taste invite you, the love of men and the hope of fame. Has it not occurred to you that you have no right to go, unless you are equally willing to be prevented from going? This is just an idea that you accept God's will. For goodness sake! "Thy will be done." Wow! You are preparing with eagerness to go and render a service to which your talent and your taste invite you, the love of men and the hope of fame. Has it not occurred to you that you have no right to go, unless you are equally willing to be prevented from going? *O, believe, as thou livest, that every sound that is spoken over the round world, which thou oughtst to hear, will vibrate on thine ear! Every proverb, every book, every byword that belongs to thee for aid or comfort, shall surely come home through open or winding passages.* He's in spirit here. He's saying "thine" and "thou." Did you hear that?

O, believe as thou livest, that every sound that is spoken over the round world, which thou oughtst to hear, will vibrate on thine ear! Every proverb, every book, every byword that belongs to thee for aid or comfort, shall surely come home through open or winding passages.

Every friend whom not thy fantastic will but the great and tender heart in thee craveth, shall lock thee in his embrace. And this because the heart in thee is the heart of all; not a valve, not a wall, not an intersection is there anywhere in nature, but one blood rolls uninterruptedly an endless circulation through all men, as the water of the globe is all one sea, and, truly seen, its tide is one.

Let man then learn the revelation of all nature and all thought to his heart; this, namely; that the Highest dwells with him; that the sources of nature are in his own mind, if the sentiment of duty is there. But if he should know what the great God speaketh, 'he must go into his closet and shut the door," as Jesus said. God will not make himself manifest to cowards. I like that. *He must greatly listen to himself, withdrawing himself from all the accents of other men's devotion. Their prayers even are hurtful to him, until he have made his own. Our religion vulgarly stands on numbers of believers. Whenever the appeal is made – no matter how indirectly – to numbers, proclamation is then and there made that religion is not. That's the same as it's up to you through your individual association; that you must undergo the experience. He that finds God a sweet, enveloping thought to him never counts his company. When I sit in that presence, who shall dare to come in? When I rest in perfect humility, when I burn with pure love, what can Calvin or Swedenborg say?*

It makes no difference whether the appeal is to numbers or to one. The faith that stands on authority is not faith. The reliance on authority measures the decline of religion, the withdrawal of the soul. The position men have given to Jesus, now for many centuries of history, is a position of authority. It characterizes themselves. It cannot alter the eternal facts. Great is the soul, and plain. It is no flatterer, it is no follower; it never appeals from itself. It always believes in itself. Before the immense possibilities of man all mere experience, all past biography, however spotless and sainted, shrinks away. Before that holy heaven which our presentiments foreshow us, we cannot easily praise any form of life we have seen or read of. We not only affirm that we have few great men, but, absolutely speaking, that we have none; that we have no history, no record of any character or mode of living that entirely contents us. The saints and demigods whom history worships we are constrained to accept with a grain of allowance. Though in our lonely hours we draw a new strength out of their memory, yet, pressed on our attention, as they are by the thoughtless and customary, they fatigue and invade. The soul gives itself alone, original and pure, to the Lonely, Original and Pure, who, on that condition, gladly inhabits, leads and speaks through it. Then it is glad, young, and nimble. It is not wise, but it sees through all things. It is not called religious, but it is innocent. It calls the light its own and feels that the grass grows and the stone falls by a law inferior to, and dependent on, its nature. Behold, it saith, I am born in the great, the universal mind. I, the imperfect, adore my own Perfect.

I am somehow receptive of the great soul, and thereby I do overlook the sun and the stars and feel them to be the fair accidents and effects which change and pass. More and more the surges of everlasting nature enter into me, and I become public and human in my regards and actions. So come I to live in thoughts and act with energies which are immortal. Thus revering the soul and learning, as the ancients said, that 'its beauty is immense,"man will come to see that the world is the perennial miracle which the soul worketh, and be less astonished at particular wonders; he will learn that there is no profane history. Wow!

Man will come to see that the world is the perennial miracle which the soul worketh, and be less astonished at particular wonders; he will learn that there is no profane history; that all history is sacred; that the universe is represented in an atom, in a moment of time. He will weave no longer a spotted life of shreds and patches, but he will live with a divine unity. He will cease from what is base and frivolous in his life and be content with all places and with any service he can render. He will calmly front the morrow in the negligency of that trust which carries God with it and so hath already the whole future in the bottom of his heart. Isn't that nice stuff, guys? Wow.

Now we will read from Circles for a moment: *The eye is the first circle; the horizon which it forms is the second; and throughout nature this primary figure is repeated without end. Everything is a circle. Skipping ahead: Permanence is a word of degrees. Everything is medial. Moons are no more bounds to spiritual power than bat-balls.*

The key to every man is his thought. Sturdy and defying though he look, he has a helm which he obeys, which is the idea after which all his facts are classified. He can only be reformed by showing him a new idea which commands his own. The life of man is a self-evolving circle, which, from a ring imperceptibly small, rushes on all sides outwards to new and larger circles, and that without end. The extent to which this generation of circles, wheel without wheel, will go, depends on the force or truth of the individual soul. Boy, is that nice! *The extent to which this generation of circles, wheel without circle, will go depends on the force or truth of the individual soul. For it is the inert effort of each thought, having formed itself into a circular wave of circumstance – as for instance an empire, rules of an art, a local usage, a religious rite – to heap itself on that ridge and to solidify and hem in the life. But if the soul is quick and strong it bursts over that boundary on all sides and expands another orbit on the great deep, which also runs up into a high wave, with attempt again to stop and bind. But the heart refuses to be imprisoned; in its first and narrowest pulses it already tends outward with a vast force and to immense and innumerable expansions.* My goodness sakes!

Every ultimate fact is only the first of a new series. Every general law only a particular fact of some more general law presently to disclose itself. There is no outside, no enclosing wall, no circumference to us. The man finishes his story – how good! How final! How it puts a new face on all things! He fills the sky. Lo! On the other side rises also a man and draws a circle around the circle we had just pronounced the outline of the sphere. Everybody's doing their own circle. Then already is our first speaker not man, but only a first speaker. His only redress is forthwith to draw a circle outside of his antagonist. I don't know if you can hear that. Somehow we just keep enlarging our associations with each other.

We meet, recognize each other and draw a bigger circle. And so men do by themselves. The result of today, which haunts the mind and cannot be escaped, will presently be abridged into a word, and the principle that seemed to explain nature will itself be included as one example of a bolder generalization. In the thought of tomorrow there is a power to upheave all thy creed, all the creeds, all the literature of the nations, and marshal thee to a heaven which no epic dream has yet depicted. Every man is not so much a workman in the world as he is a suggestion of that he should be. Men walk as prophecies of the next age. I really love this.

Step by step, we scale this mysterious ladder; the steps are actions. The new prospect is power. Once more: The steps are actions. The new prospect is power. New prospect and power are the same thing. Every several result is threatened and judged by that which follows. Every one seems to be contradicted by the new; it is only limited by the new. The new statement is always hated by the old, and, to those dwelling in the old, comes like an abyss of skepticism. But the eye soon gets wonted to it, for the eye and it are effects of one cause; then its innocency and benefit (will fit the new cause) appear and presently, all its energy spent, it pales and dwindles before the revelation of the new hour. Boy, this is what I love to have you do.

Fear not this new generalization. Why? It's something you can't understand in your own association. *Don't be afraid of it. Does the fact look crass and material, threatening to degrade thy theory of spirit? Resist it not; it goes to refine and raise the new theory of matter just as much. And it will work.*

Our moods do not believe in each other. He's writing about himself. *Today I am full of thoughts and can write what I please. I see no reason why I should not have the same thought, the same power of expression tomorrow. What I write, whilst I write it, seems the most natural thing in the world; but yesterday I saw a dreary vacuity in this direction in which now I see so much; and a month hence, I doubt not, I shall wonder who he was that wrote so many continuous pages. You too?! Alas for this infirm faith, this will not strenuous, this vast ebb of a vast flow! I am God in nature; I am a weed by the wall.*

The continual effort to raise ourselves above ourselves, to work a pitch above his last height, betrays itself in a man's relations. We thirst for approbation, yet cannot forgive the approver. Wow! *The sweet of nature is love; yet if I have a friend, I am tormented by my imperfections. The love of me accuses the other party. If he were high enough to slight me, then could I love him, and rise by my affection to new heights. A man's growth is seen in the successive choirs of his friends. For every friend whom he loses for truth, he gains a better.* Wow! This is nice stuff, guys.

Each new step we take in thought reconciles twenty seemingly discordant facts, as expressions of one law. Aristotle and Plato are reckoned the respective heads of two schools. A wise man will see that Aristotle Platonizes. And that's his trouble. O, what truths profound and executable only in the ages and orbs, are supposed in the announcement of every truth! In common hours, society sits cold and statuesque. We all stand waiting, empty – knowing, possibly, that we can be full, surrounded by mighty symbols which are not symbols to us, but prose and trivial toys. Then cometh the god and converts the statues into fiery men, and by a flash of his eye burns up the veil which shrouded all things, and the meaning of the very furniture, of cup and saucer, of chair and clock and tester, is manifest. The facts which loomed so large in the fogs of yesterday – property, climate, breeding, personal beauty and the like.

And yet here again see the swift circumscription! Good as is discourse, silence is better, and shames it. The length of the discourse indicates the distance of thought betwixt the speaker and the hearer. If they were at a perfect under-standing in any part, no word would be necessary thereon. If at one in all parts, no words would suffice at all. They would simply be whole with themselves.

Thus there is no sleep, no pause, no preservation, but all things renew, germinate and spring. Why should we import rags and relics into the new hour? Nature abhors the old, and old age seems the only disease and all others run into this one. We call it by many names – fever, intemperance, insanity, stupidity and crime; they are all forms of old age; they are rest, conservatism, appropriation, inertia; not newness, not the way onward. We grizzle every day. I see no need of it. He's speaking for himself. Whilst we converse with what is above us, we do not grow old, but grow young. Infancy, youth, receptive, aspiring, with religious eye looking upward, counts itself nothing and abandons itself to the instruction flowing from all sides. But the men and women of seventy assume to know all, throw up their hope. They have outlived their hope. That's all I would like to talk to some of the guys around me. They renounce aspiration, accept the actual for the necessary and talk down to the young. Let them then become organs of the Holy Ghost; let them be lovers; let them behold truth; and their eyes are uplifted, their wrinkles smoothed (and disappear), they are perfumed again with hope and power. This old age ought not to creep on a human mind. In nature every moment is new; the past is always swallowed and forgotten; the coming only is sacred.

Nothing is secure but life, transition, the energizing spirit. No love can be bound by oath or covenant to secure it against a higher love. No truth so sublime but it may be trivial tomorrow in the light of new thoughts. People wish to be settled; only as far as they are unsettled is there any hope for them.

Life is a series of surprises. We do not guess today the mood, and the pleasure, the power of tomorrow, when we are building up our being. We are building up our being here.

Of lower states, of acts of routine and sense, we can tell somewhat; but the masterpieces of God, the total growths and universal movements of the soul, he hideth (he protects); they are incalculable. I can know that truth is divine and helpful; but how it shall help me I can have no guess, for 'so to be" is the sole inlet of 'so to know." The new position of the advancing man has all the powers of the old, yet has them all new. It carries in its bosom all the energies of the past, yet is itself an exhalation of the morning (of the new day). I cast away in this new moment all my once hoarded knowledge, as vacant and vain. Now for the first time seem I to know anything rightly. The simplest words – we do not know what they mean except when we love and aspire.

The difference between talents and character is adroitness to keep the old and trodden round, and power and courage to make a new road to new and better goals. Don't let it go. Just let it be changed. Character makes an overpowering present; a cheerful, determined hour, which fortifies all the company by making them see that much is possible and excellent that was not thought of. Character dulls the impression of particular events. When we see the conqueror we do not think much of any one battle or success. We see that we had exaggerated the difficulty. It was easy to him. The great man is not convulsible or tormentable; events pass over him without much impression. This is going to be a description of forgiveness. People say sometimes, 'See what I have overcome; see how cheerful I am; see how completely I have triumphed over these black events.' Not if they still remind me of the black events. True conquest is the causing of the black event to fade and disappear as an early cloud of insignificant result in a history so large and advancing.

The one thing which we seek with insatiable desire is to forget ourselves, to be surprised out of our propriety, to lose our memory, and to do something without knowing how or why; in short, to draw a new circle. Nothing great was ever achieved without enthusiasm. The way of life is wonderful; it is by abandonment (that we discover this).

So how is this new? How is it new that you are being told that this is not where you're from? Every action in which you find yourself participating is totally whole and perfect and beautiful and sacred. Whether you ascribe that to be the circumstance makes no difference. But it cannot be more than you ascribe it to be. If you draw a circle around you, and you draw a circle around him, you will attempt to meet in your separate circles. Do you hear me? This must be true because you have drawn a circle that excludes him. I don't know if I can explain this to you. I would like to have you see it. But obviously, circumscribing you is a greater circle. Sometimes you may meet someone on your journey who has a larger circle into which you both enter. And in that moment you share with that teacher that greater circle of you. Yet all he can really be sharing with you is still a greater circle. It cannot not be so.

I wish I could teach this. What goes around is constantly coming around. Instead of making larger and larger circles, I convince you to make smaller and smaller circles until you stand for a moment in your own complete circle. This is A Course In Miracles. At that time, you have one perfect circle, or a moment in which you can make a comparison. Otherwise, all the circles that you draw out there will not be drawn from that one point. I have given you a point on which you can stand and expand your circles. If you will come into that, it will immediately begin to expand because it's the sharing of the individual circle with the outer dimension. It's like a cone. It's like I tried to say to this association, it is expanding outward. It's a vortex of circles of energy, being separated and entered into by you.

How can I invite someone else into my circle? Invite him in by not judging him. He cannot not enter into you if you invite him. If he doesn't respond to your judgment or to your response, what difference could that possibly make? The invitation is coming from you in the expansion of your circle. Those who want to hear you will welcome you. Those who don't, will reject you but only to the rejection of their own circle. None of this is real. If you insist on drawing a smaller and smaller circle, that's not going to have any effect on me. My circle is God. I have no circumference. You can't circumscribe me. Beyond the sun, beyond the stars, is a golden arc that I am a part of. Nothing is beyond that arc but God. But certainly I am included in that arc for the moment that I am here. You cannot prevent me from including all of space/time in me because that's what I am. If you want to limit yourself to your own body-form, do so; but the invitation, the Over-Soul invitation of what we share in the Holy Spirit, is always available to you in your individuality. We cannot not be using that together. That's what this says, and you know perfectly well that's what it says.

What advantage does it have? The advantage of the essay is that in no manner can you seek and find it. In no manner can you find it because it's already with you. Listen! It's not only already with you but it's acting totally. Not only separate from you, but including you. I really like this because each moment you are divine or you are what? Nothing! You are either divine in that moment of the sharing or you are nothing. How simple the solution if Jesus says this is nothing. When you share the divine moment, you are Godly. Otherwise you are simply nothing. What is nothing? Containment, hate, fear and death, located in you. The inevitability of your necessity to forgive should begin to occur to you. How would it not? Forgive and you will see clearly. Retain your own guilt and you will be responsible for that. Isn't that amazing? Is that what that says? That's exactly what that says! There's no distinguishing, obviously, in Emerson, between soul and spirit. He's speaking of spirit. What he says is your soul is the Holy Spirit or that whole association.

So that's what we intend to share. I have no intention of sharing your limited circle with you simply because I don't know how to do it. If you let me in, you will begin to share a larger circle. If you keep me out, you will be sharing yourself with yourself. You will be sharing yourself with nothing! And that's what is difficult for you to see. You attempt, you search desperately, to correspond to each other in your little bubbles. But all little bubbles can finally do is form foam. This is the same principle as you've got to burst the boundaries of your association, or you've got nothing but one big foam. I suppose you can describe that as links of matter somewhere in space/time. But they will prevent you from communicating in the whole. Or, at the very minimum, they will slow you down to the speed of light. Could you hear that? If you form matrices of energy, or paths that you follow, they cannot exceed the speed of light. Do you see that? If you have one bubble you can communicate through that bubble. Who can hear that?

Let me see if I can do that as quantum for you. If I'm going to teach you to communicate in quantum, I've got to get you not to try to communicate with your bubbles. Are you listening to me there? As long as you communicate in digital associations, it will be at the speed of light because you have established parameters that give you position or space. Can you hear me? So now you're going to communicate between two bubbles. You can't go faster than 186,000 miles a second. Yet you cannot become inclusive of the bubble without expressing quantum. It is literally impossible for you to communicate except in quantum. It appears to be slower, but actually you are already using the theory, whatever you call it, of quantum as the entirety of your expression – a unifying field of energy. All we're going to do in this next evolutionary step of the perception of limitation based on the correspondence of space/time is show you how to communicate in quantum. You've already got all of the tools to do it.

Not only that, I can show you how to do it mechanically. I can devise a quantum computer. In fact, look. I saw a design for quantum computing. The problem you will have with it is this: Where the hell are you going to go? Do you see? You can already travel anywhere in the universe. You pretty much are doing it right now. Can I share something with you? If you open your bubbles, you're only going to meet yourself.

Now, that does not mean that you can't open your bubbles, take on a nature and go and help little bubbles. That's called saviorship. I assure you that no alien is going to come from outer space and attack you. You are already being attacked by all of your own little bubbles, which are called space/time. Obviously, you are locked not only in your single bubble but in your accumulation of bubbles, what you call a continuum of time, based on a beginning and an end. So you keep recounting tales that actually only coincide in past references because obviously there is no such thing as creation in space/time. It can look like creation, but it cannot be creation because in eternity – what you call Creative Life – there is no separation of cause and effect. That is, the mind of eternity is what the Son is. God creates wholly, and that is what singularity is. If you separate it, you will end up with space/time or a reciprocation that is what the speed of light is – the attempt of coming from the great division, beginning with slow speed up to 186,000 miles per second.

What I'm expressing to you is a new evolutionary occurrence in whatever you think the species of man is. I just read you that man is searching for a method of communication. I guarantee you that man cannot communicate at the speed he's attempting to. And anybody but the most dumb, incredibly dumb perceptual mind, can understand that by the time he communicates, it's too late. All he can possibly do is define himself in his old relationship. That's just the truth of the matter. He can struggle with it, he can attempt to do it, and he can get old, and he can get sick, and he can die. Are you ready? This ain't Life! Life is communication. If you believe this is communication, this is the way you will communicate and you will suffer and get old and die. You cannot not because you believe you have a beginning and you believe you will have an end. And that is not true. That's what we're offering you here. However you may feel that, however you would like to express it, does not concern me. I am stopping by here to tell you, if you would like to hear it, that you are at a stage in your development, whatever the hell you thought it was, that you are ready to leave. I just read you Emerson's essay. If you persist in directing your attention to the manner by which you are arriving at this new circle, it will retain you. It will shorten your circle. It cannot not do it because there is no limit to the circle of your mind. You must stay, for the next moment, only in anticipation. Do not attempt to judge what is going to happen. If you do, you will circumscribe it in your limitation.

If you set the goal that you expect as the final thing approaches, you cannot go beyond the goal that you have set. The requirement for a leap from particle to wave is non-attention to the particle. I'm doing particle-wave physics here. Did you see that? Attention paid to the particle must attract another particle, or be converted into a wave. It cannot do both. You can Bucky it down into some sort of protein ball – I'll call it a particle. You can take it down to a carbon ball, which must begin because if you have one particle, you will have more or you will have a wave. Waves do not duplicate themselves except in the slowness of the expression of time because any wave must contain more than the speed of light. If you define it as a wave, you have reduced it to a particle, but I don't know how to tell you that. It's a quantum certainty. At no point can you tell which point you're in. That's the idea. At no point can you tell the difference between your conceptual mind and your whole mind. Whenever you try to tell the difference, you conceptualize it. But that sure as hell doesn't stop you from sharing my revelation. At least then maybe you won't kill me and attack me for offering you a solution that you don't want – or that you don't need – I don't know whether you need it or not.

If you've drawn a circle and you've got cancer and you're going to get old and die and you're going to lose all the things you love and you're satisfied with that, you don't need me. Why the hell do you need me? You will stay in that circle. But that is not to say that there is not another circle surrounding you – the Holy Spirit or whatever you call it – offering you entire relief from your own enclosure.

You know perfectly well you're trapped in space/time. When I was ten years old, I knew that. I knew that I was trapped in the past and future and didn't know where I was or where I was going – that I was in that containment. This is Emerson: I also knew that if I was contained or in prison, I had to know that there was freedom. Otherwise, how did I know I was contained? How did I know that I was locked in space/time? So I invented God as the solution, although there already was one. I invented a God to justify my containment. I literally constructed or replicated eternity and called it space/time, which is what it is. Is it a perfect replication? Yes, if there were such a thing as a perfect replication. Can you hear this? Certainly it will be perfect in your mind or you wouldn't be here.

The problem you have is you think you can tell the difference in your own perfection. I couldn't give a poop less whether you're perfect in space or time or in eternity. It's not going to make the slightest difference. What the hell difference does it make? If you're perfect in time and believe it to be time, you will sequence it in your own association and die of your own eternity – which is nonsense. But you can't die anyway. All you can do is see other things die around you while you're forced to be eternally in crap. I don't know if you can hear that. I'll do that once more for you: You can't die. You can see everything else die. Can you die? Sure. Well, let me see you do it. Everything else is dying. You see it die around you, but when you die, you won't tell me what it's like.

Do you know what bothers me the most? Some of you humans have never really heard me. I told you I saw on television three days ago, "Take good care of yourself. Protect yourself and your cholesterol..." It was from the Heart Association. And it said, "Take good care of yourself because one-third of people who have their first heart attack do not survive." Well, let's try it again: Nobody's had a heart attack. So you keep yourself in real good shape, and you do everything you can, but the statistic is that one-third of people who have their very first heart attack will not survive. Why should I worry at all? You don't get it. How will I know? Well, you couldn't possibly know. What difference will it make if I'm dead? Come on. I need somebody that will answer that. How will I know whether I'm the third that didn't survive? This is what used to make me go out and have a Jack Daniels. Can you get it? "One third of you..." He means first heart attack, not where you're all kind of static. This is preventive medicine. This says, "Let's prevent heart attacks because one-third of you are going to die when you have your first one." Well, I might as well say, "Why should I worry?"

You know what the problem is? You can't be that one-third. Do you want to look at it with me? If you were the one-third, your problems would be over. That's a true statement. Do you see what death offers you? So you say, "Well, crap, I'll be that one-third. I'll go out and live it up and be happy and do anything I want because when I'm dead I won't have to worry about it." That's what I did. "One-third of you will not survive your first heart attack." Why should I worry about it, then? I'll be that third and you guys can keep on struggling. Meanwhile, I've had all the fun. And you say to me, "Well, yeah, but you're going to be dead." And I say, "So what?" That's true. We call it Happy Nihilism. "Eat, drink, and be happy because tomorrow you'll be dead."

There's only one problem: You can't die! No one can define to you what death is except your observation of it. And there's a serious problem. Death is an idea, guys. The idea that you could get old and sick and die is going on all around you, because it's an idea in your mind. But it's impossible to prove. You can't annihilate yourself. It's impossible to prove. You can have all the evidence of it. You can say, "There's loss. I'm old. I'm getting old. I'm going to die." You can plan to exit. You can do anything you want. You can make plans to die, but you can't prove your death. You need somebody else to prove you can die. That's nuts!

Now, most of us suffered from a condition finally where we couldn't die. That's how I got this. No matter what I did, and that included trying to live or trying to die, nothing worked. The whole Course In Miracles says, "Swear not to die, you Holy Son of God." You made a bargain you cannot keep very simply because there isn't any death. Now, the acceptance of that will allow you to see that everything that you use to empower death is what death is. Do you see? So that all of the struggling you do in your existence – literally everything you do – justifies death, but yet you can't die. So that's hell. Now you're in hell. You don't like that – I don't care. Then stay in hell. The fact of the matter is you can't escape the Grim Reaper because you are the Grim Reaper. You can't kill yourself. It's impossible. The cause of death is you.

Now, since you don't believe that, because obviously you're trying to survive, you literally kill all of the things around you. That's why time seems to pass. And that's the greater picture. That's why things appear to get old and die. It's an illusion. None of this is true. This is not true! It doesn't matter what lengths you go to. Jesus says, "Why aren't you happy to hear you can't die?" Because to you "can't die" is suffering. You use death as a solution to your problem. "Oh, I'm so glad his pain and suffering is finally over." And you say to him, "Well, I've done good things and now I can lay my burden down." Screw you. I mean, I'm talking to you! You guys that are planning on death, lay up your stuff. I'm offering you freedom, eternal freedom. You store it up all you want. Why would you possibly store it up except to die? You sure as hell aren't storing it up to live. That's crazy. You're storing it up so that it lasts long enough so that you can die with it. You want to have enough left over to give to those who come after. Or if you don't want to do that, you want it to exactly coincide. That's why everybody gets charitable when they're going to die. Then they figure, "Well, I'm dead anyway. I'll go out and give it away." They didn't prove charity. They proved death. What a strange idea. Did you ever see a guy that was told he had a heart attack and was going to die and went out and gave everything away, and then he had a healing? Depending on where he is in his cycle, he'll be happy he's alive because he's alive because he gave, or he'll be pissed because he gave everything away and the x-ray turned out to be false and he'll have to go out and start all over. Or he'll quick run out and try to get it back. Not me, brother.

So those of you who will be leaving here very shortly, understand this: While you don't know it, you're only coming here and leaving each moment anyway. I'll do Course In Miracles for a moment. Most of you can hear this. At least you can read about it. Time lasted but a moment in your mind. You're always coming here and leaving. You just keep re-living the single moment when the time of terror took the place of love. You can read all about that. That's why you've got all this literature here. So you come here in a repetition of that moment, and you stretch that unreal moment to other unreal moments. So you live in that fear within your own association. I'm just showing you how not to do that. All you must do is stand in the moment of the entirety of the fear, and you'll be back in Heaven instantly.

Any moment that you spend here other than that single instant will be nothing because that single instant has already returned to Heaven. I'm not going to start teaching you A Course In Miracles. Page after page after page, this is written for you to look at. So that instant can be just as holy as you want it to be. If you've accumulated other instants of pain and death, you stand in one holy instant in your dependence on God. That link will improve immediately to the wholeness of you, and all of the attractions of the associations that you had previously rejected will enter into the new Love. Literally. I mean this literally, brother. All of the associations that are out there that are part of your mind are waiting for you to change your mind. They are products of your mind.

What we are going to share now is our new production of Christhood, our new certainty of our singleness together, our realization, as Jesus says, that "I am you, and you are me, and God is us." And that that single Self is what we are eternally. Who did we say we were? I bet you're afraid to stand up and read this. I bet you that a lot of associations here are very fearful. I don't blame you. I would be, too. This is nuts. This says what you are. I am God's Son.

How many Sons does God have? One! So if He appears to have more than one, the selves are all the same? Yes!

The reason that's done is we must start you out with singularity. If we say, He has many sons, you'll have them divided up into the twelve brothers. You will have twelve tribes, which is already the split. Do you see? Now we've got a little problem with it. Yes, God has one Son. There's only one total creating emanation from God. Okay? Is that all right with you? *I am God's Son, complete and healed and whole, shining in the reflection of His Love...* What's so lovely about this from the whole mind of Jesus is that it's a confession to the entirety of you in space/time. Obviously, if you are the living Son of God eternally, you wouldn't have to make a confession of who you are. Everybody already knows who you are because you are everybody. So this says, reflection of God's Love. And that's lovely because there's nothing really outside of that for you *...in the reflection of His Love.*

In me is His creation sanctified. I'll do sanctified for you. This is so beautiful. Obviously you are God's only Son, creating eternally. If you believe you are separate, you become a sanctuary for God. God is sanctified in you. That's the admission that there's nothing outside of you. You are a sanctuary that you can offer to the world as a place to come and find peace. "I will sanctify you" – this is Jesus – "if you will let me." Your body is sanctified through the transformation of your body – through the resurrection of your body. Paul says, "You will be a sanctuary. You will be a Jerusalem." You are sanctified and guaranteed eternal life! Sanctification is the same as the guarantee of Jesus Christ. I am a sanctuary that gives you an unconditional guarantee of salvation because I am risen. Jesus Christ risen is your guarantee of Heaven. You cannot not accept it because finally you will use that. Tell me you are going to get there another way – that's nuts. The only way that you could possibly get there is the way that you already did. And that's the guarantee.

It's nice that the New Covenant is an eternal warranty. No matter what you may do with that, it's impossible that you don't have a warrant on eternal life. You think it's a warrant out for your arrest. There's a warrant out for you, but it's for Life, not death. There's a warrant out for you!

In me is love perfected... I love it! *...fear impossible and joy established without opposite. I am the holy home of God Himself.* Once more: *I am the holy home of God Himself.* Does God abide in me? We put that great passage from Revelations into the Healing book. Did we get our Healing books? Did we get the new one, from the Healing Center? We love that passage in Revelations. God says God abides in us. "I will be your Guide. I have come to be your Guide. I am with you." I know humans that say, "How dare you tell me that God lives in me? God lives in Heaven." No, God lives in you! Without you, there is no God.

I am the holy home of God Himself. I am the Heaven where His Love abides? No, resides. Better. It doesn't just abide? It resides? It lives there. It doesn't live next door.

Is it okay if some of my cells get Godly and other of my cells are still sick? That's the way I heal. If I can get any one of your cells to admit to its own perfection, it will heal all the other cells without the necessity for specialization. Quantum healing does not occur by the addressing of the sickness at all. It occurs by reminding the cell that it's whole. You have trained the cell to specialize, it replicates itself, and it's always threatened because it's fundamentally a specialization. It cannot not be. Yet there's no single cell in you, using DNA, that doesn't contain all of the power of the single universe. So the repair job is not to send in some sort of agents, but to remind the cell through your mind that it's eternal, since you are the one that caused the specialization in the first place. That's called healing. Can you hear that? That's the way I heal. I'm not at all concerned about you determining to specialize yourself and call yourself a body. All I'm reminding you of is that you are the cause of it. If you give your body power over you, you're nuts because obviously the specialization of your body couldn't possibly be anything. All it is, is a walking-around-thing of specialization. So you occupy it and that becomes your ego. So you pretend you're not the source of it and you share your own separation, which is a body, with your ego, which is your self justifying your body. That's how that works. That's what all humans are. Yet with them eternally is the power that I just read you about by which that is performed. What is the ego? Nothing! What is the body? Nothing!

So don't let somebody tell you the Course In Miracles teaches that somehow you can take this so-called egotistical mind and make it divine. The very simple answer to what I'm offering you is that it's nothing. At no single moment does it exist. That's absurd. That led us to the following psychology of this, which is, very simply, Lesson 199 in this Workbook called A Course In Miracles. The final lesson that you learn, after learning that you are perfect, is the declaration that you make that you are not this. Otherwise you'll never get it. So the whole last 20 review lessons say only what? I am not a body. I am free. I am as God created me.

There is no peace except the peace of God. Wow. What a light! What a lovely idea! So if I'm not a body, what am I? God's only living Son. "I can never find that out." What? I'm telling you, you are. If you'll accept it, it will be true. If you reject it, you'll never get it. That's how simple it is. I am encouraging you to continue to undergo your own transformation since you can't get it by any other manner. If you read the first page of our Endeavor Academy Out of Time, the only agreement that we have in this with Master Jesus is to teach the possibility of quantum to space/time. I have no other purpose but to tell you all knowledge is gained by revelation. That's what I just read you. Do you understand me? I have no purpose here except to tell you the only way you learn is through revelation – that each moment you are taught something new if you don't reject it. If you reject it, you will be trapped in space/time.

The idea that knowledge has been gained by revelation has been accepted by man since the beginning of time very simply because he sees that the new inventions occur in moments of genius. All this really says is that it inevitably happens. And what I just read you in Emerson said it can happen with revelations of God or in sudden "Ah-ha" moments where everything changes and you suddenly know it to be new. What I am offering to you with the certainty of my own revelation is that it's going on all the time and all you've got to do is accept it. So stop trying to hold on to your own self-concept. Here's the sentence: The great barrier to this is only your own self-identity. In Chapter 31 Jesus says the only thing that could possibly keep you from knowing this is your concept of yourself. And if you persist in that, you will remain in that concept. And if you decide for an alternative, it will be there for you.

This is the Mission of Christian Science
in the teaching of A Course In Miracles:

A Journey without distance
in the space of an instant of reality...

To advance a vision for all people on earth of our divine purpose,
to be united in peace and love with all of humanity in the
recognition of our oneness and equality in the sight of God

With no regard to race, color, creed, gender, or national origin,
there is, has been, and will always be, in our species
an innate, inborn faculty of expanding self-realization
and understanding of our entire purpose for existence,
derived through and by acts of forgiveness and love.

We are certain in our hearts and minds that
this new understanding of a True Universal Relationship
must and will bring bright innovative solutions
to the often devastating problems of aggregate human existence
that have beset Mankind since the beginning of time.

Our only goal is enlightenment of mind.
The means are the consistent and uncompromising application
of the science of mind of A Course In Miracles.

Our curriculum directs, supports, enhances and accelerates
this transformation of our minds.
Our focus includes service, education, dissemination
and communication of the message that we use in Christian
Science in the manner in which we can make application of
the experience of A Course In Miracles throughout the world.

The Church
of Christian Science
in the Mission of
A Course In Miracles

The idea of utilizing the message of the resurrection of Jesus Christ in the application of the science that it is possible for me to arrive at conclusions that are best demonstrated through Jesus in the New Testament is why I am here.

Now, I am going to use, and I have been speaking for a long time, (in fact since the beginning of time) in the idea that the science of my mind will always be in a particular demonstration of what appears to be the necessity for a conversion of the wellness of the physical-ness of me in regard to being whole and perfect as I was created.

Now, what we're going to do is(and I have a little Sunday edition)... This [book] is the Sunday morning edition of Christian Science, which is fundamentally the idea of the Teachers Manual of A Course In Miracles. What it really says is, and all Jesus really says in the New Testament is that you are going to have to use the power of your mind to arrive at conclusions that will allow for change to occur immediately – in the idea of a repetition that is different than the one that you just experienced (but yet have already experienced) if Jesus is proper in his idea of resurrection. OK?

Now, what I'll do real quickly is read a little bit of it to you because I love the idea that you are using the science of your mind to admit the application of the change in you, in your body formulation. Using Jesus now in the science of the New Testament: he is not particularly concerned about how you have been in the idea... This is directly now from Jesus in the science: He is not particularly concerned in a hologram of light that you intend to be in... In the New Testament, Jesus actually underwent an experience of disappearance. All right?

Now, I am going to have to utilize the idea (and Jesus reminds you of this consistently in the New Testament) that it is going to have to come from my mind, very simply because it is a disappearance of my body formulation. And that is how I really teach healing. It is a curiosity about... I am teaching, and most of you are familiar with Christian Science. You've even heard of Mary Baker! I mean you have heard of the science of the mind. And there are lots of churches now around here. In fact I am going to send this video of the science of my mind, concerning Christian Science, as a demonstration of the purity of Christianity which is actually obvious in the idea that the science of my mind is where the requirement for the alteration of itself occurs.

Now, I am going to read just a little bit, from the Sunday edition, of the idea of Mary Baker in regard to how she came, through revelation. And most Christians... Now there is really no argument with Christian Science! You know the problem I have with Christian Science? I am going to talk about it a little bit here. Because what Mary Baker finally says about the capacity of instantaneous healing that can occur without regard to the formulation of what you formerly were in space/time, is obviously why you go to Church and call it Christian Science. And what you do is, and the reason people don't particularly want to be conformed to you, is you're teaching the science of the power of your mind to heal.

Now, actually, Mary Baker (and guys you might as well hear it), while she'll say that it is the power of my mind to heal...

Nobody really quarrels with that... What they quarrel with is the instantaneous availability of Jesus in his disappearance and re-appearance within a physical body. OK? Now, maybe I can stir up a little attention to the Course with Christian Science! Now, you..., as long as I can remember... I might as well tell you that I am a Christian Scientist that did not find approval among what we call "Protestant Congregationalists" who did not want to take the idea that they could use their mind to heal.

Now, there is nowhere that Jesus in Christian Science says that you are going to do anything but be well and perfect using your mind without regard to your physical body, and that is not going to make any difference. Now, so when somebody told me when I was back in the thirties (I am an old guy!), that in Christian Science and Mary Baker, people would refuse to go to the doctor for physical evidence of themselves because, "Well I am a Christian Scientist." That is not what Jesus taught in Christian Science. In Christian Science Jesus teaches that the love of God is so important in an individual mind that a replication of the idea of the physical-ness of you can demonstrate the wellness of you.

I'll read just a little bit. Is this little Science book of Christian Science full of the idea of the miracles that occur in the idea that suddenly there is a shift in consciousness? Yes. Will I do it? Sure. I'll read you just a little bit. If I come in to a Sunday school class, the idea of teaching A Course In Miracles, the idea of teaching the science of the mind of Jesus, which is fundamentally what Christianity is, I would have to have somewhere the idea of the necessity for a physical experience, that would involve the physical change of you, not necessarily in the application of what was mental within my mind. Now, that is what I am going to say about this, OK?

Am I all right? OK, this is called Christian Science, because it is what Mary Baker taught in the idea of a self discovery. And it happened to me when I was dying and when I went through my last death experience, as many or all of you have done. And suddenly you discovered that the application of the remedy that you used physically made you well. Now, while you are willing to admit that the mind had to do with it, the idea that it is entirely mindful if it is going to be real, is more difficult for you than the teaching of Jesus, OK? Shall we try it just for a minute?

There, this is the idea of the science of your mind to suddenly get a re-vision of how you look, a re-vision of how you look in this little Sunday school book about a course in the miracle of my mind that suddenly is demonstrable by what is happening to me. Listen with me, listen with me and watch, and watch.

Whence came to me this heavenly conviction, – a conviction antagonistic to the testimony of the physical senses? According to St. Paul, it was 'the gift of the grace of God given unto me by the effectual working of His power."

It was the divine law of Life and Love, unfolding to me the demonstrable fact that matter possesses neither sensation nor life; that human experiences show the falsity of all material things; and that immortal cravings, 'the price of learning love,' establish the truism that the only sufferer is mortal mind, for the divine Mind itself cannot suffer.

I am back with you just for the idea of beginning to point out to you in the science of the Christian idea, that when you believe that you are sick or unable to cope with the mortal mind, you actually have nothing to do with reality at all. You are not a part of what reality is. This is the teaching of Jesus. Let's look at it:

My conclusions were reached by allowing the evidence of this revelation to multiply with mathematical certainty and the lesser demonstration to prove the greater, as the product of three multiplied by three, equaling nine, proves conclusively that three times three must be nine, in the entirety of the idea – not a fraction more, not a unit less.

When apparently near the confines of mortal existence, standing already within the shadow of the death-valley, I learned these truths in divine Science: that all real being is in God, the divine Mind, and that Life, Truth, and Love are all-powerful and ever-present; that the opposite of Truth, – called error, sin, sickness, disease, death, – is the false testimony of false material sense, of mind in matter; that this false sense evolves, in belief, a subjective state of mortal mind which this same so-called mind names matter, thereby shutting out the true sense of Spirit.

I am back for just a moment because I am obviously teaching that so many now are formulating in ideas of the action of taking time each moment to practice the idea of increasing the facility of the idea that the manner in which they're viewing this world is actually only contained subjectively within their own mind.

Now, that this is the entire teaching of Christianity, in what you call the science of the mind, is a true statement. There is very little objection to the idea of the healing in Christian Science except the idea that the physical healing of the body can be accomplished by particular ideas of falsity that are contained within the mind that allow the body to be real. Now, this is not what Jesus teaches, is not what Paul teaches, it is not what the disciples teach and it is not what anyone who saw Jesus physically make an appearance here, actually teaches. Now, since you have to use it, it is going to say here, as it does in the New Testament, that the power is in your mind and there is nothing you can do about that. But that is not to say that in your mind is not contained the immediate wholeness of the idea of the relative idea of the space/time of a hologram that is all around you in the light of yourself. This is two thousand years of Christianity, OK? Will you listen with me? Listen just for a second.

When apparently near the confines of mortal existence, standing already within the shadow of the death-valley, I learned these truths in divine Science: that all real being is in God, the divine Mind, and that Life, Truth, and Love are all-powerful and ever-present; that the opposite of Truth, – called error, sin, sickness, disease, death, – is the false testimony of false material sense, of mind in matter; that this false sense evolves, in belief, a subjective state of mortal mind which this same so-called mind names matter, thereby shutting out the true sense of Spirit. And I wanted you to hear it once more.

My discovery, that erring, mortal, misnamed mind produces all the organism and action of the mortal body, set my thoughts to work in new channels of the idea that I wanted to see, and led up to my demonstration of the proposition that Mind is All and matter is naught that mind is all and matter is naught as the leading factor in Mind-science.

Christian Science reveals incontrovertibly that Mind is All-in-all, that the only realities are the divine Mind and idea. (Christian Science reveals incontrovertibly that Mind is All-in-all, that the only realities are the divine Mind and idea.) This great fact is not, however, seen to be supported by sensible evidence, until its divine Principle is demonstrated by healing the sick and thus proved absolute and divine. This proof once seen, no other conclusion can be reached.

Obviously the problem that you have with it (this is what we are going to attempt to do out in the world by the new evidence that most of you are reaching individually), is the certainty that since time is always going to be gone anyway, you don't intend to hold on to it within your own self. All right? Now, is this the science of your mind in the evidence of what you intend to do? Sure! You want to listen to a little more of what this actually says? Now, here's the idea that you can alter your association of the physical-ness of your body and it would have to involve not only time, or a moment when you are here, but the space in which you occupy the idea of a reflection of light of yourself in a hologram. What Jesus teaches throughout the New Testament is that he suddenly appears. OK. Now, is he suddenly appearing right now? Of course!

The idea that you have the power in your mind to perform this, must mean that you were successful within the idea of utilizing the science of your mind, because suddenly you saw somebody who had a terrible case of cancer, who was getting old and dying, and suddenly was well for no reason. Now, the idea that you can't accept that, which is really what Christian Science is (as a matter of fact it is what healing is), gave you the idea that he must have used a remedy, a physical remedy, within his mind of what he wanted to be. Now Jesus says, "I can do that." Jesus says, "When I decided to heal somebody I went there, I looked directly at him in a new relationship in space/time where he could see himself." Let's take another look at what the idea means: what we are really saying is that you can change the way you are looking at me right now, very simply by demonstrating a new hologram of light in which you'll be different.

Now, you say to me, "Well I know you; you are an eighty-six year old guy." Now you're saying that the idea of the physical-ness of my body being eighty-six can be altered by a factor of the idea (if what I am teaching of Christian Science is true), by the simple admission that (I don't seem to be) using the power of my mind through Jesus Christ, (and I suggest that you do) I can heal the sick and raise the dead. Now, say to me, "Can you heal the sick and raise the dead?" How else would I be able to do it physically? Now, you don't object to the idea that I can heal with my mind; what you object to, is the idea that I can heal you physically very simply because the nature of Christian Science in the idea of A Course In Miracles is that the healing is going on continuously with what is going on with you.

You listen with me. Here is the science of your mind in the miracle of utilizing the power of God to demonstrate a vertical idea of a horizontal *and* vertical idea of a variation of suddenly appearing out of nowhere! [Song: *You Came To Me From Out Of Nowhere...*] Are you suddenly appearing out of nowhere? Sure! Are you listening to that song, You came to me from out of nowhere? Sure! Is that a Christian song? Oh sure. Do you like the idea that when you go out and say, "You should have seen who came up to me on the corner, and I know that he has been dead for four hundred years or five or a thousand, or I know he is not due within my sequence of time for another hundred years." That is what science of mind is. Listen:

The physical effects of fear illustrate its illusion. Gazing at a chained lion, crouched for a spring, should not terrify a man. The body is affected only with the belief of disease produced by a so-called mind ignorant of the truth which chains disease. Nothing but the power of Truth can prevent the fear of error, and prove man's dominion over error.

Many years ago the author made a spiritual discovery, the scientific evidence of which has accumulated to prove that the divine Mind produces in man health, harmony, and immortality. (Gradually this evidence will gather momentum and clearness, until it reaches its culmination of scientific statement and proof.) Nothing is more disheartening than to believe that there is a power opposite to God, or good, and that God endows this opposing power with strength to be used against Himself, against Life, health, harmony. And you know it is not true.

Every law of matter or the body, supposed to govern man, is rendered null and void by the law of Life, God. Ignorant of our God-given rights, we submit to unjust decrees, and the bias of education enforces this slavery. Be no more willing to suffer the illusion that you are sick or that some disease is developing in the system, than you are to yield to a sinful temptation on the ground that sin has its necessities.

I am going to leave you for a moment in the idea that Christian Science has actually been a lot more successful at teaching the science of the mind than the idea of Christianity, necessarily, and that is why those in Christianity say, "Well I am not..., I can't do that, because I would have to admit to the possibility of the entire wellness of myself in an instant conversion of how I look physically." All right, can you see that with me?

Now, I am going to leave you and I am going to come back in the idea that who is going to appear here... Watch me now. Here... [*takes off sweater*] Did you do that physically with your body? Sure! Can you do it physically with the idea that when I took off my sweater I was able to present to you the certainty that in our Course In Miracles, we teach you that the idea that I was wearing that sweater a moment ago is over and gone, and if it is over and gone I don't have to be concerned in Christian Science, as Mary Baker would tell you, about how I can be whole and well in the idea of what I am. I'll be back in just a moment. You stay here with the love that I am feeling for you in the idea that as soon as I took off my sweater you went, "Wow, I am glad he took off his sweater, because the appearance of him in a reflection of light is the science of my mind in the love that Jesus expresses for me!

I'll be back in just a moment; I'll be back in just a moment, just a moment.

Music and Song: In the Garden

I come to the garden alone
While the dew is still on the roses
And the voice I hear falling on my ear...

Now, the change that occurred just then was very important in the science of your mind in how you heal.

...The Son of God discloses
And He walks with me, and He talks with me
And He tells me I am His own
You are looking very different than you did in the other

place that you were in. And what you really learned from me, from Jesus, is that the place that you are in, has been resurrected by the idea of your mind in Christian Science.

> *...And the joy we share as we tarry there*
> *None other has ever known*
> *He speaks, and the sound of His voice*
> *Is so sweet the birds hush their singing*
> *And the melody that He gave to me...*

The idea that you are going to listen to me and we are going to send this to, what do you call them, Christian Scientists? We are going to send the Christian Scientists the story about Jesus, because the place that he is in is different than the place that you are in. Because the place that he is in is different than the place that you are in. Now, does he bring the new place with him when he comes into this science of the idea of your mind? Sure!

> *Within my heart is ringing*
> *And He walks with me and He talks with me*
> *And He tells me I am His own*

Now, you can say, "Well he looks very much the same to me." You could say the same thing about me if you wanted to! You could say to me that the continuum that you are representing to me, is a reflection of the idea of cause and effect in the notation that there is a variation between what we teach with God, through Jesus Christ, in what I am certain is in my own mind.

> *And the joy we share as we tarry there*
> *None other has ever known*
> *None has ever known*

Now, what I am going to do in this idea of the science of my mind is offer you a physical demonstration of the manner in which I can perform a new idea of what I intend to do. This is Christian Science now. You say, "Well you are able to do it with the power of your mind." I don't understand that. The only power of mind I have is the singularity of a representation of a reflection of light that allows me to see what I believe I am within myself and if I believe, this is now directly from Jesus, that I can get sick, if I believe that in my mind there is an idea of a physical capacity of hatred, the idea that I don't have to love you, the idea that I am going to starve, the idea I am going to hate my enemy, actually what I am, are you ready, is nothing.

The entire teaching of the science of mind through Jesus teaches you, and we are going to read just a little bit about it from Christian Science so you can get an idea in your mind that either you are going to be whole and absolutely real as the song would indicate or you simply won't be anything. Do you have it with me? Do you have it? Yes. You say, "Well I came here, I am occupying this body and I am going to get old and I am going to die." That has no meaning to me anymore than it really has any meaning to you. Let's look at it from a Christian Science standpoint. OK? You listen with me:

Mind is the I AM, or infinity. Mind never enters the finite. I love that idea. Intelligence never passes into non-intelligence, or matter. Good never enters into evil, the unlimited into the limited, the eternal into the temporal, nor the immortal into mortality. The divine Ego, and this we use a lot in our Course In Miracles, this is Christian Science, or individuality, is reflected in all spiritual individuality from the infinitesimal to the infinite.

Immortal man was and is God's image or idea, even the infinite expression of infinite Mind, and immortal man is coexistent and coeternal with that Mind. He has been forever in the eternal Mind, God; but infinite Mind can never be in man, but is reflected by man in the idea of the perfection in which he can enter with Jesus. The spiritual man's consciousness and individuality are reflections of God. They are the emanations of Him who is Life, Truth, and Love. Immortal man is not and never was material, but always spiritual and eternal. One more idea, listen to me.

God is indivisible. A portion of God could not enter man; neither could God's fullness be reflected by a single man, else

291

God would be manifestly finite, lose the deific character, and become less than God. Allness is the measure of the infinite, and nothing less can express God. Now, listen:

God, the divine Principle of man, and man in God's likeness are inseparable, this according to the Jesus teaching and of Christian Science, harmonious, and eternal is the idea of how you are by utilizing your idea of any reflection of light. The Science of being furnishes the rule of perfection, and brings immortality to light. God and man are not the same, but in the order of divine Science, God and man coexist and are eternal. God is the parent Mind, and man is God's spiritual offspring.

I love that. The idea that you are learning with me the reasonableness of the fundamental idea of a comparison of lightness and darkness are the manner in which you successfully altered your idea, all right, in my last death experience. Now, you say to me, "Well I believe that with Jesus that when I die, all right, I am going to be able to enter the Kingdom." And all Jesus really says in the science of mind and what he says to you is, "There is not any such thing as death." You could not possibly die, very simply because when you think you are dying the reflection of light you are getting is actually nothing. All right?

Now, this is the science of the mind of the manner in which you practice, if you are going to..., this is from Mary Baker incidentally who is very successful. You know what is going to surprise me and we are going to send this out to Christian Science, is the idea that they won't really question the idea of the manner in which the miracles are manifested by a voice that spoke through Mary Baker, if you'd like to use her, in the idea that Jesus spoke to her. Did Jesus speak to Mary Baker? Of course. Did Jesus speak to Christian Science people about the idea of an alteration of time within themselves where they recognize that they suddenly were sick and that they were not only not sick but are in a totality of a reflection of light that is different than the one they were in just a moment ago. OK?

Let's listen together shall we? Let's listen just a little bit to the idea of what we are saying about this.

It is ignorance and false belief, based on a material sense of things, which hide spiritual beauty and goodness. Understanding this, Paul said: "Neither death, nor life, nor things present, nor things to come, nor height, nor depth, nor any other creature, shall be able to separate us from the love of God." This is the doctrine of Christian Science: that divine Love cannot be deprived of its manifestation, or object; that joy cannot be turned into sorrow, for sorrow is not the master of joy; that good can never produce evil; that matter can never produce mind nor life result in death. The perfect man—governed by God, his perfect Principle—is sinless and eternal.

Harmony is produced by its Principle, is controlled by it and abides with it. Divine Principle is the Life of man. Man's happiness is not, therefore, at the disposal of physical sense. Truth is not contaminated by error. I love that. Harmony in man is as beautiful as in music, and discord is unnatural, unreal.

We are going to demonstrate, we have twelve minutes here, oK, in which the science of the idea of Christian Science is going to demonstrate, so beautifully put by Mary Baker, the possibility that a miracle can actually occur and it really does not have anything to do with your physical body. You say, "Well that certainly..., well I know you just read me that everything is controlled by my mind." Yes, and I am going to include the notation that if there is only one mind, the source of my reality is God and that I therefore cannot be excluded as the Son of God from the perfection that I am. OK, will you listen with me? Let's do it from a Mary Baker standpoint in the idea that the presence of Christian Science when you came in here on this idea of the science of your mind, oK, in Sunday school, to practice the idea of healing the sick and raising the dead, using the power of your mind was a teaching of Jesus and while you don't mind admitting it you say to me, "Well I am not a Christian Scientist," and of course you are a Christian Scientist. Everything that you do in the idea of Christianity is the certainty that the power of your mind to be whole and perfect has been endowed to you by the perfection of a physical re-appearance of the resurrection of Jesus Christ, for goodness sake! OK, now, you don't like the idea that somewhere I am telling you that it means I don't have to use any physical sense. I didn't say that. I said you don't have to use any physical sense because you are not physical. This world that you believe that you occupy was actually over a long time ago and you know there is a whole universe out there, and you know perfectly well that the idea of the separation of cause and effect in yourself can only produce ideas of reflection of light that will have no meaning. Let's listen together just a little more about the catechism of the Mind Training of Christian Science.

Boy, you look good. Did you see how you....here, the... some of you...People are stopping in here, somebody said, "Did you see that what's my name again is teaching Christian Science?" And I said to him, "All Christians actually teach Christian Science or con-science or consciousness of yourself in relationship with the idea that you can be healed through the power of mind by Jesus Christ." And there is nowhere, there is no sense in arguing with me, the reason you can't argue with me is you either are whole and perfect as you were created, oK, which is the sense that you have in your mind, or this is going to be hateful and real in which case you are going to be forever condemned to this idea and that is why we teach this. Listen:

The Scriptures say, "In Him we live, and move, and have our being." What then is this seeming power, independent of God, which causes disease and cures it? What is it but an error of belief that you could have been sick in the first place, a law of mortal mind, wrong in every sense, embracing sin, sickness, and death? It is the very antipode of immortal Mind, of Truth, and of spiritual law. It is not in accordance with the goodness of God's character that He should make man sick, then leave man to heal himself; it is absurd to suppose that matter can both cause and cure disease, or that Spirit, God, produces disease and leaves the remedy to matter.

John Young of Edinburgh writes: "God is the father of mind, and of nothing else." Such an utterance is "the voice of one crying in the wilderness" of human beliefs and preparing the way of Science for the idea that the materialism of you is always going to be over and gone within your idea of yourself.

Christian Science demonstrates that none but the pure in heart can see God, as the gospel teaches. In proportion to his purity is man perfect; and perfection is the order of celestial being which demonstrates Life in Christ, Life's spiritual ideal.

The true idea of man, as the reflection of the invisible God, is as incomprehensible to the limited senses as is man's infinite Principle.

The reason that I am talking about that in the idea of Science is the most perfect that I can get you to recognize, is that the solution to what you want to find is going to be in you. Is that so? Now, the idea that it is going to be in you in Christian Science is the notation that suddenly, although you may not even know why you are well, there may have been no remedy for you, what you had in you was the inevitability of the perfection of you in the notation in idea that you lasted only for that moment in your own mind. Let's look at what time offers you through Jesus in the idea that he is going to tell you in the science of your mind that he can alter your association by a physical re-appearance that he is going to do, I understand it is going to be about three minutes. You mean Jesus is coming into this idea of Christian Science? Sure, sure!

Now, do you know what will amaze you? He does not look the way you think he looks and that is really not what is important. What is important is the manner in which you as a teacher, as a remedy for the idea of the power of Jesus mind, as a disciple of mind, will teach the science of your mind in the notation that the reflection of light that you are getting is going to be singular and whole no matter what you do with it, and in any particular sense it won't make any difference. And you say to me, "Well…" Shall I try a little bit with you in what happened here just about twenty minutes ago?

The idea…, here, I am going to read you a little bit about the science of your mind in the power of the hologram of yourself which is what Christian Science actually is. Listen to what Mary Baker has to say about the idea that Jesus made a physical appearance for her. Oh, sure. Now, can you prove that within your mind? How could you possibly prove it? The reason you can't prove it is because it is in your mind. Jesus reminds you in Christian Science that the power of your mind to make a decision about what you want to see is one that you must make and the idea that you make it must have been possible or how can it be past tense in your mind? Listen, listen with me, from the entirety of our teaching of Christian Science.

All Things I Think I See Reflect Ideas

This is salvation's keynote: What I see reflects a process in my mind, which starts with my idea of what I want. From there, the mind makes up an image of the thing the mind desires, judges valuable, and therefore seeks to find. These images are then projected outward, looked upon, esteemed as real and guarded as one's own. From insane wishes comes an insane world. From judgment comes a world condemned. And from forgiving thoughts a gentle world comes forth, with mercy for the holy Son of God, to offer him a kindly home where he can rest a while before he journeys on, and help his brothers walk ahead with him, and find the way to Heaven and to God.

Our Father, Your ideas reflect the truth in the science of my mind, and mine apart from Yours but make up dreams. Let me behold what only Yours reflect, for Yours and Yours alone establish truth.

The idea that you have decided on an individual basis, here and now, to have that experience could only mean that you have had it. Now, the story of how Paul, all right, described to Jesus the certainty that the voice from Jesus actually spoke to him is nothing that is mysteriousness about Christianity. You know perfectly well it is true. What is hard for you to say is that in the science of your mind when it is demonstrated, as it is going to be in this new attitude of the performance of you, you won't be able necessarily to describe it in the nature of the power of the concept that you use to describe yourself.

Now, the reason that is true is because the only time you can really describe it is when you had the experience yourself and that experience is over and that is why it is called resurrection. It is called resurrection because obviously when the Christians tell you, "Well we are all going to have to die," there is nowhere in Christian Science and there is certainly nowhere in Paul where Paul says that you have to die in order to know that Jesus is with you. OK, let's look real quick at a little bit of it and we'll be able to see that while you know perfectly well that what I am teaching is the idea that you can have the experience, what I am trying to demonstrate to you in the science of the power of my mind is that it seems to you reasonable that if there is a universe out there that there is a manner in which I can come to know it must be contained within me. OK? You listen with me, listen with me right now.

Behold, I shew you a mystery; We shall not all sleep, but we shall all be changed, in a moment, in the twinkling of an eye, at the last trump: for the trumpet shall sound, and the dead shall be raised incorruptible, and we shall be changed.

I Am Surrounded By The Love Of God.

Father, You stand before me and behind, beside me, in the place I see myself, and everywhere I go. You are in all the things I look upon, the sounds I hear, and every hand that reaches for my own. In You, the idea of who you thought you were will disappear, because it has disappeared, time disappears, and place becomes a meaningless belief. For what surrounds Your Son and keeps him safe is Love Itself. There is no Source but This, and nothing is that does not share Its holiness; that stands beyond Your one creation, or without the Love Which holds all things within Itself.

Father, Your Son is like Yourself. We come to You in Your Own Name today, to be at peace within Your everlasting Love.

Our time is up in the Christian Science of my mind, oK, but I want to impress on you the teaching of Jesus in the reflection of light that you appeared to get from somebody other than yourself. Now, Jesus says that in a particular way. I just have time to read a reflection of the idea of the light that you believe is different from what you are. Listen with me:

Thou shalt love the Lord thy God with all thy heart, and with all thy soul, and with all thy mind. This is the first and great commandment. And the second is like unto it, Thou shalt love thy neighbour as thyself.

Thou shalt love thy neighbour as yourself, since the reflection of thought that you are getting can be an accumulation of the science of your mind in the idea that, in the new continuum of time, there are appearing from outside of this frame ideas in the science of your mind, all right, of the certainty that you were suddenly healed, all right. Now, the idea that you have to have a reason for it really doesn't concern me, because if you decide with Jesus that you want to be whole and well you can literally be in a different idea of association of where you thought you were. This is how you are going to get out into the universe, isn't it? This is how you are going to come in the science of your mind to the certainty that in the idea of changing your mind you suddenly were healed of sickness and death.

Now, am I a Christian Scientist? Of course! Are you a

Christian Scientist? You could not, not be. You could not, not have in you the idea that is contained in you is the idea that there is a vast universe out there that is not connected to the limitation you impose on yourself in the faculty of reflection of light where there is a variance from one idea to another. And that is what you call a neighbor. That is why Jesus 2000 years ago when he made an appearance with you, demonstrated very emphatically to you that he could heal the sick and raise the dead. Now, Christian Science teaches you, as Jesus teaches you in the science of your mind, that you are the cause of the disease within your own mind and you can't possibly be the cause of it if there is such a thing as the idea of the entirety of the source of your reality and the source of your reality is with us now in the idea that you are going to allow for the idea...

We are going to send it to all of the Christian Scientists. What it is, is very simply like Mary Baker, you might as well use her, teaches the idea that miracles occur. Now you are perfectly willing to admit that miracles occur, but you do not want to illuminate the necessity to use medicine. What do I care whether you use medicine. The medicine you are using will be how you feel about yourself physically and you will be directly well to the degree that you would accept the idea from Jesus that you are whole and perfect as you were created no matter what you think.

And I love you as Christian Science. And I love you as a neighbor in the appearance that Jesus, here he came, in the appearance that Jesus just came in, oK, to a Christian Science meeting, actually it is a Presbyterian. Ha, ha, ha!! The idea that..., Presbyterian is the idea of a repetition that is very similar to the idea of Christian Science, since it is a re-incarnation of the idea of the formulation of you in the perfection of Jesus.

I'll be with you, I'll be with you in the certainty of the love that we are feeling for each other in the idea of having Christian Science, all right. I can practice it on a moment by moment basis, using Jesus, and not reveal it to anybody. That is what a course in the Mind Training actually is, isn't it? You can drop me a line about it as a Christian Scientist; I would love to authenticate with you the certainty that what Jesus says is absolutely true. Did he say it two thousand years ago when he made a physical appearance? Yes. Did he say it ten minutes ago when he made a physical appearance? Of course! That is why you are being provided with the idea of alterations of yourself in escaping from earth to Heaven in the certainty of who you are.

And I'll see you in just a moment, and I'll see you in just a moment, and I'll see you here and now in that certainty of the science of my mind in the acceptance of the entirety of the responsibility for what is going on in the illusion that it was possible for me to be in this little place in space/time.

.

www.ingramcontent.com/pod-product-compliance
Lightning Source LLC
Chambersburg PA
CBHW070342090426
42733CB00009B/1255